Inside

The

Illuminati

Evidence, Objectives, and
Methods of Operation

Inside

The

Illuminati

Evidence, Objectives, and Methods of Operation

Mark Dice

The Resistance
San Diego, CA

Table of Contents

Also by Mark Dice:

-*The Illuminati in Hollywood*
-*The Illuminati: Facts & Fiction*
-*The New World Order: Facts & Fiction*
-*Illuminati in the Music Industry*
-*The Resistance Manifesto*
-*Big Brother: The Orwellian Nightmare*
-*The Bilderberg Group: Facts & Fiction*
-*Bohemian Grove: Facts & Fiction*

Connect with Mark on:

Facebook.com/MarkDice
Twitter.com/MarkDice
Instagram.com/MarkDice
YouTube.com/MarkDice
MarkDice.com

Introduction

The Illuminati is either called a "conspiracy theory" or a "conspiracy fact," depending on who you talk to. Those familiar with the Illuminati secret society may tell you that it is a criminal and diabolical network of some of the world's most wealthy, educated, and elite bankers, businessmen, and politicians, who work behind the scenes to gain and maintain high levels of power, enormous wealth, and wield control over the world.

The list of claims that come along with this monstrous conspiracy are vast, and range from the Illuminati being an elite good-old-boy network looking out for their own interests (often at the expense of others and in unscrupulous ways), to claims that they are actually alien beings from another galaxy who masquerade as humans, drink people's blood to survive, and are working to prepare planet earth for the arrival of the Antichrist who will rule the New World Order as a god, offering those who worship him "eternal life" through transhumanist technology merging man with machine.

In this book I will help you get to the core of the conspiracy by providing you with some of the original evidence proving the existence and activities of this infamous group, dating back to the late 1700s in the state of Bavaria, Germany, and as more and more evidence is piled up, we will slowly move into the present day, proving beyond a reasonable doubt that the Illuminati is

1

still fully operational, and many of the "conspiracy theories" are actually true.

This analysis is a supplement for my previous book, *The Illuminati: Facts & Fiction* and will continue to investigate and examine the many allegations and conspiracy theories associated with the Illuminati. Since the subject matter is so vast, this second volume was required to continue my analysis of the wide-ranging claims and evidence connected to the "Illuminati conspiracy." I am dedicated to separating the facts from the fiction, since buried within the mountain of "conspiracy theories" circulated on this subject, there is a considerable amount of irrefutable evidence that there is indeed a powerful "Illuminati" secret society that is operating today in America and around the world.

There is also a large amount of wild speculation, half-truths, and out-right lies about what the Illuminati is doing, who is involved with them, and what evidence is available. Some people dismiss the idea that there is a "conspiracy" at all, and do not even believe such a thing exists, because when an educated and rational person comes across some of the more outrageous (and clearly false) allegations stemming from the Illuminati conspiracy, they just shake their head in disbelief and get the impression that all the allegations and "conspiracy theories" must be false as well; thinking such claims must have come from equally mentally deranged people who purport some of the more far-fetched and fabricated information as "evidence" and "proof."

In this book I will present to you a rational approach to the idea of an "Illuminati conspiracy" and I will discuss the historical evidence of the original, admittedly real, Bavarian Illuminati and the roots of this secret society that has spawned countless tales of its power and reach. I will also cover many of the affiliated secret societies that were not examined in my previous book and will continue to investigate various people who claim to be actual former members. We will also look at some political elite insiders and see what they have to say about the Illuminati and the idea that a secret society of powerful men is posing a danger to the world and to our freedoms. Skeptics of an Illuminati conspiracy will be very surprised to learn the names of some prominent people throughout history who have made startling statements clearly revealing their conviction that the Illuminati is real and poses a danger to us all.

I don't like to use the word "conspiracy" because it has a negative connotation that this material is just a "conspiracy theory," when in fact, I do very little *theorizing* at all. The terms "conspiracy theory" and "conspiracy theorist" have become a pejorative, which means they have a negative connotation and are used to insult people and shut down the discussion, similar to someone screaming "racist" at someone in attempts to bypass critical thinking and cause a knee jerk reaction to paint them as such, when in reality they simply have an opposing political ideology on a particular issue. Much to some people's surprise, many "conspiracies" are actually real, and the dictionary definition of a conspiracy is simply, "an agreement by two or more persons to commit a crime, fraud, or other wrongful act." People are actually charged with "conspiracy" in criminal courts every day for simply "conspiring" or planning to commit a crime. Conspiracies happen on a small scale such as when two people conspire to rob a bank, and on a large scale when the leadership of a powerful country fabricates a reason to go to war. Conspiracies are a fact of life. When researchers such as myself point out real, solid, irrefutable evidence that reveals a conspiracy, we are often attacked as "crazy tinfoil hat wearing conspiracy theorists," because the term causes people to immediately dismiss the claims as a paranoid delusion imagined by someone on the Internet who lives in their mother's basement. The reality is that actual conspiracy theorists can be found in high positions of power and conspiracy theories are put forth by well-educated people. Let's not forget that Hillary Clinton publicly claimed that a "vast right wing conspiracy" was fabricating allegations that President Bill Clinton had sexual relations with intern Monica Lewinski.[1] Hillary Clinton was being a conspiracy theorist, when in reality her husband Bill *was* having sexual relations with the intern, and there was no *conspiracy* trying to bring him down—it was only people reporting on the facts.

The Bush administration put forth a conspiracy theory that Iraq had weapons of mass destruction and were planning to use them on America and our allies, strong-arming the public into invading the country based on this conspiracy theory which was later proven to be 100%

---

[1] *Washington Post* "First Lady Launches Counterattack" by David Maraniss (January 28, 1998)

false.[2] Not only was it false, but to be more accurate, it was actually a lie concocted to justify the invasion and war. As everyone now knows, there were no weapons of mass destruction at all, and Americans had been duped into going to war based on a conspiracy theory constructed by the US government.

Until the twenty-first century, most Americans had never heard of the Illuminati. Dan Brown's novel *Angels & Demons* introduced millions of people to the group in 2003 (although his version was far from the truth and more like a purposeful disinformation campaign). And with the rise of the information age and social media, YouTube videos a click away, and countless websites popping up dedicated to the subject, more and more people became interested in this mysterious subject.

The 2004 presidential election in America brought John Kerry and George W. Bush together to face off for the presidency, both of whom are members of the Skull & Bones secret society headquartered at Yale University, which added fuel to this growing fire. I say that they *are* members, not *were* members, because Skull & Bones is not just a fraternity like they would have you believe, but is instead a post-graduate organization that gives its members access to one of the most powerful social networks in the world. This is how two Skull & Bones members were able to secure the nominations for both the Republican and Democrat party in the same election, so

---

[2] *CBS News* "White House Admits WMD Error" by Lauren Johnston (July 9th 2003)

no matter which one of them won (George W. Bush or John Kerry), it would be a victory for Skull & Bones.

It was around this same time that "9/11 conspiracy theories" were growing, and the cover story for the War in Iraq continued to fall apart. The official story of the September 11th attacks and the expanding "war on terror" just wasn't adding up. For the first several years after the World Trade Center was destroyed, so-called "9/11 conspiracy theories" were contained to the Internet, but around 2005 and 2006 they boiled over into the mainstream and found many high-profile supporters whose comments about 9/11 being an "inside job" couldn't be ignored by the mainstream media.[3]

When people interested in investigating the massive inconsistencies in the official story tried piecing together what really happened that day, it inevitably took many "down the rabbit hole" to discover the various secret societies that all led back to the Illuminati. 9/11 would lead to Skull & Bones, which would lead to the Bilderberg Group, which would lead to the Bohemian Grove, which would lead to the Illuminati and a whole can of worms that raised many more questions about what the shadowy elite of our world are doing behind the scenes was opened.

When one quiets their mind from the buzz of pop culture and mainstream media and steps back from their self-absorbed lifestyle and looks deeper into world events and the power structure directing society, they begin to

---

[3] *New York Times* "500 Conspiracy Buffs Meet to Seek the Truth of 9/11" by Feuer, Alan (June 5, 2006)

see the world very differently. Once someone begins to understand that there is more than meets the eye in our world, and they discover the different branches of elite ruling class networks that all converge under one umbrella, their life is often never the same. People describe it as their awakening to what's really happening in the world or "going down the rabbit hole," or having their eyes finally opened.

If one truly wishes to learn about the history of the world, and about the driving force behind major world events, the economy, and even our very culture, then one must look into the Illuminati. At one point in history, in the late 1700s, when the Illuminati was first exposed, most people knew about them and the dangers they posed but as time went on and generations have passed, most people had forgotten about them. Sports entertainment and celebrity news had come to dominate most people's minds and many had fallen asleep at the wheel thinking everything was just fine.

Just as many people used to doubt and deny that the Italian Mafia even existed, the same is true of the modern Illuminati. Ancient secret societies are admitted by mainstream historians to have existed and were not just social clubs for men looking to keep themselves entertained after work. They had a powerful function, even back then. Manly P. Hall, a very well respected secret society insider, explains, "The esoteric organizations of ancient times were for the most part religious and philosophical. In the medieval world they were philosophical and political. In the modern world, political and social."[4]

He goes on to say plainly, "It is beyond question that the secret societies of all ages have exercised a considerable degree of political influence," and that "a second purpose for secret societies was to create a mechanism for the perpetuation from generation to generation of policies, principles, or systems of learning, confined to a limited group of selected and initiated persons."[5]

For years, FBI director J. Edgar Hoover denied that the La Cosa Nostra or Italian Mafia even existed. Some believe the mob was actually blackmailing Hoover with compromising photos of him and his boyfriend Clyde Tolson, but for whatever reason, even the head of the FBI publicly denied there was any such thing as an organized criminal business network that had police, judges, lawyers, and other public officials on their payroll. All the denials changed in 1957 after a major mafia meeting on a farm in Apalachin, New York (about 200 miles northwest of New York City) was discovered, now known as the Apalachin Meeting.

The property was owned by gangster Joseph Barbara and the suspicious gathering of fancy cars and men in suits got the attention of a state trooper. Police surrounded the property and ended up detaining fifty-eight men, and for the first time there was indisputable

---

[4] Hall, Manly P. - *The Secret Destiny of America* page 53-54

[5] Hall, Manly P. - *The Secret Destiny of America* page 54

evidence that the Italian Mafia did, in fact, exist. Many of the men were suspected or wanted criminals who claimed they were just meeting for a weekend barbecue. Of course police had a decent idea of what was really going on and the Mafia began to be unmasked. Some of the men tried to flee into the nearby woods, but most were apprehended. "Don Vito" Genovese, the leader of the Genovese crime family, had organized the meeting to delegate various gambling, loansharking, and drug trafficking operations.

More shocking revelations were to come a few years later in 1963 when a mobster named Joe Valachi, who worked for Lucky Luciano and the Genovese Crime Family for 30 years, testified before the McClellan Congressional Committee on Organized Crime and revealed in detail many of the Mafia's operations. Valachi had hoped his testimony would help him avoid a death sentence for murder. His testimony shocked most people who could have never imagined how far-reaching the Mafia was, and how they regularly paid police and judges to look the other way. Joe Valachi's congressional testimony also introduced the world to the term La Cosa Nostra.

Many people wonder if the Illuminati Mafia actually call themselves "the Illuminati." I highly doubt it, although perhaps occasionally in jest. The Italian Mafia referred to themselves as La Cosa Nostra, which means "this thing of ours," or "our thing," so the Italian Mafia literally had no name. They didn't call each other up and say "hey we're having a Mafia meeting tonight, why don't you stop by?" No. They just said, "we have to do our thing" and they knew what each other meant. While you will learn, the Illuminati did at one time call themselves "the Illuminati," they have most likely abandoned this term long ago, and have expanded into various front groups to further their aims, and—like the Italian Mafia—speak in a language that is understood by each other, but doesn't betray its true meaning to outsiders.

Many scholars, reporters, and government officials say that conspiracies "never work" because "it's too difficult to keep a secret" and point to events like Watergate to justify their claims, but it's foolish to believe that every major conspiracy which is attempted is botched, or that word of it would leak out somehow. It's preposterous to assume that *every* group of conspirators are so foolish that they haven't planned plausible deniability for their actions to convolute any investigation to the point of confusion if any suspicion is aroused or if any outsiders were to take a closer look into their activities.

The Manhattan Project (the atomic bomb program) began in 1939 and was kept secret for six years until the world witnessed the mushroom cloud rising up from what was the Japanese city of Hiroshima in 1945. The project cost $2 billion dollars (adjusted for inflation, that's $26 billion in 2014 dollars) and 130,000 people worked on it in several different states,[6] making it the largest project in American history, but it was still completed in secret.

---

[6] http://energy.gov/management/office-management/operational-management/history/manhattan-project

Lieutenant Leslie Groves of the Army Corps of Engineers who directed the project would later reveal in his book *Now It Can Be Told: The True Story of the Manhattan Project,* that, "compartmentalization of knowledge, to me, was the very heart of security. My rule was simple and not capable of misinterpretation—each man should know everything he needed to know and do his job and nothing else."[7]

By giving different groups of scientists and engineers separate tasks and fabricating cover stories for what they were actually working on, those in the know were able to pull off their plan without any outsiders seeing the big picture. President Harry Truman, who was the Vice President under FDR, only became aware of the program after President Roosevelt's death in April of 1945, when Truman was then sworn in as his replacement—that's how well kept the secret was! Not even the vice president knew of this enormous and expensive life-altering plan! Four months after Truman was sworn in as president and let in on the secret, the bomb was dropped on the Japanese city of Hiroshima on August 6, 1945, and then three days later, the second one destroyed Nagasaki.

While enormous secrets can be kept by the political elite, they also sometimes leak out. The political elite often become arrogant because of their power and think they can get away with anything. How else could you explain John Edwards running for president in 2008, when he knew he had a newborn illegitimate child from

---

[7] Groves, Lesley - *Now it Can Be Told: The Story of the Manhattan Project* (1962) page 140

an affair with his campaign's photographer while his wife Elizabeth was dying of cancer? The Illuminati see themselves as the Gods of Mount Olympus, as literally having evolved into gods thanks to their occult knowledge, which often leads to arrogance and carelessness, causing some of their secrets to be revealed.

How did this "Illuminati" start, and how did they operate in the past, and more importantly, what are they doing right now? In short, the "priest class"—or what is considered to be the ancient Illuminati—dates back thousands of years to ancient Egypt and Greece, where Man's unfolding intellect was kept hidden from the general public and reserved for "the elect" or the "sages" in what were called Mystery Schools. These fraternities taught the various sciences and philosophies to the intellectual elite who benefitted tremendously from this knowledge. Many believe that at one time in the ancient past, the Mystery Schools had the best of intentions but were hijacked and taken over by selfish and wicked men who used their superior intellect, not to help mankind, but to take advantage of people, morphing the once noble fraternities into a Gnostic mafia of sorts, keeping the majority of humans in the dark about the true nature of reality.

33rd degree Freemason Manly P. Hall claims, "With the decline of virtue, which has preceded the destruction of every nation of history, the Mysteries became perverted. Sorcery took the place of the divine magic."[8] There is a belief in esoteric circles that God or Gods, or

---

[8] Hall, Manly P. – *The Secret Teachings of All Ages* page 40

extra-terrestrials, or even Satan, gave an ancient human (or small group of humans) some kind of secret knowledge, allowing him (or them) the ability to activate incredible powers latent in the mind, enabling them to become the first priests and kings. Many occultists believe this power can be traced back to the Atlanteans, the supposed demigods, who—according to the theory—are believed to have literally inhabited the Lost City of Atlantis.

These ideas, fraternities, and philosophies will be examined throughout this book. We'll look into dozens of interconnecting esoteric circles from the ancient Mystery Schools of the Eleusians and Dionysians to the Gnostics, the Knights Templar, Jesuits, Freemasons, Skull & Bones, Bilderberg Group, Bohemian Grove, the Federal Reserve, and many lesser-known, but critically important, pieces of the puzzle as well.

What are the facts and what is fiction? How did it all start? What is the evidence for the Illuminati's existence? What are their goals? Are they in communication with alien beings from another galaxy that secretly work with them and guide them in their evil ways? Are they themselves alien beings disguised as humans? You are about to find out as you dive head first *Inside the Illuminati.*

Early Evidence

When we talk about the Bavarian Illuminati, we're talking about the group that a man named Adam Weishaupt founded in Bavaria, a southern state in Germany, back in 1776. Specifically he founded it on May 1st 1776, which is called May Day or Walpurgis Night, a date celebrating an old meeting of witches and sorcerers. May Day is also a major Communist holiday that celebrates the "workers of the world." Almost 200 years after Adam Weishaupt ceremoniously founded the Illuminati on this day, Anton LaVey ritualistically shaved his head and founded the Church of Satan on May 1st 1966 as his way of celebrating this occult holiday.[9]

The Bavarian Illuminati was basically a reorganization and modernization of the corrupted ancient Mystery Schools. Weishaupt was a lawyer like so many corrupt politicians today, and in 1772 when he was twenty-four-years-old, he became a law professor at Ingolstadt University in Bavaria, Germany. A few years later he became the dean of the law department and began formulating his plan to launch the Illuminati.

He received his inspiration for forming his secret society from both the Rosicrucian manifestos and from the Jesuits (the zealous elite Catholic Society of Jesus founded in 1540). The Rosicrucian manifestos were books that first appeared in 1614 in Germany, and

---

[9] Baddeley, Gavin - *Lucifer Rising* page 71

described an "invisible brotherhood" dedicated to the pursuit of knowledge and Hermetic and alchemical magic. No such secret society actually existed, but the Rosicrucian manifestos planted the seeds for such a thing in men's minds, which was the author's purpose (although not the tyrannical kind of organization that Adam Weishaupt conceived).

Weishaupt used his position at the university to begin recruiting students and others to join him in his quest to overthrow the ruling monarchs of his day and install a global communist system with him and his inner circle of associates as the new rulers. Originally he called his group the Perfectabilists, meaning they aimed to "perfect" man by facilitating his "evolution," but the name Perfectabilists was quickly changed to the Illuminati to fit in with the "enlightenment" theme of the era, since Illuminati is Latin for "the enlightened ones." While he was growing increasingly successful at expanding his network and influence, it was only a matter of time before his secrets began to slowly leak out.

Original Writings Found

It's indisputable that original copies of Adam Weishaupt's writings were discovered and published for all to read. This is fully admitted in mainstream history books and encyclopedias, although few people care to take the time and actually look. Today, well over one hundred original documents are kept at the State Museum in Ingolstadt, Germany, where they are on public display.

Founder, Adam Weishaupt, wrote under the pseudonym "Spartacus" and all other members used pseudonyms as well, although many were identified after their letters were found and some defectors came forward. In 1784, eight years after the Illuminati were formed, a defector named Joseph Utzchneider gave a bunch of documents to Duchess Dowager Maria Anna, warning her of the organization and their goals of overthrowing the government and destroying religion. The Duchess, who was the sister-in-law of the Duke, handed them over to her brother-in-law Duke Karl Theodore, the leader of Bavaria.

A seemingly farfetched tale regarding the discovery of more original writings involves a story about how an Illuminati member was struck by lightning and killed, and when his body was examined the coroner discovered some documents that had been stuffed in a hidden pocket sewn into his clothes. Adam Weishaupt fled Bavaria in 1785 and headed to a neighboring province when he saw the writing on the wall that authorities were closing in on him. He and his friend Jakob Lanz were riding on horseback on their way to Regensburg when Lanz was struck by lightning and killed.[10]

While this story is so bizarre, it's understandable for people to dismiss it as a myth, but multiple historical sources report that this is exactly what happened.[11] But

---

[10] July 20th, 1785

[11] http://www.bavarian-illuminati.info/2008/11/lang-or-lanz-myths-about-the-myths/

regardless, a treasure trove of documents were also discovered by other means as well.

On October 11th 1786 police searched the home of Xavier von Zwack, located in the city of Landshut (45 miles from Ingolstadt), where they found over two hundred letters including membership lists, symbols, carvings used to fake various wax seals used by princes, nobles, clergymen, and merchants; instructions on counterfeiting, committing suicide, recipes for poison, an abortion tea, invisible ink, and instructions for building an explosive strongbox that would blow up and destroy everything inside if it was opened by someone who didn't know how to disarm it. One paper listed a method for filling a room full of a deadly gas in case they wanted to kill someone without getting their hands dirty.[12] These documents were soon published by the government in a report titled *Some Original Works of the Order of the Illuminati* [Einige Originalschriften Des Illuminaten Ordens in German].

The following year in 1787 police searched the castle of Baron de Bassus and discovered more papers which were then published as a *Supplement of Further Original Works*.[13] The next year in 1788 Johann Faber published *The Genuine Illuminati* [*Der ächte Illuminati*] which revealed the rituals for the Preparation, Novitiate Degree, Minerval Degree, the Minor and Major Illuminati Degrees.

---

[12] Robison, John – *Proofs of a Conspiracy* p. 79

[13] Full name: Thomas Maria Baron de Bassus

In 1789 a French journalist named Jean-Pierre-Louis de Luchet published a book titled *Essay on the Sect of the Illuminists* [*Essai sur la Secte des Illuminés*] which denounced the Illuminati and said they controlled Masonic lodges throughout Europe.

In 1794 Illuminati whistleblower Ludwig Adolf Christian von Grolmann published *The Latest Work Of Spartacus and Philo* (Weishaupt's and Baron von Knigge's code names) *[Die Neuesten Arbeiten Des Spartacus Und Philo]*, exposing the secrets of the Illuminati Dirigens degree (Scottish Knight degree) which appointed men to run Masonic lodges so they could recruit new members from within Freemasonry.

In 1797 a French Jesuit priest named Abbe Barruel published a series of books on the French Revolution because he believed it was the result of the Illuminati, saying, "The third conspiracy, which I am now about to investigate, is that of the atheistical Illuminati, which at my outfit I denominated the conspiracy of the Sophisters of Impiety and anarchy against every religion natural or revealed, not only against kings, but against every government, against all civil society, even against all property whatsoever."[14]

Barruel pondered, as others still do today, as to whether Weishaupt was the mastermind behind the conspiracy, or whether he was working with or for someone else. "It is not known, and it would be difficult to discover, whether Weishaupt ever had a master, or

---

[14] Barruel, Abbe – *Memoirs Illustrating the History of Jacobinism* Volume III page v

whether he is himself the great original of those monstrous doctrines on which he founded his school," he wrote.[15]

A man named John Robison, a science professor (called natural philosophy back then), living in Scotland published a lengthy book about the Illuminati in 1798 titled *Proofs of a Conspiracy*, which was one of the first books written in English about the organization. Before writing his book, he was actually asked to join them, but after looking into the group he realized he didn't want to have anything to do with them and then decided to write his book hoping to expose them. In *Proofs of a Conspiracy*, he also included English translations of many of the confiscated Illuminati papers.

Robison wrote that, "A collection of original papers and correspondence was found by searching the house of one Zwack (a member) in 1786. The following year a much larger collection was found at the house of Baron Bassus; and since that time Baron Knigge, the most active member next to Weishaupt, published an account of some of the higher degrees, which had been formed by himself."[16]

He warned, "An association has been formed for the express purpose of rooting out all the religious establishments and overturning all the existing governments of Europe. I have seen this association

---

[15] Barruel, Abbe – *Memoirs Illustrating the History of Jacobinism* Volume III page 5

[16] Robison, John – *Proofs of a Conspiracy* p. 76

exerting itself zealously and systematically, till it has become almost irresistible." He continued, "I have seen that this association still exists, still works in secret, and that not only several appearances among ourselves show that its emissaries are endeavoring to propagate their detestable doctrines among us, but that the association has Lodges in Britain corresponding with the mother Lodge at Munich ever since 1784."[17]

Original 5 Members

Adam Weishaupt   (codename: Spartacus)
Andreas Sutor   (Erasmus Rotero-damus)
Bauhof or Baubof   (Agathon)
Franz Anton von Massenhause (Ajax)
Max Elder von Merz (Tiberius)

Primary Goals

The original top five goals of the Illuminati were: 1) Abolish the Monarchy and replace all governments. 2) Abolish private property and inheritance. 3) Abolish patriotism along with people's national identity and national pride. 4) Abolish the family, marriage, morality, and then have the government raise and indoctrinate the children. 5) Abolish all religion. These are basically the same goals that would be outlined around seventy years later in the Communist Manifesto (1848) and make up the

---

[17] Robison, John - *Proofs of a Conspiracy* page 7.

foundation of communism since Weishaupt no doubt inspired Karl Marx. More on this later.

More modern goals include a universal one world digital currency; a Big Brother Orwellian surveillance state; the elimination of the second Amendment and ending citizens' gun ownership (leaving only police and military to be armed); implementing an all-powerful nanny state socialist government; all leading up to the unveiling of a "messiah" who will claim to be God and offer people eternal life here on earth, saying he has "restored mankind" to our "pre-fallen" state so we can live forever through the use of cybernetic Transhuman technology on the new "Heaven on earth" he has created.[18]

Deposition for the Court

In 1785 three former members, Joseph Utzschneider, George Grunberger, and Johann Cosandey wrote out a joint deposition for the court where they provided information about some of the Illuminati's goals and philosophies that men in the first few degrees were taught. First of all, "The Illuminee who wishes to rise to the highest degree must be free from all religion; for a *religionist* (as they call every man who has any religion) will never be admitted to the highest degrees."[19]

---

[18] See my previous book, *The New World Order: Facts & Fiction*

[19] Barruel, Abbe -*Memoirs Illustrating the History of Jacobinism* page 685

The second principle revealed to the initiates was that the ends justify the means. "The welfare of the Order will be a justification for calumnies [defamatory statements], poisonings, assassinations, perjuries, treasons, rebellions —in short, for all that the prejudices of men lead them to call crimes.   One must be more submissive to the Superiors of the Illuminati, than to the sovereigns or magistrates who govern the people; and he that gives the preference to sovereigns or governors of the people is useless to us.   Honor, life, and fortune, all are to be sacrificed to the Superiors. The governors of nations are despots when they are not directed by us. They can have no authority over us, who are free men."[20]

What they called the Patet Exitus, or the "doctrine of suicide," was also taught as an honorable way anyone who was caught could escape prosecution and prevent themselves from revealing the Order's secrets.

Thirdly, the deposition revealed, "The Superiors of the Illuminati are to be looked upon as the most perfect and the most enlightened of men; no doubts are to be entertained even of their infallibility."[21]

"It is in these moral and political principles that the Illuminati are educated in the lower degrees; and it is according to the manner in which they imbibe [assimilate] them and show their devotion to the Order, or are able to

---

[20] Ibid

[21] Barruel, Abbe - *Memoirs Illustrating the History of Jacobinism* page 687

second its views, that they are earlier or later admitted to the higher degrees."[22]

"In consequence of our acquaintance with this doctrine of the Illuminati, with their conduct, their manners, and their incitements to treason, and being fully convinced of the dangers of the Sect, we the Aulic Counsellor Utzschneider and the Priest Dillis left the Order. The Professor Grünberger, the Priest Cosandey, Renner, and Zaupfer, did the same a week after."

Their testimony continues, "It [the Illuminati] spread through almost every province under the cloak of Freemasonry; because it sows division and discord between parents and their children, between Princes and their subjects, and among the most sincere friends; because on all important occasions it would install partiality on the seats of justice and in the councils, as it always prefers the welfare of the Order to that of the state, and the interests of its adepts to those of the profane."[23]

"Experience had convinced us, that they would soon succeed in perverting all the Bavarian youth. The leading feature in the generality of their adepts were irreligion, depravity of morals, disobedience to their Prince and to their parents, and the neglect of all useful studies. We saw that the fatal consequence of Illuminism would be, to create a general distrust between the prince and his subjects, the father and his children, the minister and his

---

[22] Ibid.

[23] Ibid

secretaries, and between the different tribunals and councils."[24]

"We abandoned, one after the other, this Sect [the Illuminati], which under different names, as we have been informed by several of our former Brethren, has already spread itself in Italy, and particularly at Venice, in Austria, in Holland, in Saxony, on the Rhine, particularly at Frankfort, and even as far as America. The Illuminati meddle as much as possible in state affairs, and excite troubles wherever their Order can be benefited by them."[25]

"After we had retired from the Order, the Illuminati calumniated us on all sides in the most infamous manner. Their cabal made us fail in every request we presented; succeeding in rendering us hateful and odious to our superiors, they even carried their calumnies [defamatory statements] so far as to pretend that one of us had committed murder."[26]

---

[24] Ibid.

[25] Barruel, Abbe - *Memoirs Illustrating the History of Jacobinism* page 687-688

[26] Barruel, Abbe - *Memoirs Illustrating the History of Jacobinism* page 688

Original Illuminati Structure

The Nursery (Entry Level)

Preparatory Literary Essay

Novitiate (Novice)
Minerval (Brethren of Minerva, Academy
of Illuminism)
Illuminatus Minor

Symbolic Freemasonry

Apprentice
Fellow Craft
Master
Scots Major Illuminatus
Scots Illuminatus Dirigens (Directory)

The Mysteries (Higher Level)

Lesser

Presbyter, Priest
Prince or Regent

Greater

Magus
Rex or King

The 1st Edict Against the Illuminati

An edict is an act of law issued by a monarchy, (much like an executive order issued by a president today) and on June 22, 1784, Duke Karl Theodore, the Elector of Bavaria [the ruler of the state], issued the first edict against the Illuminati after his sister-in-law Duchess Dowagar Maria Anna was given some documents by an early defector named Joseph Utzschneider, and then passed them onto the Duke.[27]

The edict reads, in part, "Whereas all communities, societies and associations without approval from a public authority and the confirmation of the Monarch are illegal, prohibited by law, suspect and dangerous things in [and] of themselves. His Electoral Highness [the Duke] has decided not to tolerate them in his State, whatever their designation and interior constitutions, ordering categorically…one and all subjects to withdraw from any association or secret assembly of this kind…those societies [have] drawn the attention of the public and awakened its fears…"[28]

---

[27] Stauffer, Vernon - *New England and the Bavarian Illuminati* page 176

[28] Rene, Le Forestier - *Les Illuminés de Bavière et la franc-maçonnerie allemande* page 453 [Paris: 1914], Arche reprint, 2001. (Quote translated in English in *Perfectabilists: The 18th Century Bavarian Order of the Illuminati* by Terry Melanson page 27)

The 2nd Edict Against the Illuminati

The following year in 1785, Duke Karl Theodore issued a second edict, which was much more threatening and specifically named the Illuminati and Freemasonry as the perpetrators of a conspiracy against the government. In this edict the Duke also announced that if anyone were to come forward and reveal who was involved or specifically which masonic lodges had been infiltrated and were being used in this conspiracy—that informant could remain anonymous and even keep half the money that was confiscated as a result of their confession. The other half [of the money], the edict said, would be given to the poor.

It reads in part, "We [the government]...have been deeply affected and displeased to learn that the various Lodges of so-called Freemasons and Illuminati, who are still in our States, have taken so little heed of our General Prohibition issued on June 22nd of last year against all fraternal societies clandestine and unapproved, as to not only continue to hold meetings in secret, but to raise funds, and to recruit new members, seeking to further increase the already large numbers of adepts."[29]

It continues, "We had deemed this society, very much degenerated and of primitive institution, too suspect, both as regards to religious concerns and from a social and political point of view, so that we could no longer tolerate

---

[29] Rene, Le Forestier - *Les Illuminés de Bavière et la franc-maçonnerie allemande* page 468-469 [Paris: 1914], Arche reprint, 2001. (Translated in English in *Perfectabilists: The 18th Century Bavarian Order of the Illuminati* by Terry Melanson page 29)

it in our States…we command that all authorities must execute our orders exactly and secretly inform us of any disobedience. We declare that all money and any funds collected illegally [by the lodges] shall be confiscated [and] half will be given to the poor, while the other half will go to the denunciator [informant], even if he is a member of one of those societies, with a promise to keep his name confidential."[30]

The edict concludes, "We hope that each of our subjects value enough of our favor and his own honor and happiness so that everywhere we can count on due obedience to our orders and be excused from having to take more severe measures."[31]

The 3rd Edict Against the Illuminati

On August 16, 1787, not long after the castle of Baron de Bassus was searched, where more papers were discovered, the third edict against the Illuminati was issued by the Duke of Bavaria saying the penalty would be death for any Illuminati members discovered meeting or recruiting anyone to join them. "Any so charged and

---

[30] Rene, Le Forestier - *Les Illuminés de Bavière et la franc-maçonnerie allemande* page 468-469 [Paris: 1914], Arche reprint, 2001. (Translated to English in *Perfectabilists: The 18th Century Bavarian Order of the Illuminati* by Terry Melanson page 29)

[31] Rene, Le Forestier - *Les Illuminés de Bavière et la franc-maçonnerie allemande* page 468-469 [Paris: 1914], Arche reprint, 2001. (Translated to English in *Perfectabilists: The 18th Century Bavarian Order of the Illuminati* by Terry Melanson page 29)

found guilty are to be deprived of their lives by the sword; while those thus recruited are to have their goods confiscated and themselves to be condemned to perpetual banishment from the territories of the Duke. Under the same penalties of confiscation and banishment, the members of the order, no matter under what name or circumstances, regular or irregular, they should gather, are forbidden to assemble as lodges."[32]

"As more time passes it is further realized how harmful and dangerous the Order of the Illuminati will be for the State and religion if allowed to flourish here and beyond. It is impossible to predict the deplorable effects that would result for posterity if we stand back, if not handled very seriously while there is still time to forcefully eradicate a disease which is far more daunting than the plague itself."[33]

"...for the recruiter he is to be deprived of life by the sword, and for the recruited he will be sentenced to have his property confiscated and banished for life from all States of His Electoral Highness, with a promise of never being allowed to return. Under the same penalties of forfeiture and expulsion, the prohibited Lodges of the

---

[32] Rene, Le Forestier - *Les Illuminés de Bavière et la franc-maçonnerie allemande* page *507-508* [Paris: 1914], Arche reprint, 2001. (Translated to English in *Perfectabilists: The 18th Century Bavarian Order of the Illuminati* by Terry Melanson page 40)

[33] Rene, Le Forestier - *Les Illuminés de Bavière et la franc-maçonnerie allemande* page 507-508 [Paris: 1914], Arche reprint, 2001,pp 507-508. (Translated to English in *Perfectabilists: The 18th Century Bavarian Order of the Illuminati* by Terry Melanson page 40)

Illuminati, under whatever name they may hide and carefully present themselves, in all places, must be subject to rigorous surveillance. Those in lodge attire will be held and treated as if they had attended meetings in secret, in suspect places such as hotels or particular houses, and we will not allow the futile excuse usually given—an honest society of good friends—especially when those present have already been suspected of impiety and Illuminism."[34]

The 4th Edict Against the Illuminati

Most mainstream sources (including the often inaccurate and completely unreliable Wikipedia) claim that shortly after the third edict was issued in 1787, the Illuminati were completely irradiated and weren't much of a concern after that. The problem is—the Duke of Bavaria actually issued a *fourth* edict a few years later in 1790 saying that the Illuminati was not only still active but were continuing to recruit new members!

On November 15, 1790, the following announcement against the Illuminati was issued by the Duke, saying, "The Elector has learned, partly by the spontaneous confession of some members, party by sound intelligence, that despite the Edicts of July 14, 1784 and August 16th 1785 (and in the same month in 1787), the Illuminati still

---

[34] Rene, Le Forestier - *Les Illuminés de Bavière et la franc-maçonnerie allemande* page 507-508 [Paris: 1914], Arche reprint, 2001 pp 507-508. (Translated to English in *Perfectabilists: The 18th Century Bavarian Order of the Illuminati* by Terry Melanson page 40)

hold, albeit in smaller numbers, secret meetings through the Electorate, but especially in Munich and the surrounding area; they continue to attract young men to the cause and have maintained a correspondence with [secret] societies and with members in other countries."[35]

It goes on, "They continue to attack the State and especially religion, either verbally or through pamphlets...Every speech, every printed book or manuscript against religion and the state must be reported to the authorities or the Elector [Duke] himself, as well as any secret meetings. Those who have remained silent on these issues, having indeed been proven to have possessed information, will be severely punished. The denunciator, even if he was an accessory to the crime, will receive a cash reward along with the other, and his identity will be kept confidential."[36]

The fourth edict clearly warns, "Any member who has assisted in a secret meeting, has recruited new members or corresponded with [secret] societies or brothers in other countries, will be mercilessly punished by death. Any civil servant or [those in the] military, any holder of a beneficial office, a parish priest, etc., must swear that he

---

[35] Rene, Le Forestier - *Les Illuminés de Bavière et la franc-maçonnerie allemande* page 614-615 [Paris: 1914], Arche reprint, 2001. (Translated to English in *Perfectabilists: The 18th Century Bavarian Order of the Illuminati* by Terry Melanson page 56)

[36] Rene, Le Forestier - *Les Illuminés de Bavière et la franc-maçonnerie allemande* page 614-615 [Paris: 1914], Arche reprint, 2001. (Translated to English in *Perfectabilists: The 18th Century Bavarian Order of the Illuminati* by Terry Melanson page 56)

has not and will never form a part of the sect or they'll be convicted of perjury and shall be punished accordingly."[37]

Taking Over the Government

One of the original Illuminati defectors named Joseph von Utzschneider, who gave a deposition to the court about the Illuminati plans, warned that they planned to "introduce a worldwide moral regime which would be under their control in every country. This council would decide on all matters concerning pardons, appointments and promotions, as well as rejections...This would give it the unlimited right to pronounce final judgment over the honesty and usefulness of an individual."[38]

The confiscated correspondence between members confirms this allegation. One of the letters reads, "The Order must possess the power of life and death in consequence of our oath; and with propriety, for the same reason, and by the same right, that any government in the world possesses it—for the Order comes in their place, making them unnecessary. When things cannot be otherwise, and ruin would ensue if the association did not employ this mean, the Order must, as well as public

---

[37] Rene, Le Forestier - *Les Illuminés de Bavière et la franc-maçonnerie allemande* page 614-615 [Paris: 1914], Arche reprint, 2001. (Translated to English in *Perfectabilists: The 18th Century Bavarian Order of the Illuminati* by Terry Melanson page 56)

[38] Koselleck, Reinhart - *Critique and Crisis: Enlightenment and the Pathogenesis of Modern Society* Cambridge, Mass MIT Press (1988) page 92-32

rulers, employ it for the good of mankind; therefore for its own preservation."[39]

Many letters clearly revealed their intent to deceive people in order to "insure their happiness."[40] Weishaupt's megalomaniacal goals of world domination become clear with such statements as, "the Order will, for its own sake, and therefore certainly, place every man in that situation in which he can be most effective. The pupils are convinced that the Order *will* rule the world. Every member therefore becomes a ruler."[41]

"The great strength of our Order lies in its concealment; let it never appear in any place in its own name, but always covered by another name, and another occupation."[42] This has effectively happened with private organizations like the Council on Foreign Relations, the Bilderberg Group, and the Federal Reserve—basically taking over the key power centers in society. It must be pointed out that the Founding Fathers of America wrote down their grievances with the Monarch in the Declaration of Independence and 56 men signed their names to it and sent it off to the king of England. They didn't hide their intentions or deceive people hoping to further their aims. They were open and honest about their beliefs, tactics, and goals—unlike Weishaupt and the

---

[39] Robison, John – *Proofs of a Conspiracy* p. 124-125

[40] Robison, John – *Proofs of a Conspiracy* p. 134

[41] Robison, John – *Proofs of a Conspiracy* p. 123

[42] Robison, John – *Proofs of a Conspiracy* p. 112

Illuminati—who used deception and fraud as a standard practice.

Similarly, when theologian Martin Luther opposed the tyrannical control of the Catholic Church over 250 years before Weishaupt, he wrote down his grievances and nailed them on the front door of his local church in 1517. He didn't lie or deceive anyone about his hopes of breaking the Catholic Church's stranglehold on society, but fellow German, Adam Weishaupt, was power-hungry himself, and instead of wanting to free society from the tyranny of the Jesuits and the Catholic Church, he wanted to be the tyrant himself.

Inducting New Members

Various venues were used for recruiting new members. Once someone expressed interest to a current member about his desire to overthrow the monarch, that person was "carefully observed in silence," and if, after consideration by the council, "the Novice" as they were called, were thought to be a possible asset, he would be appointed a mentor and invited to a conference.[43]

One correspondence between members reads, "I shall therefore press the cultivation of science, especially such sciences as may have an influence on our reception in the world; and may serve to remove obstacles out of the way...Only those who are assuredly proper subjects shall be picked out from among the inferior classes for the

---

[43] Robison, John – *Proofs of a Conspiracy* p. 66

higher mysteries…And in particular, every person shall be made a spy on another and on all around him."[44]

Once given initial approval by the council, the Novice would be shown "certain portions" of the goals and rules of the Order and was instructed to give a weekly account in writing of his progress in carrying out his directives. At this point he was not allowed to take physical possession of any material and had to read it in the Mentor's house just to make sure they wouldn't turn it over to authorities, giving them concrete evidence of the conspiracy.[45]

High level member Baron Von Knigge would later admit, "As a rule, under the veil of secrecy, dangerous plans and harmful teachings can be accepted just as well as noble intentions and profound knowledge; because not all members themselves are informed of such depraved intentions, which sometimes tend to lie hidden beneath the beautiful facade…because for the most part, unknown superiors lie in ambush and it is unworthy of an intelligence man to work according to a plan, which he does not fully see."[46]

Another original correspondence brags, "Nothing can escape our sight; by these means we shall readily discover

---

[44] Robison, John – *Proofs of a Conspiracy* p. 77

[45] Robison, John – *Proofs of a Conspiracy* p. 67

[46] Quoted in Steven Luckert, *Jesuits, Freemasons, Illuminati and Jacobins: Conspiracy theories, secret societies and politics in late eighteenth-century Germany*, Ph.D dissertation, State University of New York at Binghamton, pages 285-286.

who are contented, and receive with relish the peculiar state-doctrines and religious opinions that are laid before them; and, at last, the trustworthy alone will be admitted to a participation of the whole maxims and political constitution of the Order...In a council composed of such members we shall labor at the creation of means to drive by degrees the enemies of reason and of humanity out of the world, and to establish a peculiar morality and religion fitted for the great society of mankind."[47]

In perhaps the most sinister initiation to the higher levels, a prospect was told they had to show their loyalty to the Illuminati by killing someone who betrayed the Order. The candidate was taken before a man bound and gagged who was said to have betrayed their oaths and then handed a knife and blindfolded before being positioned in front of the supposed traitor who they were then ordered to stab. Once the prospect stabbed the "person" in front of them, the blindfold was removed to reveal that the "traitor" had been swapped with a sheep, and the entire charade was a test of their loyalty.[48]

If the candidate refused to carry out the "murder" of the supposed "traitor," then they were told they passed the test anyway but were then never allowed to proceed to a higher level and never trusted with any deeper secrets because they had shown they wouldn't kill for the Order.

---

[47] Robison, John – *Proofs of a Conspiracy* p. 77

[48] Robison, John – *Proofs of a Conspiracy* page 224

Contingency Plans if Discovered

A lot of people claim that because some Illuminati members were discovered and many of their writings published, that they simply gave up and ceased to exist from that point on, but common sense, the Duke of Bavaria's 4th Edict, and the Illuminati's own writings suggests otherwise. Weishaupt wrote, "By this plan we shall direct all mankind. In this manner, and by the simplest means, we shall set all in motion and in flames. The occupations must be so allotted and contrived, that we may, in secret, influence all political transactions...I have considered everything, and so prepared it, that if the Order should this day go to ruin, I shall in a year re-establish it more brilliant than ever."[49]

"There must not be a single purpose that ever comes in sight that is ambiguous, and that may betray our aims against religion and the State. One must speak sometimes one way and sometimes another, but so as never to contradict ourselves, and so that, with respect to our true way of thinking, we may be impenetrable."[50]

"This can be done in no other way but by secret associations, which will by degrees, and in silence, possess themselves of the government of the States, and make use of those means for this purpose."[51]

---

[49] Robison, John - *Proofs of a Conspiracy* p. 84

[50] Robison, John – *Proofs of a Conspiracy* p. 85

[51] Robison, John – *Proofs of a Conspiracy* p. 106

Shortly after the Illuminati were discovered, and believed by many to have been destroyed, Joseph Willard, President of Harvard University, warned, "There is sufficient evidence that a number of societies of the Illuminati have been established in this land of Gospel light and civil liberty, which were first organized from the grand society, in France. They are doubtless secretly striving to undermine all our ancient institutions, civil and sacred. These societies are closely leagued with those of the same Order in Europe; they have all the same object in view. The enemies of all order are seeking our ruin. Should infidelity generally prevail, our independence would fall of course. Our republican government would be annihilated."[52]

Willard was just one of many Americans, including George Washington, who believed the Illuminati survived the intended purge and continued to work under the cover of Freemasonry and other organizations.

The Eradication of Christianity

Unlike theologian Martin Luther who famously nailed his ninety-five grievances on the door of the Castle Church of Wittenberg, Germany in 1517, thus starting the Protestant Reformation with the hopes of ending the Catholic Church's hold on power and their corrupt un-

---

[52] A Sermon Preached in Lancaster ... on the Anniversary of Our National Independence ... Before the Washington Benevolent Societies of Lancaster and Guildhall (Windsor, Vermont: Thomas M. Pomroy, 1812), pp. 14–15 (July 4, 1812)

Christian practices and perversion of Jesus' message—Adam Weishaupt didn't appreciate Christianity at all, and instead wanted it completely destroyed. Despite his strong differences with the Church, Martin Luther still respected Jesus and his teachings and simply wanted to reform the Church, but Weishaupt wanted the Church *and* Christianity entirely eradicated.

John Robison wrote, "It surely needs little argument now to prove that the Order of Illuminati had for its immediate object the abolishing of Christianity (at least this was the intention of the Founder) with the sole view of overturning the civil government, by introducing universal dissoluteness and profligacy [reckless] manners, and then getting the assistance of the corrupted subjects to oversee the throne. The whole conduct in the preparation and instruction of the Presbyter and Regens [degrees] is directed to this point."[53]

Another letter written by Baron von Knigge said, "I have been at unwearied pains to remove the fears of some who imagine that our Superiors want to abolish Christianity; but by and by their prejudices will wear off, and they will be more at their ease." He goes on to write that he made sure not to let them know that "our General [Weishaupt] holds all Religion to be a lie, and uses even Deism, only to lead men by the nose."[54]

Weishaupt explains, "But I assure you this is no small affair; a new religion, and a new state-government, which

---

[53] Robison, John – *Proofs of a Conspiracy* p. 124

[54] Robison, John – *Proofs of a Conspiracy* p. 124

so happily explain one and all of these symbols, and combines them in one degree, you may think that this is my chief work; but I have three other degrees, all different, for my class of higher mysteries; in comparison with which this is but child's play."[55]

Weishaupt even boasts, "Who would imagine that I was to be the founder of a new religion,"[56] and continues, "We must, first gradually explain away all our preparatory pious frauds. And when persons of discernment find fault, we must desire them to consider the end of all our labor…Second, we must unfold, from history and other writings, the origin and fabrication of all religious lies; and then, third; we give a critical history of the Order."[57]

The plan to destroy Christianity can clearly be seen today with the liberal media and the gay mafia pushing homosexuality in everyone's face and then accusing Christians of "hate speech" and "bigotry" if they simply disagree with gay marriage or homosexual couples adopting children. There is clearly a double standard in the mainstream media in terms of what is considered "hate speech" because when popular musicians or liberal political commentators spew hateful anti-Christian rhetoric on a continuous basis, such vicious attacks are touted as "justifiable payback" for the Inquisition hundreds of years ago. Imagine if major media figures

---

[55] Robison, John – *Proofs of a Conspiracy* p. 85

[56] Robison, John – *Proofs of a Conspiracy* p. 86

[57] Robison, John – *Proofs of a Conspiracy* p. 89

were to make the same vicious statements about Jews as they do Christians. Their careers would be over before the end of the day and they would be forever branded an "anti-Semite" and never work again.

A popular reverend named Jedediah Morse preached a series of sermons between 1798 and 1799 in New England where he warned about the Illuminati's assault on Christianity in Boston and the surrounding area, saying, "Practically all of the civil and ecclesiastical establishments of Europe have already been shaken to their foundations by this terrible organization; the French Revolution itself is doubtless to be traced to its machinations; the successes of the French armies are to be explained on the same ground. The Jacobins are nothing more nor less than the open manifestation of the hidden system of the Illuminati. The Order has its branches established and its emissaries at work in America. The affiliated Jacobin Societies in America have doubtless had as the object of their establishment the propagation of the principles of the illuminated mother club in France...I hold it a duty, my brethren, which I owe to God, to the cause of religion, to my country and to you, at this time, to declare to you, thus honestly and faithfully, these truths. My only aim is to awaken you and myself a due attention, at this alarming period, to our dearest interests. As a faithful watchman I would give you warning of your present danger."[58]

---

[58] Morse, Jedediah, A Sermon Exhibiting the Present Dangers, and Consequent Duties of the Citizens of the United States of America Delivered in Charlestown, 1799

Regardless of your personal religious beliefs, you must admit that Christians have been (and continue to be) the primary opposition to the Illuminati and the New World Order, (not to mention the coming Mark of the Beast), and are the final obstacle standing between the Illuminati and their remaining goals. Christians have long warned about the "satanic conspiracy" being perpetuated by the Illuminati and have been on the front lines of the culture war being waged by Hollywood, which aims to destroy what little morality remains in society.

Using Feminism to Breakdown Families

Since one of the Illuminati's original goals was to break up the traditional family unit so children would be raised and indoctrinated by the government, they planned on manipulating women through what would later be known as feminism, encouraging them to rebel against their duties of domestic management and motherhood.

"There is no way of influencing men so powerfully as by means of the women," the original writings read. "These should therefore be our chief study; we should insinuate ourselves into their good opinion, give them hints of emancipation from the tyranny of public opinion, and of standing up for themselves; it will be an immense relief to their enslaved minds to be freed from any one bond of restraint, and it will fire them the more, and cause them to work for us with zeal, without knowing that they do so; for they will only be indulging their own desire of personal admiration."[59]

What this means is they planned on transforming women into self-centered, narcissistic, pleasure seeking sluts, and promote this behavior under the banner of "freedom," so instead of raising their children and keeping their families in balance, they would have the government raise their kids while turning against their husbands and disrupt the family unit in hopes of redirecting people's loyalty and love to the State instead of each other.

In more modern times this same method has been applied to promote the feminist movement in the 1970s through the creation of Ms. Magazine and the push to demonize stay-at-home moms. Kim Kardashian and other skilless skanks are promoted as role models even though they have no real value, and are worthless and talentless false idols advertised by the mainstream media as modern day royalty. The hypocrisy of feminism is astounding. For example, feminists who cry about sexism and the "culturally programed gender roles" only want to give up the roles society expects of *them*, while still demanding men to continue following theirs.

Women who whine about "equal rights" still expect men to always pay for dates and buy them expensive gifts. Women who don't feel it's their duty to know how to cook still feel men should fix things around the house and diagnose their car problems. And of course, feminist women who proclaim they want to end the gender roles

[59] Robison, John – *Proofs of a Conspiracy* p. 111

still expect their man to cough up thousands of dollars on a diamond engagement ring when the courtship is on the road to marriage. Feminism is a one-way hypocritical double standard street that not only targets men, but also other women who resist giving in to this cultural Marxism.

Mothers who choose to be stay-at-home moms and raise their own children or who enjoy cooking for their family are labeled "victims" of a "male-dominated ideology." Feminism pressures women to turn their children over to daycare centers and trade in working around the home for being stuck in a cubicle sitting in front of a computer all day. Feminism has led to an entire generation being raised in single parent homes with many mothers turning to government assistance, costing the taxpayers countless dollars—not to mention tens of millions of children growing up without the guidance and supervision of two parents.

Adam Weishaupt himself was an unfaithful husband who actually impregnated his wife's sister, which he revealed in one of his correspondences. In hopes of killing the baby to hide his adulterous behavior he gave his sister-in-law an "abortion tea," and it appears from his letter about the issue that he also repeatedly punched his mistress in the stomach hoping to abort the child.

"I am now in the most embarrassing situation; it robs me of all rest, and makes me unfit for everything. I am in danger of losing at once my honor and my reputation, by which I have long had such influence. What think you— my sister-in-law is with child," he wrote.

He continues, "We have tried every method in our power to destroy the child; and I hope she is determined on everything—even d — [believed to mean *death*]. But alas! Euriphon is, I fear, too timid. Alas! poor woman, thou art now under the *disciplina arcani* [the Discipline of the Secret] and I see no other expedient [convenient yet immoral way]."[60]

Using Schools to Indoctrinate the Youth

Tyrants throughout history have known that if they are to effectively maintain their power they must indoctrinate the youth with their brand of propaganda to ensure as the children come of age, they will blindly support the leader and his ideologies. Adolf Hitler used the Nazi Youth program to brainwash children beginning at a young age; the Taliban in Afghanistan banned girls from going to school at all to keep them ignorant; and North Korea's strict control of their education system are just a few examples of this in our modern era.

"We must win the common people in every corner," the original Illuminati writings read. "This will be obtained chiefly by means of the schools, and by open, hearty behavior, show, condescension, popularity, and toleration of their prejudices, which we shall at leisure root out and dispel."[61]

---

[60] Robison, John – *Proofs of a Conspiracy* p. 94

[61] Robison, John – *Proofs of a Conspiracy* p. 111

The indoctrination of students by the public school system is clear today with programs like Common Core and the promotion of the Big Government nanny state and the gay lifestyle while demonizing the second Amendment right to bear arms and belief in God. Being a Christian in public schools is not only frowned upon, but out right ridiculed, and favorably mentioning the word "God" or "Jesus" has basically been banned.[62]

Charlotte Iserbyt who was the head of policy at the Department of Education during the Reagan administration discovered how tax-exempt foundations were shaping the American education system to eliminate critical thinking and innovation by turning students into zombies who only regurgitate what they're told. She published her findings in her book *The Deliberate Dumbing Down of America.* Iserbyt and others assert that Skull & Bones runs the Department of Education, which dictates what is taught to the kids. Skull & Bones also controls the American Historical Association which dictates the "official" version of American history by carefully crafting an often one-sided and biased view of what really happened.

While the vast majority of students who attend public schools are primarily concerned with the latest teen idol, their favorite professional sports teams, or simply getting drunk and high, children of the elite are taught team building, networking skills, and other tools to prepare

---

[62] *Fox News* "School: We Have a Right To Ban God" by Todd Starnes (July 11th 2014)

them to rapidly advance up the social hierarchy once they enter the "real world."

Philips Exeter Academy is just one example of a private boarding school which was set up for the children of the elite to prepare them for life in the upper class. The Illuminati has largely funded this school and used it to educate their children and prepare them for their duties later in life. In 1930 Edward Harkness (a member of Skull & Bones' sister organization Wolf's Head) donated $5.8 million dollars to the school under the condition that their method of teaching students would change to what he called the Aristotelian method of antiquity.[63] Harkness was the second largest shareholder in Rockefeller's Standard Oil in the early 1900s and was in John D. Rockefeller's inner circle.

The Rockefeller family has been one of the most powerful Illuminati families for generations and the "Aristotelean method of antiquity" that Edward Harkness paid to implement at Philips Exeter Academy was based on the ideology of the Greek philosopher Aristotle (a student of Plato) who believed that most people were too stupid to govern themselves, and that society should be structured in a way that "philosopher kings" should rule and decide what was best for the people.

Controlling the Media

Weishaupt knew the power of information, and back in his time there was obviously no television, radios or

---

[63] http://www.exeter.edu/admissions/109_1220_11688.aspx

Internet, but there were books, libraries, and reading clubs, and he knew how important it was to control them if he wanted to manage what information reached the minds of the public. In one correspondence he wrote, "By establishing reading societies, and subscription libraries, and taking these under our direction, and supplying them through our labors, we may turn the public mind which way we will."[64] [*Which way we will*, meaning the direction they desired.]

He goes on to write, "In like manner we must try to obtain an influence in the military academies (this may be of mighty consequence); the printing-houses, booksellers shops, chapters, and in short in all offices which have any effect, either in forming, or in managing, or even in directing the mind of man."[65]

Another letter written by a different member identified as Cato [real name Xaver von Zwack] points out, "We get all the literary journals. We take care, by well-timed pieces [articles], to make the citizens and the Princes a little more noticed for certain little slips."[66] What this means is they planned to use the newspapers to attack their enemies. "A little more noticed for certain little slips" means to highlight and reinforce anything officials have said or done that can be used against them.

---

[64] Robison, John – *Proofs of a Conspiracy* p. 112

[65] Ibid.

[66] Robison, John – *Proofs of a Conspiracy* p. 113

Author Terry Melanson explains in his excellent book, *Pefectibilists*, that, "Without having to ascend a series of initiations and meaningless rituals—such as those of Freemasonry and Rosicrucianism—like-minded individuals could gather in reading societies, form an intellectual social circle, and discuss the literature of the Enlightenment and the politics of the day. Those who directed these societies had control of the material being read and discussed. It became a perfect vehicle to instill radical or subversive views."[67]

Today, much of the American mainstream media and other outlets in countries around the world are under the control of the government. In some countries the State-controlled television is clearly evident, but in places like America such control is done more covertly, leading many to believe that it is a "free and independent" press. In 1975 a congressional investigation discovered the CIA had virtually every editor from the major news outlets in their pocket.[68] The Church Hearings, as they were called, uncovered the government was spending a billion dollars a year (in 2014 dollars) to secretly pay editors and reporters to work as gatekeepers and propagandists for the

[67] Melanson, Terry - *Perfectibilists: The 18th Century Bavarian Illuminati* page 60

[68] Final Report of the Select Committee to Study Government Operations With Respect to Intelligence Activities. April 1976. pp. 191–201

establishment.[69]   The program was dubbed Operation Mockingbird.

Of course, after it was exposed, the CIA claimed to have ended their media manipulation, which is a laughable lie. Even the former President of CBS, Sig Mickeson, admitted that CIA continued to maintain relationships with top media figures, "…but because of all the revelations of the period of the 1970s, it seems to me a reporter has to be a lot more circumspect when doing it now or he runs the risk of at least being looked at with considerable disfavor by the public. I think you've got to be much more careful about it."[70]   In more recent times, the Operation Mockingbird program has been adapted to social media as well.

President Obama appointed a Harvard Law professor named Cass Sunstein to a cabinet level position in order to set up countless fake social media accounts and "troll" the comments section of news articles, YouTube videos, and Facebook pages in attempts to discredit news stories the White House thought were damaging to the establishment.[71]   One of Edward Snowden's leaks

[69] Final Report of the Select Committee to Study Government Operations With Respect to Intelligence Activities. April 1976. pp. 191–201

[70] *YouTube* "CIA Admits Using News To Manipulate the USA" (1975)

[71] Sunstein, Cass R & Vermeule, Adrian "Conspiracy Theories: Causes and Cures" 17 Journal of Political Philsophy 202 (2008) page 22

revealed that the NSA took things even further by having paid trolls harass and defame people online who the establishment thought were causing too much trouble for the government's well-controlled narrative in attempts to erode their credibility and fan base.[72]

The NSA also developed technology to spoof e-mails, SMS messages, inflate or deflate the view count on YouTube videos, adjust the ranking of websites, manipulate the outcome of online polls, or simply shut down someone's social media presence all together for phony "terms of service" violations.[73]

For decades both the Pentagon and the CIA have had entire divisions dedicated to working with Hollywood in order to literally help produce major television shows and movies. When studios want access to expensive military equipment like aircraft and tanks or actual Army bases, they approach these government television and film liaisons and if the storyline is seen as portraying a current war or a particular military branch or government agency in a favorable light, then the projects are approved and producers are given access to consultants, equipment, uniforms, military bases, and even given active duty servicemen and women to work as extras.

---

[72] *TechDirt.com* "New Snowden Doc Reveals How GCHQ/NSA Use The Internet To 'Manipulate, Deceive And Destroy Reputations' by Mike Masnick (February 25th 2014)

[73] *The Guardian* "GCHQ has tools to manipulate online information, leaked documents show" by James Ball (July 14th 2014)

As *Fortune* magazine once pointed out in article titled Hollywood's Military Complex, "Even in an age of special effects, it's exponentially cheaper to film on actual military ships with real military advisers...The fulcrum of Hollywood's unlikely partnership is Phil Strub, a former film school student and Navy videographer, now the entertainment liaison at the Department of Defense."[74] Strub is just one of several such men who work full-time with the television and film studios on behalf of the government.

In the 1990s the CIA assigned Chase Brandon to be their liaison to Hollywood in order to establish a mutually beneficial relationship between the entertainment industry and the CIA.[75] These government entertainment liaisons maintain script approval and have been known to make dramatic changes to screenplays before they are approved in order to achieve the government's propaganda goals. *The Recruit* (2003), *The Sum of All Fears* (2002), *Argo* (2012), *Lone Survivor* (2013), and many, many other popular films and television shows have all been produced with the consent, oversight, and input of the CIA or the Pentagon.[76]

---

[74] *Fortune Magazine* "Hollywood's Military Complex" by Soo Youn (December 19, 2013)

[75] *The Guardian* "Hollywood reporter: The caring, sharing CIA: Central Intelligence gets a makeover" by John Patterson (October 5th 2001)

[76] *Cinema Review Magazine* "The Recruit: About the Production" (2003)

Infiltration of Freemasonry

Illuminati frontman Adam Weishaupt loved the idea of using existing secret societies to help grow his organization, saying, "Nothing can bring this about but hidden societies. Hidden schools of wisdom are the means which will one day free men from their bonds. These have in all ages been the archives of nature, and of the rights of men; and by them shall human nature be raised from her fallen state."[77]

One of the primary vehicles used to conceal and further their agenda was (and still is) Freemasonry. Already an established occult organization in his time, Weishaupt had goals of using the fraternity for his own means, and in July 1782 he infiltrated Freemasonry and introduced what he called Illuminated Freemasonry.[78] Using the existing structure of Freemasonry he created factions which were dedicated to his cause and with their ruthlessness and obsession, his supporters quickly took control of the highest levels within lodges across Europe.

In his own words Weishaupt explains the importance of using this pre-existing fraternity as the ideal cover, saying, "None is fitter than the three lower degrees of Freemasonry; the public is accustomed to it, expect little from it, and therefore takes little notice of it."[79] "I declare

[77] Robison, John – *Proofs of a Conspiracy* p. 91

[78] Ridley, Jasper – *The Freemasons* p. 181

[79] Robison, John – *Proofs of a Conspiracy* p.112

and I challenge all mankind to contradict my declaration, that no man can give any account of the order of Freemasonry, of its origin, of its history, of its object, nor any explanation of its mysteries and symbols, which does not leave the mind in total uncertainty on all these points. Every man is entitled therefore, to give any explanation of the symbols and a system of the doctrine that he can render palatable."[80]

Knowing the power of claiming to have possession of a great secret, he knew how men could be manipulated into doing his bidding, hoping to have the great secret someday revealed to them. "Of all the means I know to lead men, the most effectual is a concealed mystery. The hankering of the mind is irresistible; and if once a man has taken it into his head that there is a mystery in a thing, it is impossible to get it out, either by argument or experience. And then, we can so change notions by merely changing a word."[81]

A certificate from an Illuminati infiltrated Freemason lodge in Munich contains a pyramid with the sun over the capstone and the seal on the certificate shows the Owl of Minerva, a symbol of wisdom to the Illuminati, and the mascot of the Bohemian Grove.[82]

One of the most popular books on the definitions of Freemasonry's symbols also confirms that Weishaupt

[80] Robison, John – *Proofs of a Conspiracy* p. 63

[81] Robison, John – *Proofs of a Conspiracy* p. 129

[82] Lodge of Saint Theodore vom guten Rat in Munich from 1780

successfully infiltrated the fraternity and introduced his plot to the inner circle. *The Lexicon of Freemasonry* was first published in 1845 by Albert G. Mackey, a 33rd degree Freemason, who was one of the most prominent scholars on the subject of Freemasonry in his day. The book contains an alphabetized list of most Masonic symbols accompanied by a detailed explanation of their esoteric meaning.

In the entry on the Illuminati, Mackey admits, "Weishaupt was a radical in politics, and an infidel in religion; and he organized this association, not more for purposes of aggrandizing himself, than overturning Christianity and the institutions of society. With the view of carrying his objects more completely into effect, he united himself with a lodge of Freemasons in Munich, and attempted to graft his system of Illuminism upon the stock of Freemasonry...Many Freemasons, misled by the construction of his first degrees, were enticed into the order."[83]

Popular 20th century occult writer Alice Bailey, who claimed her books were dictated to her by a supernatural entity, wrote that, "There is no dissociation between the One Universal Church, the sacred inner Lodge of all true Masons, and the innermost circles of the esoteric societies...It must not be forgotten that only those souls who are on the Probationary Path or the Path of

---

[83] Macky, Albert – *The Lexicon of Freemasonry* page 201

Discipleship will form the nucleus of the coming new world religion."[84]

The role of Freemasonry in the Illuminati will be expanded on later in this book, along with a history of this fascinating fraternity and their transformation from a stonemason trade union to the spiritual secret society it is today.

Connections to Yale's Skull & Bones

Skull & Bones, the secret society at Yale University, is often said to be simply a fraternity, but it's far from it. It is actually not only a secret society, but its what's called a senior society, meaning students aren't full-fledged members until their senior year. It was the first senior society at the university and the first secret society as well. Students don't just pledge to join hoping to get chosen like they do at fraternities—instead they are recruited if they are seen as possible valuable servants.

Skull & Bones members are responsible for creating the CIA, the Federal Reserve, the Department of Education, the American Historical Society, and various media monopolies. Skull & Bones doesn't just have identical symbols, ideologies and goals in common with the Illuminati, there are some other very specific pieces of evidence that show a direct link between the two groups.

William Huntington Russell, one of the two founders of Skull & Bones, was studying abroad in Germany just before he returned to America and founded the

---

[84] Bailey, Alice - *Externalization of the Hierarchy* page 513

organization in 1832 using the same symbols, riddles, initiation practices, and having essentially the same goals as the Bavarian Illuminati.

Of course the very emblem of Skull & Bones or the "Brotherhood of Death," as they are often called, is a sinister skull and cross bones, identical to the Death's Head (totenkopf) pin that Nazis operating the death camps wore during World War II. The skull and cross bones (Jolly Roger) emblem was also used by the Knights Templar, and was the symbol of pirates due to its intimidating look and was meant to convey that they hold the power over life and death. Many Freemasons have a human skull (real or a replica) on their desk in their office or in the "chamber of reflection" in the Lodge.

In 1876 a group of Yale students broke into the Skull & Bones headquarters to investigate this shady organization and then published a detailed newsletter titled *The Fall of Skull and Bones* about what they discovered inside. The burglars called themselves "File & Claw," partly to mock Skull & Bones, but also because they used a file and crow bar to remove several security bars that covered the boarded up windows in the group's headquarters, a building that looks like, and is called, "the Tomb." One of the more interesting things they found once inside was a framed card on the wall that read, "From the German Chapter, Presented by Patriarch D.C. Gilman of D. 50."

I'll point out again that founder William Huntington Russell was in Germany, the hotbed of Illuminati revolutionaries, and the File & Claw intruders reported an open burial vault inside that contained four human skulls and a plaque written in German reading, "Wer war der Thor, wer Weiser, Bettler oder Kaiser? Ob Arm, ob Reich, im Tode gleich," which in English says, "Who was the fool, who was the wise man, beggar or king? Whether poor or rich, all is the same in death." This is extremely interesting when you learn this same cryptic riddle is virtually identical to the one given at the initiation ritual of the Bavarian Illuminati.

In his 1798 book *Proofs of a Conspiracy*, one of the first books to contain English translation of the confiscated Illuminati writings, John Robison describes the initiation ceremony into the "Regent Degree" of Illuminism, in which the initiate would be placed in front of a skeleton that had a crown and a sword at its feet, and the men were asked whether it was the skeleton of a king, nobleman, or a beggar. No matter their answer, the lodge president would explain, "The character of being a man is the only one that is of importance."[85]

This means they don't believe in an afterlife or a divine judgment by God and is used to instill a Social Darwinistic might is right world view. More on this philosophy and the history of Skull & Bones later.

What Ever Happened to Adam Weishaupt?

Adam Weishaupt's fate is often forgotten in the wake of the Illuminati since the man himself was overshadowed by the monstrous conspiracy he gave birth to. In 1785 he was fired from his job at Ingolstadt University where he

---

[85] Robison, John - *Proofs of a Conspiracy* page 110

was the head of the law department.[86]   At this time authorities didn't know he was involved with the Illuminati (let alone the leader and founder) but soon the Bavarian government began to learn about the Illuminati and tighten the noose in their quest to eliminate them, so Weishaupt later fled Bavaria dressed as a craftsman to avoid detection since authorities were now on the lookout for him.   He was given exile in Gotha (a city in the German state of Thuringia, located just north of Bavaria) which was under control of Illuminati sympathizer Duke Ernest II.   There he worked as a legal advisor for the Duke's court until he died in 1830 at the age of 82.

After Weishaupt fled Bavaria to avoid capture, a book printer named J.J.C. Bode would take the lead as the head of the Illuminati, and used his printing shop to continue to spread Enlightenment philosophies throughout Europe. Bode traveled from Germany to France and imported the Illuminati into French masonic lodges which later became instrumental in the French Revolution. After J.J.C. Bode, the leader was Karl Leonard Reinhold, a Freemason who believed Moses incorporated secrets from the Egyptian priesthood into the fraternity.

After Weishaupt's first wife died, he married her sister (the one who he impregnated while his wife was still alive and tried to kill the baby). He and his new wife had their first son Wilhelm the following year in 1784, who died at the age of eighteen in 1802.

Adam himself died when he was eighty-two and was survived by his second wife, Anna Maria, and six

---

[86] http://freemasonry.bcy.ca/texts/illuminati.html

children, two daughters (Nanette and Charlotte), and his four sons Ernst, Karl, Eduard, and Alfred, who all went on to serve as officers in the military.

French Revolution Connections

There are still whispers that the French Revolution was the work of the Illuminati, specifically the work of "Illuminated Masonic lodges" that were infected with Adam Weishaupt's revolutionary goals. While many historians argue that the French Revolution was the result of a random and organic uprising of the French people against the oppressive Monarchy, others saw the strings being pulled from behind the scenes by the Illuminati.

While head of the Illuminati, J.J.C. Bode took two trips to Paris not long before the French Revolution, where he introduced the Illuminati to French Freemason lodges under the new name of the Philadelphes. Revolutionary and radical Enlightenment ideologies grew under the cover of various French Masonic lodges, reading societies, and Jacobin clubs, all of which were influential in organizing the French Revolution.

Bode wrote in his journal on June 30, 1787 that he met with French Freemason Charles-Pierre-Paul, marquis de Langes Savalette who would soon be involved with the revolution, and on July 3rd he made an entry about meeting with French Revolution National Assembly member Francois-Antoine Lemoyne Daubermesnil to specifically discuss the Illuminati![87]

Historian Charles Porset of the National Scientific Research Center in France confirmed that Bode's journal was authentic, saying, "the Journal has now been published by a German scholar, Hermann Schuttler, and it confirms in all respects the idea put forward by Rossberg of collusion between the Illuminati and the Philadelphes. Moreover, a 'secret lodge is then created'—the Lodge of the Philadelphes...The unedited correspondences found in the Kloss archives housed in the Library of Grand Orient of the Netherlands, between Bode, von Busch and the Landgrave of Hesse-Darmstadt, which I've published, prove it. 'We agreed,' wrote Bode, 'that for France, we would adopt the name Philadelphes instead of Illuminati.'"[88]

Another clear piece of evidence linking masonic lodges to the French Revolution is a letter from Duke Philip of Orleans that was sent out to all French Masonic lodges which reads, "all the Lodges are summoned to confederate together, to unite their efforts to maintain the revolution; to gain over it, in all parts, friends, partisans, and protectors; to propagate the flame, to vivify the spirit,

---

[87] Schüttler, Hermann - *Die Mitglieder des Illuminatenordens [Members of the Illuminati 1776–1787/93.* Ars Una, München 1991

[88] Melanson, Terry - *The Perfectabilists: The 18th Century Bavarian Order of Illuminati* page 72

to excite zeal and ardor for it, in every state, and by every means in their power."[89]

In 1791 a book titled *The Veil Withdrawn* was published which was one of the first books to connect Freemasonry to the French Revolution. In 1792 a booklet titled *The Tomb of Jacues Molay* was released by Cadet de Gassicourt that linked the revolution to the Knights Templar. A few years later in 1803 a German man named Johann Starck published *Triumph of Philosophy* where he too claimed the Illuminati used Masonic lodges as a cover for organizing the French Revolution.

[Author's Note: Please take a moment to rate and review this book on Amazon.com or wherever you purchased it from to let others know what you think. This also helps to offset the trolls who keep giving my books fake one-star reviews when they haven't even read them. Almost all of the one-star reviews on my books are from NON-verified purchases which is a clear indication they are fraudulent, hence me adding this note. These fraudulent ratings and reviews could also be part of a larger campaign trying to stop my message from spreading by attempting to tarnish my research through fake and defamatory reviews, so I really need your help to combat this as soon as possible. Thank you!]

---

[89] Barruel, Abbe - *Memoirs Illustrating the History of Jacobinism* page 780

The Thirteen Bloodlines Theory

People sometimes refer to the "Illuminati bloodlines" or the "top thirteen bloodlines of the Illuminati" as the ruling elite within the pyramid of power that controls our world. A dozen or two names are thrown around and said to be Illuminati families who interbreed with each other to retain their wealth and power among the small group of ruling elite. The most common alleged thirteen bloodlines are: Astor, Bundy, Collins, DuPont, Freeman, Kennedy, Li, Onassis, Rockefeller, Rothschild, Russell, Van Duyn, and the Merovingian bloodline.

One of the more popular promoters of this theory is Fritz Springmeier, who in 1999 published *Bloodlines of the Illuminati*, where he wrote, "The goal of this book is to lay out the historical facts about these elite bloodlines...once one understands these bloodlines, wars between kings no longer appear as wars between elite factions, but often can be recognized as contrived wars created to control the masses of both sides by their greedy Machiavellian masters."[90]

---

[90] Springmeier, Fritz – *Bloodlines of the Illuminati* page 1

Springmeier continues, "The Illuminati themselves decided to elevate 13 bloodlines. The number 13 is extremely important magically, and these 13 occult tribes mock the 13 tribes of Israel (remember the 13th tribe, the Tribe of Joseph was split into Ephraim & Manasseh). This does not mean that only 13 Illuminati bloodlines are powerful. There are other families that have risen to prominence. Further, worldwide there are other families of great oligarchical power who have allied themselves to the Illuminati in the political and economic realms without having to intermarry into the Illuminati."[91]

While Fritz's book appears on the surface to be an impressive analysis of the supposed thirteen bloodlines, it is clear that he bought into several known hoaxes and reprinted them as fact, such as the widely debunked claims of John Todd, a man who in the 1970s claimed to be an Illuminati "defector" belonging to one of the "Illuminati bloodlines."[92] Springmeier also claims that the Illuminati have been operating a space station on Mars, which he says they began colonizing in the late 1990s.[93]

A much more credible researcher, Antony Sutton, who was given a Skull & Bones membership list in the early 1980s by the daughter of a member, has a much more

---

[91] Springmeier, Fritz – *Bloodlines of the Illuminati* page 1

[92] See my previous book, *The Illuminati: Facts & Fiction* to read my complete analysis of John Todd.

[93] Lecture *The Top 13 Illuminati Bloodlines* produced by Prophecy Club, available on YouTube

accurate and rational approach. In his excellent analysis, *America's Secret Establishment*, Sutton has stated that twenty to thirty families have dominated the Skull & Bones society since its creation in 1832 and his book provides a scholarly overview of their activities.

The thirteen bloodlines theory is essentially a more modern version of the ancient "divine right of kings" theory, which was perpetuated for thousands of years, claiming that God ordained families of monarchs and kings to rule. In many cases, as with Egyptian Pharaohs, the Caesars of Rome, and the Chinese Dynasties, kings believed (or at least claimed to believe) that they themselves *were* Gods or literal descendants of the Gods, which in turn, they thought, gave them the divine right to rule. This is not just an ancient idea. The Nazi's actually believed that white people were the descendants from the (supposed) God-like inhabitants of the Lost City of Atlantis.

Adolf Hitler and his inner circle of Nazi officers, including Heinrich Himmler, Rudolph Hess, and Joseph Goebbels, literally believed that white people (the Aryan race, as they liked to call them) were descendants of Gods that once inhabited the Earth, who supposedly lived in the City of Atlantis. The Nazis thought the myth of the "Lost City" was literal history and when the city allegedly sunk into the sea, according to their beliefs, several of the demigods fled to the Himalayas of Tibet where they were said to have started the Nordic and Aryan races.

According to Nazi philosophy, the Jews, claiming to be "God's chosen people," were preventing the Aryans from their "divine right" to rule the earth, and race-mixing was weakening the magical power of the Aryan race. Hitler was largely inspired by Helena Blavatsky's 1888 book, *The Secret Doctrine*, which claims that Satan helped free Man in the Garden of Eden, thus allowing humans to "evolve" into gods ourselves. "Satan will now be shown, in the teaching of the Secret Doctrine, allegorized as Good, and Sacrifice, a God of Wisdom," the book reads.[94] "Blessed and sanctified is the name of the Angel of Havas—Satan," Blavatsky wrote.[95]

Mainstream historians focus on the racial aspects of the Nazis quest for power, but often ignore the root of their ideology which was a twisted occult doctrine and literally based on Satanism and the belief that they had divine blood in their veins and were descendants of gods. A German secret society called the Thule Society gave birth to the Nazi party and operated much like the Skull & Bones society does in America, working to groom the country's future leaders. The Thule Society's logo was a swastika with a dagger in front of it.

The "most royal candidate" theory is the belief that every presidential election in the United States has been won by the candidate with the most royal blood, thus having the closest ties to the kingship bloodline of Europe.[96] Proponents of the theory claim that every U.S. president since George Washington can have their

[94] Blavatsky, H.P. - *The Secret Doctrine v. II* p. 237)

[95] Blavatsky, H.P. - *The Secret Doctrine v. II* p. 235)

[96] *New York Times* "Chronicle" by Nadine Brozan (October 28th 1996)

bloodline traced back to European royals, and say at least thirty-three presidents are descendants of Alfred the Great and Charlemagne.[97]

But this begs the question of why a small group of families would consider themselves to have "royal blood." What exactly does "royal blood" mean? Well, it means that they believe they are direct descendants of the Gods. People who subscribe to this theory often point to a passage in the Book of Genesis in the Bible as evidence. Genesis 6:1-2 reads, "And it came to pass, when men began to multiply on the face of the earth, and daughters were born unto them, That the sons of God saw the daughters of men that they were fair; and they took them wives of all which they chose." Genesis 6:4 continues, "There were giants in the earth in those days; and also after that, when the sons of God came in unto the daughters of men, and they bare children to them, the same became mighty men which were of old, men of renown."

Some Christians and Biblical scholars believe that the "Sons of God" which came and took the daughters of men and had children with them, were an alien race called the Annunaki. Some versions of the Bible clearly say that the Sons of God were "supernatural beings" and clearly refers to some kind of alien creatures who came to earth and mated with human females, creating some kind of alien/human hybrid called the Nephilim.

---

[97] *The Daily Mail* "Is ruling in the genes? All presidents bar one are directly descended from a medieval English king" (August 4th 2012)

Some believe that God caused the great flood hoping to destroy these Nephilim creatures and then have Noah, his sons and their wives, later repopulate the earth after they emerged safely from the Ark. According to some beliefs, those supposed hybrid creatures survived and went on to become the first kings and queens, and later evolved into what we refer to as the Illuminati today.

The myth that Jesus Christ secretly had a child with Mary Magdalene was brought into the mainstream through Dan Brown's 2003 book *The Da Vinci Code*, which was inspired by the widely debunked *Holy Blood, Holy Grail* (1982). Dan Brown's novel was made into a film in 2006 starring Tom Hanks, which carried the idea to a much larger audience who wholeheartedly believed the hoax of the "Jesus bloodline."

According to the myth, the Knights Templar and Freemasons are the guardians of the Holy Grail, which according to this theory, the Grail refers to the descendants of Jesus and Mary Magdalene, thus the "Holy Grail" is the divine bloodline whose supposed members have to live in secret to protect themselves from being killed by the Catholic Church, which allegedly will do anything to prevent this "secret truth" from being known, because it would undermine their power.

This Jesus bloodline myth may very well be unveiled at some point in time as "evidence" of the Illuminati's supposed "divine right to rule" by claiming they are the literal descendants of Jesus. It may very well culminate with the appearance of the antichrist who will claim to be the long awaited messiah of the world and cite his alleged genetic connection to Jesus as evidence that he is the return of Christ.

When looking into the supposed "bloodlines of the Illuminati" you will often come across people talking about "the Reptilians" who believe the Illuminati are literally a group of "shape shifting extraterrestrials" or demonic inter-dimensional entities masquerading as humans in order to work towards enslaving the human race. The "Reptilian" theory is widely ridiculed, although a sizable portion of the population has no doubt that famous politicians and celebrities are "impostors," only pretending to be human.[98] Many of the Reptilian claims are something straight out of the *X-Files*, the popular paranormal thriller from the 1990s, and are virtually identical to the plot of a 1980s mini series titled *V* (for visitors).

A British conspiracy theorist named David Icke is largely responsible for spreading this theory, and claims these "Reptilian Illuminati" have to drink human blood, "because they are drinking the person's life-force and because they need it to exist in this dimension in a human form."[99] More recently Icke seems to have distanced himself from "Reptilians" and began focusing on the Archons, which refer to supernatural agents of the evil Gnostic creator God, the Demiurge. Icke is also a big proponent that these "Reptilian Illuminati" families have

---

[98] *The Wire* "12 Million Americans Believe Lizard People Run Our Country" by Philip Bump (April 2nd 2013)

[99] Icke, David - *The Biggest Secret* page 295

interbred with each other throughout history to maintain their unique bloodline and hide their secret from outsiders.

In ancient times it was fairly easy to control who would marry whom, and keep royal families breeding with other royal families. Most people marry others in the same socioeconomic level because they run in the same circles, attend the same prestigious universities, and grow up in the same wealthy neighborhoods. While the ancient alien/nephilim bloodline theory is interesting on its surface, there is little to no evidence that people from these supposed royal or divine/alien/reptilian families have any significant difference in their DNA from "regular" people, or "commoners" as we are called. In more modern times the regulation of who marries whom through arranged marriages has become nearly impossible to control, so if this theory were true, then the "alien" DNA would be so widely spread that we would be seeing it pop up in medical reports around the world.

One likely reason for a small number of families rising to power in the ancient past is that they just so happened to be living on fertile land, allowing them to have healthy and strong offspring due to an abundance of food and easily accessible water. As they say in real estate—location, location, location. These issues are explored in detail in the Pulitzer Prize winning book *Guns, Germs, and Steel: The Fates of Human Societies* (1997), written by Jared Diamond. His research presents the case that a variety of environmental factors, not any genetic or intellectual superiority, has been the reason certain cultures have dominated most others around the world.

I certainly wouldn't rule out the possibility that some kind of extraterrestrial (or demonic) race is secretly working with the Illuminati leadership and directing them in their affairs, but the subject of aliens is beyond the scope of this book and in most cases the "evidence" of such beings is impossible to verify (at least at this point) or limited to interpretations of ancient art or "video evidence" of unidentified flying objects—most of which are top secret experimental aircraft or hoaxes. Aliens (or demons) working *with* the Illuminati is one thing—a handful of families interbreeding with each other to keep their "alien family tree" a secret amongst themselves is something totally different.

Affiliated Secret Societies

Secret societies entered popular culture in the 21st century, thanks in part to Dan Brown's novels and Hollywood films like *The Skulls* (2000) and *National Treasure* (2004). As the 2004 United States presidential election approached, it was reported in mainstream news that both George W. Bush and his opponent John Kerry were members of Skull & Bones, the now somewhat well-known secret society based at Yale University. The correct terminology is actually that they "are" members, not that they "were" members, since it's a lifetime membership starting their senior year of college.

While many people have now heard of Skull & Bones, most falsely believe it's just an elite fraternity for rich kids, but Skull & Bones differs from a fraternity in several key ways. First of all, nobody "pledges to join" the club hoping to get accepted. Instead they recruit people who are seen as worthy to be members. The club doesn't do any charity work, which is common with most fraternities, and their entire focus is geared for members' postgraduate life which is why someone doesn't become an official member until their senior year, as opposed to rushing a fraternity freshman year like most other college clubs.

While there are countless secret societies on college campuses around the world, Skull & Bones is in a league of their own in terms of their power and influence. While they are perhaps one of the more well-known secret societies (thanks to the Internet), there are certainly other powerful (and dangerous) ones that are lesser known.

There are secret societies of businessmen, politicians, and media moguls, (like the Bilderberg Group and the Allen & Company Sun Valley Conference); there is a secret society of scientists (the Jasons); there's even a secret society of *secretaries* (the Seraphic Society), who cater to men in other secret societies. Few people know that there is a secret society of women modeled after the Bohemian Grove who call themselves the *Belizean* Grove. Many of these mysterious groups have overlapping members, and at the higher levels work in concert with each other in one giant compartmentalized pyramid-shaped power structure. In this chapter I'll take you back to the beginning, thousands of years ago, and we'll slowly move forward in time tracking the evolution of this invisible empire.

Mystery Schools

The first secret societies were called the Mystery Schools, which meant they taught the Ancient Mysteries of life and death. The word "mystic" means one who studied the mysteries, and ancient inquisitive men formed groups or "schools" to study and ponder life's biggest questions. Certain supposed answers were discovered or myths developed which aimed to help man make sense of his existence here on this planet.

Some see the secret occult knowledge stemming from these Mystery Schools not as evil, but as a tool that can be used for either good or evil, similar to "the Force" in *Star Wars*. Just as men gather into associations based on common interests like car meets, model airplane clubs and countless other kinds of clubs, men in ancient times who found they had a common interesting pondering the mysteries of life found themselves coming together in these Mystery Schools.

Various Mystery Schools popped up in the ancient world, claiming to, or seeking to, discover the powerful secrets of life, and looking to get in harmony with the divine in order to fully receive the blessings the Universe offers or explain the human condition. While these groups appear to have at one time had the best intensions, many believe they were eventually corrupted and taken over by sinister men who turned the once noble schools into a mafia of madmen who used their superior intellect and social networks to enslave society. Illuminati insider Manly P. Hall explains, "The masses, deprived of their birthright of understanding and groveling in ignorance, eventually became the abject slaves of the spiritual impostors. Superstition universally prevailed and the black magicians completely dominated national affairs, with the result that humanity still suffers from the sophistries [fallacious arguments, especially with the intention of deceiving] of the priestcrafts of Atlantis and Egypt."[100]

The esoteric tradition, as it is sometimes called, appears to have begun in Mesopotamia, the oldest human civilization and the first to develop a written language. From there it can be traced to ancient Egypt and the Isis cults (3100 B.C.) and then over to Greece in the Eleusinian Mysteries (1500 BC) involving the Demeter and Persephone cults. During this time the Dionysian Mysteries were practiced in ancient Greece and Rome and included the use of intoxicants and other trance-inducing techniques in attempts to come into a greater understanding of the Mysteries. The Dionysian mysteries were based on Dionysus, one of the Twelve Olympians in Greek mythology, who was the God of wine and ecstasy.

If you keep following the chain, you progress to the Pythagoreans (5 B.C.) and onto other Greek mystery cults like Mithrasim (100 A.D.), then to the Gnostics (1-300 A.D.), to the Knights Templar (1118) and on to the Cathars in the 13th Century, and then to the Jesuits (founded in 1540), continuing to the Rosicrucians (1614), then to Freemasonry (1717) and continuing to the Illuminati (1776); and if you keep moving ahead—when you get to more modern times you'll see organizations like Skull & Bones (1832), Bohemian Grove (1872), the Federal Reserve Bank (1913), the Council on Foreign Relations (1921), the Bilderberg Group (1954), and so on.

While you may be familiar with some of these major Illuminati organizations, each piece of the puzzle contains

---

[100] Hall, Manly P. - *The Secret Teachings of All Ages* page 316

countless details and when meticulously assembled, creates a mosaic that reveals a clear and common theme. They are all hierarchical fraternities who use various rituals and pageants to instill in their members that they are a special elite group of masters who know "the truth" that will enable them to become gods among men.   In order to preserve their secrets to a select few, initiates often swear blood oaths to never reveal their knowledge to outsiders or those in the lower levels of the hierarchy.

The Knights Templar

At this point in time, many people have heard about the Knights Templar and may be familiar with a little bit of the story surrounding them and the accusations levied against them by the Catholic Church, but few people have taken an extended look into the organization and their activities.   While most people believe the accusations of devil worshiping and blasphemous rituals were fabricated by the Catholic Church as an excuse to seize the Templar's wealth and put them out of commission, you may be very surprised to discover who admits the accusations were actually true.

The Knights Templar name basically means they were the knights of Solomon's Temple, and were a group of (supposed) Christian knights who volunteered to protect Jerusalem from the Muslims who were trying to seize the land.   The Templars were founded in 1118 in France by a man named Hugues de Payens who recruited around nine others, mostly members of his own family, who then offered to protect pilgrims traveling from the coast of the Mediterranean to the Holy Land.

While they were supposedly dedicated "warrior monks" who wanted to supposedly protect the Holy Land, it appears the founders had an ulterior motive, and while the majority of the growing Templar organization may have been wholly dedicated to protecting the Holy Land, the inner circle were busy secretly excavating the site of Solomon's Temple for treasure and rare artifacts.

Among the most damning allegations made against the Templars was that their inner circle performed satanic homosexual rituals involving a demonic idol called Baphomet. While most people believe these allegations were fabricated by the Catholic Church to demonize the Templars, others have a different view. Eliphas Levi, a popular occultist in the 19th century, explains, "Did the Templars really adore Baphomet? Did they offer a shameful salutation to the buttocks of the goat of Mendes? What was actually this secret and potent association which imperiled Church and State, and was thus destroyed unheard? Judge nothing lightly; they are guilty of a great crime; they have exposed to profane eyes the sanctuary of antique initiation. They have gathered again and have shared the fruits of the tree of knowledge, so they might become masters of the world."[101]

He continues to say, "Yes, in our profane conviction, the Grand Masters of the Order of the Templars worshipped the Baphomet, and caused it to be worshipped

---

[101] Levi, Eliphas – *Transcendental Magic* p. 7-8

by their initiates."[102]   In the infamous *Satanic Bible*, published in 1966 by Anton LaVey (real name Howard Levy), Baphomet is listed as the demon the Knights Templar worshiped.[103]   So even the Church of Satan's founder accepts the allegations made against the Templars as true.

Manly P. Hall, a 33rd degree mason best known for his revealing book *The Secret Teachings of All Ages*, wrote, "The famous hermaphroditic Goat of Mendes was a composite creature formulated to symbolize this *astral light*. It is identical with Baphomet, the mystic *pantheos* of those disciples of ceremonial magic, the Templars, who probably obtained it from the Arabians."[104]

So, according to Hall and others, it is believed the Templars not only found physical treasure like gold and silver in their executions, but also informational treasure as well, in the form of ancient scrolls where they learned their strange secret doctrine.

Researchers Knight and Lomus, who are certainly not considered "conspiracy theorists," explained that according to their findings, "Hence it follows that the mysteries of the craft are in reality the mysteries of religion.   The Knights were, however, careful not to entrust this important secret to any whose fidelity and discretion had not been fully proved.   They therefore

---

[102] Levi, Eliphas – *Transcendental Magic* p. 307

[103] LaVey, Anton - *The Satanic Bible* page 136

[104] Hall, Manly P. – *The Secret Teachings of All Ages* p. 316

invented different degrees to test their candidates, and gave them only symbolical secrets without explanation, to prevent treachery and solely to enable them to make themselves known to each other. For this purpose it was resolved to use different signs, words and tokens in each degree, by which they would be secured against the Saracens, cowans or intruders."[105]

In *The History of Magic* (published in 1860), Eliphas Levi reveals, "The Templars had two doctrines; one was concealed and reserved to the leaders, being that of Johannism [Gnosticism]; the other was public, being Roman Catholic doctrine. They deceived in this manner the enemies that they hoped to supplant. The Johannism of the adepts was the Kabalah of the Gnostics, but it degenerated speedily into a mystic pantheism carried even to idolatry of Nature and hatred of all revealed dogma... They went even so far as to recognize the pantheistic symbolism of the grand masters of Black Magic, and the better to isolate themselves from obedience to a religion by which they were condemned before, they rendered divine honors to the monstrous idol Baphomet."[106]

Lynn Picknett and Clive Prince also confirm the secret doctrine accusations in their book *The Templar Revelation*, writing, "It is likely that the majority of the Knights Templar were no more than simple Christian solders they appeared to be, but the inner circle was different. The inner circle of the Templars appears to

---

[105] Night & Lomas – *The Book of Hiram* p. 434

[106] Levi, Eliphas – *History of Magic* p. 211

have existed in order to further active research into esoteric and religious matters. Perhaps one of the reasons for their secrecy was the fact that they dealt with the arcane aspects of the Jewish and Islamic worlds. They sought, literally, the secrets of the universe wherever they suspected they might be found, and in the course of their geographic and intellectual wanderings came to tolerate— perhaps even to embrace—some very unorthodox beliefs."[107]

These "unorthodox beliefs" appear to have involved what's called sex magic (often spelled sex magick with a "k" on the end), which is the practice of incorporating various sex acts into secret rituals in the belief that the sexual energy produced is transformed into spiritual power, allegedly enabling participants to activate dormant supernatural abilities. Theodore Reuss [co-founder of the Ordo Templi Orientis] revealed that sex magic was the greatest secret of occult fraternities, saying, "Our order possesses the key which opens up all Masonic and Hermetic secrets, namely, the teachings of sexual magic, and this teaching explains, without exception, all the secrets of Freemasonry and all systems of religion."[108] He also said that sex magic was the big secret of the Knights Templar.[109]

---

[107] Picknett & Prince - *The Templar Revelation* page 106

[108] King, Francis - *The Magical World of Aleister Crowley* page 78

[109] Picknett & Prince - *Templar Revelation* page 176

In his companion book to *The Secret Teachings of All Ages*, titled *Lectures on Ancient Philosophy*, Manly P. Hall again reveals some amazing occult secrets that few people have discovered about the Templars. He wrote, "It was not the physical power of the Templars, but the knowledge which they had brought with them from the East, that the church feared. The Templars had discovered part of the great Arcanum; they had become wise in those mysteries which had been celebrated in Mecca thousands of years before the advent of Mohammed; they had read a few pages from the dread book of the Anthropos, and for this knowledge they were doomed to die."[110]

Eliphas Levi writes in agreement, "It was the memory of this scientific and religious absolute, of this doctrine summarized in a word, of this word alternately lost and recovered, which was transmitted to the elect of all antique initiations…it was this same memory handed on to secret associations of Rosicrucians, Illuminati and Freemasons which gave a meaning to their strange rites, to their less or more conventional signs, and a justification above all to their devotion in common, as well as a clue to their power."[111]

This "occult power" wasn't the only thing that led to their downfall. The Templars, with the help of other secrets they likely learned from the rare scrolls they acquired, ultimately became wealthy bankers who issued

---

[110] Hall, Manly P. - *Lectures on Ancient Philosophy* page 439

[111] Levi, Eliphas - *History of Magic* page 31-32

loans, not only to people, but to governments and monarchs. The Catholic Church wouldn't allow people to charge interest on money they lent to someone else because it was considered a sin (called usury), but the church looked the other way when the Templars did it, likely because they needed their protective services in the Holy Land.

Through lending money with interest, the Templars had exploited one of the most powerful and mysterious concepts in the world today. The same tactic is used by the Illuminati banking cartel through their front groups like the Federal Reserve, the World Bank, and the International Monetary Fund. More on the magic of making money and collecting interest on loans later.

The Jesuits

Fast forward a few hundred years and we can see the Catholic Church following the same pattern of the Templars hoarding knowledge, power, and wealth, so insiders can live like kings by taking advantage of the ignorant masses. Ignatius of Loyola founded the Society of Jesus (aka the Jesuits) in 1540, whose members are also known as the "Pope's Marines" because of their militant support of the Catholic Church. The Jesuits were founded to fight against the Protestant Reformation with hopes of keeping the Catholic Church in power by any means necessary. While supposedly being a Christian group, the Jesuits' activities have been anything but.

Some believe that Illuminati founder Adam Weishaupt was covertly working for the Jesuits, but his correspondences reveal he deeply despised the Jesuits, although he did adopt their "ends justifies the means" tactics in hopes of replacing them with his own similar kind of tyranny.

A document titled *The Secret Instructions of the Jesuits,* was published in the early 1600s, allegedly written by a general in the society, and revealed the supposed tactics and "ends justifies the means" code of the Jesuits. The Church claims the documents are a forgery designed to defame the Jesuits, of course, but when one becomes aware of the ruthless and criminal activities Church insiders have engaged in to gain and maintain their power, it doesn't really matter if they're a forgery or not, because the tactics of the Jesuits and the Vatican have become widely known.

The Catholic Church's crimes are legendary, from imprisoning Galileo for (correctly) declaring the earth revolved around the sun, to the Spanish Inquisition where officials tortured and killed anyone who dared disagree with them. And everyone is familiar with their institutional pedophile problem and the generations of cover-ups they have engaged in to protect the perpetrators.

These actions continue to give Christians a bad name with most anti-Christian bigots apparently unaware (or willfully ignoring) the millions of non-Catholic Christians (like Protestants, Lutherans, Methodists, Baptists, non-denominational groups, etc.) which were (and still are) appalled by the actions of the Catholic Church who, for centuries, held a monopoly on Christianity, albeit their twisted and un-Biblical brand of it.

Jesuits were responsible for the 1605 Gunpowder Plot in England, which was an assassination attempt where the perpetrators, including Guy Fawkes, tried to blow up the House of Parliament to kill King James and the Protestant aristocracy. Every November 5th, bonfires and fireworks are used to commemorate the failure of the plot, an event that has come to be known as Guy Fawkes Night.

Vatican City in Rome is not just a city, but a completely sovereign country owned and operated by the Catholic Church that was established in 1929 by the Lateran treaty. It is only 110 acres and has a population under a thousand people and has over $8 billion dollars in assets.[112]   The Pope, of course, is the head, and is protected by his own personal army, the Swiss Guard.

The Popes, Bishops and Priests of the Catholic Church are basically the same as the Pharisees who Jesus denounced over 2000 years ago for their hypocrisy and pride due to their spiritual knowledge. One needs to look no further than the Inquisition or the massive institutional cover-up of countless pedophile priests to see the Catholic Church is corrupt to the core. The Catholic Church also diverts and perverts the teachings of Jesus in numerous ways, such as having people confess their sins to a priest instead of to God himself, as well as having sold indulgences, which, if you don't know, means that people used to pay money to the church and in return a priest would forgive that person's sins and tell them they could then get into Heaven. Some indulgences were even sold

---

[112] *NBC News* "Inside the Vatican: The $8 billion global institution where nuns answer the phones" (Feb 14, 2013)

for sins people would commit in the future.   Such a practice was clearly a shameful abuse of power and completely contradictory to the teachings of Jesus.

The Catholic Church basically took the freeing messages of Jesus and packaged them up and then sold them to the public, when Jesus had intended them to be accessible to all for free.   This is the same thing the Jewish Pharisees did with Judaism causing Jesus to publicly denounce them.   It is for these reasons and more that the Vatican, and specifically the Pope is looked at with suspicion regarding the New World Order and is believed by some to one day be the false prophet spoken about in the Bible.

According to Biblical prophecy, the counterfeit Christ (the Antichrist) will be a political figure and the leader of the world, who will be accompanied by the false prophet, a global religious leader that will (wrongfully) confirm to the world that the messiah has arrived when the Antichrist announces he is God.   Since the Catholic Church is trying to reinstate itself as the *only* Christian authority in the world, many see the Pope as a prime candidate for this false prophet.

In 2007 Pope Benedict proclaimed that the Catholic Church was the only place that can offer salvation and held the only key to Heaven.[113]   He didn't mean Christianity is the only path to salvation, which is a primary tenant of the faith.   He meant specifically that the Catholic Church was the only way to God and that all

---

[113] *Associated Press* "Pope affirms Catholicism as only way to salvation" By Nicole Winfield (July 11, 2007)

other Christian denominations were basically leading people astray and were not "true" churches.[114]

This is the same Pope who, when he was still a Cardinal (then named Cardinal Ratzinger), was in charge of covering up the extensive pedophile priest network which has been operating within (or perhaps in charge of) the Catholic Church for generations.[115] A 69-page document typed in Latin and taken from the Vatican's Secret Archives bearing the seal of Pope John XXIII, was sent to every Bishop in the world in 1962 and contained detailed instructions and policies regarding keeping allegations of sexual abuse a secret.

The title of the documents in Latin, *Crimine Solicitationies*, translates to "*Instruction on proceeding in cases of solicitation*" and was basically identical to an earlier set of instructions issued in 1922.[116] The documents were confirmed authentic by the Roman Catholic Church in England and Wales.[117]

Bishops were instructed to deal with child abuse allegations "in the most secretive way" and were reminded of their commitment to "perpetual silence" for what the documents called the "secret of the Holy

[114] *NBC News* "Pope: Other denominations not true churches" (July 10, 2007) .

[115] *BBC* Documentary"Sex Crimes and the Vatican" (October 2006)

[116] Thomas Doyle, The 1922 instruction and the 1962 instruction "Crimen sollicitationis" promulgated by the Vatican

[117] *The Guardian* "Vatican told bishops to cover up sex abuse: expulsion threat in secret documents" by Antony Barnett (August 17, 2003)

Office."[118]   They go on to say, "The oath of keeping the secret must be given in these cases also by the accusers or those denouncing the priest and the witnesses."[119] Anyone who speaks of the "secret of the Holy Office" or who admits publicly that any victims have come forward were threatened with excommunication.

All complaints about sexual abuse were stored in the Secret Archives of the Vatican. Daniel Shea, a lawyer for abused children said, "It proves there was an international conspiracy by the Church to hush up sexual abuse issues. It is a devious attempt to conceal criminal conduct and is a blueprint for deception and concealment."[120]

Another attorney for abused children, Richard Scorer, said, "We always suspected that the Catholic Church systematically covered up abuse and tried to silence victims. This document appears to prove it. Threatening excommunication to anybody who speaks out shows the lengths the most senior figures in the Vatican were prepared to go to prevent the information getting out to the public domain."[121]

This leads to the dark road of what is called *sex magic,* which is the most sinister secret of Satanism and is

---

[118] *Crimine solicitations* documents *"Instruction on proceeding in cases of solicitation"* page 3 paragraph 11.

[119] *Crimine solicitations* documents *"Instruction on proceeding in cases of solicitation"* page 4paragraph 13

[120] *The Guardian* "Vatican told bishops to cover up sex abuse: expulsion threat in secret documents" by Antony Barnett (August 17, 2003)

[121] Ibid.

covered in the chapter titled *Spiritual Beliefs*. The leader of the Jesuits is officially called the "Superior General," often nicknamed the "Black Pope," and is believed by many to be the actual leader of the Catholic Church who wields his power from behind the scenes.

The Rosicrucians

The Rosicrucians are an interesting secret society-type of group, because the "group" started off as a hoax, really, which then inspired people to actually form such a group (or factions) based on the teachings of the mysterious Rosicrucian Manifestos, the first of which was published in Germany in 1614. Two other manifestos later appeared, one the following year in 1615, and another the year after that, said to have come from a secret brotherhood that made up an Invisible College which was preparing to reveal themselves to the world.

There are various theories as to who the author or authors of these mysterious books were. Many believe they were written by Johann Valentin Andrea, a German Lutheran theologian who was allegedly hoping they would help break the Catholic Church's stranglehold on power.

Whoever wrote the manifestos chose to release them under the pseudonym Christian Rosencreutz as a symbol for the work because the name translates to *Rosy Cross*— a rose having been an alchemical symbol of heavenly perfection and paradise. The first manifesto tells a story of how "Christian Rosencreutz" went on a journey to the Middle East to study the occult and the ancient mysteries.

The books are said to contain hidden meanings and esoteric knowledge which could only be revealed to a select few.

In the texts, "Christian Rosencreutz" wrote about a future utopia where people of different religions would all worship the same God in their own style while having tolerance for all other views. Of course, the Catholic Church condemned the manifestos and anyone who supported them.

The books also forecasted a coming age of enlightenment resulting from the revelation of ancient Hermetic secrets. Some believe surviving Knights Templars were behind the mysterious manifestos, and some also credit Rosicrucianism for changing stone mason guilds into the philosophical Freemasonry we are familiar with today.

Rosicrucian researcher Christopher McIntosh wrote, "It has often been suggested that the Hiramic legend in Masonry might be linked with the legend of Christian Rosenkreuz and his tomb...It is not impossible, therefore, that an impulse of a Rosicrucian nature (using the word "Rosicrucian" in its widest sense) was responsible for the transformation of operative into speculative Masonry."[122] The transformation from "operative" masonry to "speculative masonry" means changing from a mere stone mason trade union to the philosophical and spiritual form of Freemasonry that exists today. The 18th degree of Scottish Rite Freemasonry is called the Knight of the

---

[122] McIntosh, Christopher – *The Rosicrucians* p. 43

Rose-Croix (Rose Cross), clearly showing a connection between the two groups.

The Mormon Church, or the Church of Latter Day Saints, as they prefer to be called, contains several parallels with Rosicrucianism. First, both stem from books said to have been "discovered" or mysteriously appeared, which cleverly mix occult myths and rituals with Christian philosophy. Mormonism founder Joseph Smith Jr. most likely knew of the Christian Rosencreutz legend (which was two hundred years old in his time) when he concocted his tale of "finding" a supposed ancient text himself. Since Joseph Smith was a Freemason, he certainly would have been familiar with the Legend of Enoch, which claims that the true name of God was carved into a golden delta (triangle), and hidden before the great flood so that it would be preserved (and discovered) by a future generation.

These myths of ancient "lost and found" divine texts speaking of past cultures and mystical secrets were the inspiration for *The Book of Mormon* which Joseph Smith claimed to have "found" written on a stack of Golden Plates in the 1820s, which of course aren't in a museum somewhere because he said an angel took them back to heaven for safe keeping! Smith was a Freemason who mixed Masonic mythology with Christianity to create Mormonism which he claimed "restored" the lost secrets from the ancient past with his "discovery" (fabrication) of the Book of Mormon, again, which he magically "translated" from "Golden Plates" that are nowhere to be found.

The name "R. C. Christian" appeared in 1980 surrounding the creation of an enormous and mysterious occult monument in the small town of Elberton, Georgia —a structure known as the Georgia Guidestones. The name was chosen as a pseudonym by the individual who designed and paid for this bizarre monument. "R.C. Christian," obviously standing for Rose Cross Christian, and the Brotherhood of the Rose Cross, which was a popular calling card of early Rosicrucians. The Georgia Guidestones monument stands nineteen feet tall and displays ten different commandments in eight different languages as the New World Order's ten commandments. The first of which is to maintain the human population under 500 million people. The monument is said to be the "Guidestones to an age of reason" and has several astrological markings in the design, including a hole in line with the North Star.

It wasn't just Mormonism founder Joseph Smith and the man behind the Georgia Guidestones who received inspiration from the Rosicrucians, but also the early founders of Freemasonry and even the father of the Illuminati, Adam Weishaupt. Many Rosicrucians in his time actually denounced Weishaupt and the Illuminati for taking what they considered to be a noble concept of an enlightened brotherhood, and turned it into a mechanism to exercise his own tyrannical goals.

Freemasonry

Often said to be just a men's club of old guys who want to get away from their wives much like the Moose

Lodge or Knights of Columbus—Freemasonry is quite a bit different from most men's clubs and is actually often included when talking about the grand "Illuminati conspiracy." What most people don't know, and what high level masons have openly admitted, is that there is a secret society *within* this secret society.

Manly P. Hall, considered one of Freemasonry's greatest philosophers, openly admitted that, "Freemasonry is a fraternity within a fraternity—an outer organization concealing an inner brotherhood of the elect...the visible society is a splendid camaraderie of 'free and accepted' men enjoined to devote themselves to ethical, educational, fraternal, patriotic, and humanitarian concerns. The invisible society is a secret most august [respected and impressive] fraternity whose members are dedicated to the service of a mysterious arcanum arcanorum [secret of secrets.]"[123]

You'll sometimes hear people say that their grandfather was a "master mason" and dismiss any talk of a "conspiracy" because all grandpa did was engage in cheesy rituals and attend boring meetings. A "master mason" sounds quite impressive if you don't know much about masonry. George Washington was a master mason and a considerable number of the Founding Fathers of America were masons, so they can't be that bad, right? Out of the fifty-six signers of the Declaration of Independence, eight of them were confirmed to be Freemasons and at least sixteen U.S. presidents have also been masons, including James Madison, James Monroe,

---

[123] Hall, Manly P. - *Lectures on Ancient Philosophy* page 433

Andrew Jackson, James Polk, Theodore Roosevelt, William Howard Taft, Franklin D. Roosevelt, Harry Truman, Lyndon B. Johnson, and Gerald Ford.

While sounding like an impressive title, a master mason is only the 3rd level (or degree) of a 33 level hierarchy. The first degree is called entered apprentice, the second is fellow craft, and the third is a master mason; but there are thirty-three degrees in the Scottish Rite. A rite is "a formal or ceremonial act or procedure prescribed or customary in religious or other solemn use."[124]

The Scottish Rite is the most popular brand of Masonry and within the higher levels each degree is given a mysterious sounding name like Secret Master (4th Degree), Knight of the Rose-Croix (18th degree) and Grand Pontiff (19th degree). In the 32nd degree (the second highest level), the initiate is called a Sublime Knight Commander of the Royal Secret or Master of the Royal Secret.

The "Scottish Rite" actually started in France and was based on legends that originated from Scotland that were told by Scotts who fled to France in the late 1700s when the British Isles were having problems. Regardless of where the name originated, Scottish Rite Freemasonry is the most popular esoteric hierarchy of the fraternity.

The 33rd degree of the Scottish Rite is the highest level and is awarded by invitation only. Each of the degrees represents the different vertebrate in the human spine and symbolize the member's ascent in their quest for Enlightenment within the fraternity. On top of the

---

[124] dictionary.com

33rd vertebrate of the spine sits the skull, which holds the brain, so the 33rd degree signifies that the initiate has become fully enlightened with the secret gnosis (knowledge) of the ancient mysteries. Freemasonry evolved out of stone masonry, whose ancient tradesmen used a series of secret handshakes and code words to identify each other and their level of skill. Over time, various philosophies started arising out of those trade unions and used popular stone mason tools as symbols to represented various aspects of their philosophy. As their theology grew, the stonemasons morphed from what was called *operative* masonry (meaning men who worked with stones) to *speculative* masonry, which refers to the philosophical and spiritual Freemasons today.

While the operative (or stone masons) built cathedrals out of stone, the speculative (or Freemasons) built their intellect. The term "Freemason" likely comes from freestone masonry. Freestone is a softer stone used for cathedral faces that is intricately carved by higher skilled masons and is used as a metaphor to describe the development of a man's character and abilities. Some say that "free" means they are free from ignorance or free from the chains of darkness that once enslaved them.

Evidence indicates that the Knights Templar either assimilated with Freemasonry or directly created it. Most American's came to hear about Freemasonry as a result of Dan Brown's 2003 novel *The Da Vinci Code*, and then in the following few years the History Channel, Discovery, National Geographic and other networks produced shows looking into this fascinating group. The 2004 film

National Treasure starring Nicholas Cage capitalized on the hype, and portrayed them as the secret guardians of America.

It officially came into its modern form in 1717 with the creation of the Grand Lodge of England and has been shrouded in mystery ever since. Much of the controversy surrounding Masonry stems from allegations that the higher-level members worship Satan and that they deceive lower level members about its purpose. "Anti-Masons" don't just come up with these allegations out of thin air though; they often point to Masonic texts written by highly revered Masons as their evidence.

The "Bible of Freemasonry," a book titled *Morals and Dogma*, written by Albert Pike in 1871 explains Masonic philosophy and is read primarily only by dedicated Freemasons. Part of this philosophy, Pike explains, is, "Masonry, like all the Religions, all the Mysteries, Hermeticism and Alchemy, *conceals* [emphasis in original] its secrets from all except the Adepts and Sages, or the Elect, and uses false explanations and misinterpretations of its symbols to mislead those who deserve only to be misled; to conceal the Truth, which it [the Mason] calls Light, from them, and to draw them away from it."[125]

He reaffirms this deception later in the book, saying, "The Blue Degrees are but the court or portico (porch) of the Temple. Part of the symbols are displayed there to the initiate, but he is intentionally misled by false interpretations. It is not intended that he shall understand

---

[125] Pike, Albert - *Morals and Dogma* p. 104-105

them; but it is intended that he shall imagine that he understands them...their true explication [explanation and understanding] is reserved for the Adepts, the Princes of Masonry [those of the 32nd and 33rd Degrees]."[126]

Pike even makes several statements appearing to support the Devil, saying, "Satan is not a black god, but negation of God ... this is not a Person, but a Force, created for good, but which may represent evil. It is the instrument of Liberty or Free Will. They [Freemasons] represent this Force...under the mythological and horned form of the God Pan; thence came the he-goat of the Sabbat, brother of the Ancient Serpent, and the Light-bearer."[127]

Later in the book he wrote, "Lucifer, the Light-bearer! Strange and mysterious name to give to the Spirit of Darkness! Lucifer, the Son of the Morning! Is it he who bears the Light, and with its splendors intolerable, blinds feeble, sensual, or selfish souls? Doubt it not!"[128]

I have personally spoken with a 32nd degree Mason who is a friend of a friend, and at first he dodged my insinuations that he worshiped Lucifer, but I pressed him and he started praising Lucifer and criticizing Christians saying they were morbid for worshiping a dead man hanging on a cross, and that they were judgmental and intolerant of other religions.

---

[126] Pike, Albert - *Morals and Dogma* page 819

[127] Pike, Albert - *Morals and Dogma* page 102

[128] Pike, Albert - *Morals and Dogma* p. 321

Satanist Aleister Crowley seems to agree that there is some great mystical secret held by the inner circle when he said, "Although I was admitted to the thirty-third and last degree of Freemasonry so long ago as 1900, it was not until the summer of 1912 that my suspicion was confirmed. I speak of my belief that behind the frivolities and convivialities of our greatest institution [Freemasonry] lay in truth a secret."[129]

In his book autobiography *The Confessions of Aleister Crowley*, he wrote, "...for Freemasonry asserts that every man is himself the living, slain and re-arisen Christ in his own person. It is true that not one mason in ten thousand in England is aware of this fact; but he has only to remember his 'raising' to realize the fundamental truth of the statement."[130]

Albert Pike was a lawyer who became a Confederate General in the Army, fighting against the northern colonies during the Civil War trying to ensure slavery was kept in place. He is believed to have been the leader of the Knights of the Golden Circle, a secret society of Confederates that included notorious outlaw Jesse James and John Wilkes Booth, the man who assassinated President Lincoln. The Lincoln assassination was not the action of a lone gunman, but was part of a larger plot hatched by the Knights of the Golden Circle with hopes of securing a victory for the south. John Wilkes Booth and other Knights of the Golden Circle planned to assassinate

---

[129] Grant, Kenneth – *Aleister Crowley and the Hidden God* page 174

[130] Crowley, Aleister - *Confessions of Aleister Crowley* page 669

the vice president and the secretary of state that same night, thus eliminating three of the top officials in the United States government, hoping that would ensure the Confederates could take over.

Aside from being a key member of the KGC, it is rumored that Albert Pike founded the KKK as well, which isn't far-fetched at all, considering it's obvious he was a racist who saw black people as slaves. When African Americans first wanted to become part of the Masonic fraternity, Pike wrote, "I took my obligations to white men, not to Negroes. When I have to accept Negroes as brothers or leave Masonry, I shall leave it."[131]

Pike owned the *Daily Appeal*, a newspaper in Tennessee, where on April 16, 1868 he published an editorial saying, "The disenfranchised people of the South...can find no protection for property, liberty or life, except in secret association...We would unite every white man in the South, who is opposed to negro suffrage [the right to vote], into one great Order of Southern Brotherhood, with an organization complete, active, vigorous, in which a few should execute the concentrated will of all, and whose very existence should be concealed from all but its members."[132]

A larger than life statue of Albert Pike stands in Judiciary Square in Washington D.C. alongside Abraham Lincoln, and Pike's body is kept in a tomb inside the Masonic headquarters in Washington D.C., a building

---

[131] William H. Upton - *Negro Masonry*, New York: AMS Press, 1975

[132] Brown, Walter Lee - *A Life of Albert Pike* page 439-440

called the House of the Temple, which is the home of the "Supreme Council" of Freemasonry.

Theosophist teacher and occult writer Alice Bailey, who claimed her books were dictated to her telepathically by an entity she called the Master of Wisdom, wrote that, "The Masonic Movement when it can be divorced from politics and social ends and from its present paralyzing condition of inertia, will meet the need of those who can, and should wield power. It is the custodian of the law; it is the home of the Mysteries and the seat of initiation. It holds its symbolism the ritual of Deity, and the way of salvation is pictorially preserved in its work. The methods of Deity are demonstrated in its temples, and under the All-seeing Eye the work can go forward. It is a far more occult organization than can be realized, and is intended to be the training school for the coming advanced occultists. In its ceremonials lies hid the wielding of the forces connected with the growth and life of the kingdoms of nature and the unfoldment of the divine aspects in man."[133]

Many Muslims are against Freemasonry partly because one of Freemasonry's ultimate goals is to rebuild the Temple of Solomon on its original site in Jerusalem, where the Al-Aqsa Mosque currently stands. This spot is claimed by both Muslims and Jews as their religion's holy place, and a primary aim of both Palestinians and Jews is to once and for all claim this spot as their own.

Muslims are also critical of Freemasonry's secretive nature. Sheikh Ahmad Kutty, a prominent Muslim

---

[133] Bailey, Alice - *Externalization of the Hierarchy* page 511

scholar at the Islamic Institute of Toronto, explains, "As far as I know, Freemasonry is a secret organization whose beliefs and practices are totally kept confidential except from those who are initiated into it. They have levels of secrets which are not divulged to those who are at lower levels. A Muslim should never fall prey or give allegiance to something which cannot be scrutinized by the firm criteria of the Quran and the Sunnah. Whoever joins Freemasonry is like a person who writes a blank check; by doing so he agrees to give allegiance blindly to an authority to comply with their wishes no matter what they are."[134]

In 1998 a law was enacted in Britain ordering police, judges, and other government employees in the UK to reveal whether they were Freemasons after it was believed a Masonic Mafia was operating within the government.[135] Ten years later the law was reversed but the controversy continued. A secret Metropolitan Police report written in 2002 and leaked to the press in 2014 reveals that an internal investigation by Scotland Yard, the police agency of London, discovered that an organized criminal network of Freemasons largely controlled the police department.[136] The investigation, called Operation

---

[134] http://askthescholar.com/AskTheScholar2.aspx?q=1098

[135] *The Independent* "Anger at 'cloak of secrecy' for Freemason judges" (November 10th 2009)

[136] *The Independent* "Revealed: How gangs used the Freemasons to corrupt police" (January 13th 2014)

Tiberius, found that the Metropolitan Police were infested with corrupt Freemasons who used their position within the department to engage in organized crime, destroy evidence, and recruit other corrupt officers.[137]

While Freemasonry is primarily a men's organization, there is a woman's branch called the Eastern Star, whose logo is literally an upside down pentagram. There is even a branch for young girls called Job's Daughters (or Rainbow Girls) and one for boys called the DeMolays—named after Jacques de Molay, the last Grand Master of the Knights Templar. President Bill Clinton was a DeMolay as a child, which many believe served as a prep school to groom him to later take his place as an Illuminati insider.

As noted earlier, it's important to highlight that in 1782 Adam Weishaupt successfully infiltrated Freemasonry at the Congress of Wilhelmsbad, Germany, which was the largest, most important Masonic gathering of the eighteenth century.[138] There he assigned men to oversee the implementation of "Illuminated Masonry" and recruit new supporters from Masonic lodges throughout Europe who would work on behalf of the Illuminati.

---

[137] Ibid.

[138] Macky, Albert - *The Encyclopedia of Freemasonry,* Entry on Illuminati of Bavaria

Skull & Bones Society

Even if you're familiar with Skull & Bones and some of the allegations about them (many of which are true, by the way), the deeper you look into this group, the more apparent it becomes that they are anything but an ordinary college fraternity. Since it has already been touched upon earlier in this book, I won't repeat most of what has already been covered, but I will add a few more pieces to the puzzle that most people are not familiar with so you can get a more complete picture of them.

Skull & Bones was the FIRST secret society at Yale and the first *senior* society—meaning someone doesn't become a member until their senior year at Yale. There were fraternities at Yale, but Skull & Bones started a new chapter in the school's history in 1832 when they created the first secret society, soon to be followed by Scroll & Key and then later Wolf's Head, which are the top three senior (and secret) societies. The three clubs even hold regular "inter-council meetings" several times a year to coordinate their activities.

Each year fifteen new members are recruited (or "tapped," as they say) to join. They are chosen during the last few weeks of the semester their Junior year in order to prepare them to replace the outgoing seniors who lead them through the elaborate and satanic initiation ceremony where they are given a new name (Long Devil, Machiavelli, Baal, Beelzebub are just a few examples).[139] During part of the initiation, they lay in a coffin and give

---

[139] Robbins, Alexandria - *Secrets of the Tomb* page 127

a detailed history of their sexual experiences up to that point in a ritual called Connubial Bliss.

Members consider the world "their realm" and call outsiders "Barbarians." Once initiated the men (and now some women) are considered "bonesmen" or Knights of Eulogia, which is Greek for "Knights of the Blessing." They even hold a special Skull & Bones wedding ceremony when one of their members gets married to initiate the new wife into the "Bones Family." Behind every corrupt man, there's usually a woman willing to look the other way. They also own a 40-acre island located on the St. Lawrence River in Alexandria Bay, called Deer Island, which is used as a private vacation spot for "bonesmen" and their families.

After the summer, when the new school year begins, and the new initiates are then seniors, they meet every Thursday and Sunday night for a fancy dinner (often steak and lobster) that is followed up with what are called "sessions" which include various lectures and debates. It is believed that they eat using Adolf Hitler's silverware that a "bonesmen" somehow obtained. Skull & Bones has its own collection of books in its library located in the Tomb [headquarters] to help new members learn the ways of the world. There is even a "Bones Bible" and other black books kept in the clubhouse library. They operate as a 5013c organization under the Russell Trust Association (or RTA Incorporated) and their 2012 filings with the IRS (which must be available for "public review" if you know just where to look and how to get them) shows they spent $469,000 dollars that year on "personal development" for their members.[140]

No alcohol is allowed inside the Skull & Bones Tomb clubhouse, that's how serious they are. This is not a party. Taking over the world is serious business. Another difference between Skull & Bones and ordinary fraternities is that frats usually do community service and help with local fundraisers, but this strange group only looks out for themselves. In fact, the men (and now women) who are recruited into Skull & Bones are never engineers or mathematicians, because these careers hold little power compared to those in business, banking, media, politics, and law, which are the dominant careers of the members.

By now I'm sure you're familiar that the most famous member is President George W. Bush, but what most people don't know is that his family has a long history with the group. Aside from his father George Herbert Walker Bush being a member, Prescott Bush, George W.'s grandfather was a member, as well as his uncles Jonathan Bush, John Walker, and his other uncle George Herbert Walker III. So was his great-uncle George Herbert Walker Junior, and his cousin Ray Walker.[141]

After George W. Bush became president in January 2001, he appointed several of his fellow bonesmen to various high level positions within the government. For example, he nominated William H. Donaldson (Bones

---

[140] IRS Form 990 RTA Incorporated OMB no 1545-0047 line 18

[141] Robbins, Alexandria - *Secrets of the Tomb* page 164

1953) as chairman of the Securities and Exchange Commission; Edward McNally (Bones 1979) was given a position in the Department of Homeland Security.[142] Robert D. McCallum was appointed to Assistant Attorney General; Roy Austin was made the ambassadorship to Trinidad and Tobago; Victor Ashe was given a spot on the board of directors of Fannie Mae (the Federal National Mortgage Association), America's biggest home mortgage financier, and so on.[143]

The list of Skull & Bones members who have risen to the pinnacles of power is long. Co-founder Alfonzo Taft became the head of the Department of War, which was the name of the Department of Defense until the government changed the name in true Orwellian double-speak fashion. Alfonzo Taft's son, William Taft became President of the United States. Pierre Jay was the first chairman of the New York Federal Reserve Bank; Winston Lord became chairman of the Council on Foreign Relations. Percy Rockefeller was on the board of Brown Brothers Harriman & Company, which had its assets seized in 1942 under the Trading with the Enemy Act after it was discovered the firm was helping fund Adolf Hitler.[144] John Kerry, who ran for president against George W. Bush

---

[142] *Yale Daily News* "Yalie joins Homeland Security" By Michelle Rosenthal (January 29, 2002)

[143] Robbins, Alexandria - *Secrets of the Tomb* pages 181-182

[144] *The Guardian* "How Bush's grandfather helped Hitler's rise to power" by Ben Aris and Duncan Campbell (September 25, 2004)

in the 2004 election, later became Secretary of State under President Obama.

The list of key power players in government just goes on and on. Raymond Price (1951) was a speechwriter for Presidents Nixon, Ford, and Bush. Christopher Taylor Buckley (1975) was the chief speechwriter for George H. W. Bush when he was the Vice President. Austan Goolsbee (1991) became President Barack Obama's chief economic advisor, etc., etc. It's interesting to also point out that the father of American football, Walter Camp, was a bonesman. Football, as you may know, serves as a modern day bread and circus distraction for the majority of Americans, channeling their energy and aggression into watching a bunch of men chasing after a ball instead of paying attention to important social issues. This is all part of the plan because it keeps most people out of the way so the elite can carry out their agenda.

Skull & Bones members created the American Historical Association, the American Psychological Association, the American Chemical Society; and the American Economic Association. The atomic bomb was basically a Skull & Bones project involving William Averell Harriman, Governor of New York (class of 1913), Henry Stimson, Secretary of War (class of 1888), Robert Lovett, Secretary of Defense (class of 1918), McGeorge Bundy, U.S. Intelligence Officer (class of 1940) and George L. Harrison, advisor to the Secretary of War and President of the New York Federal Reserve Bank (class of 1909).

I guess it shouldn't be surprising that an organization whose symbols and themes revolve around death would ultimately be responsible for creating the most deadly weapon in the history of mankind. The group's obsession with death is extremely disturbing and all the death symbolism is meant to serve as a continuous reminder of their own mortality, and since they don't believe in an afterlife, they are urged to become gods on earth during their short time here by any means necessary.

We often think of the society "ruling the world" in terms of politicians and business, but they have also dominated the faculty of Yale University as well. Some reports claim that four out of five faculty members between 1865 and 1916 were bonesmen.[145] In 1873, a student newspaper called *The Iconoclast*, published an article denouncing Skull & Bones control of Yale. "Out of every class Skull and Bones takes its men...They have obtained control of Yale. It's business is performed by them. Money paid to the college must pass into their hands, and be subject to their will....It is Yale College against Skull and Bones!"[146]

Aside from being accused of dominating the faculty at Yale and power positions in politics and business, they are often accused of worshiping Satan and conducting extraordinary disturbing rituals. The group's favorite number, 322, possibly holds a secret satanic meaning. Many people believe the number 322 is a reference to the Book of Genesis chapter 3 verse 22 which talks about Adam and Eve eating the Forbidden Fruit from the Tree

---

[145] Robbins, Alexandria - *Secrets of the Tomb* pp. 48, 50, 127

[146] *The Iconoclast* (1873)

of Knowledge of Good and Evil and employing this number is seen as a reference to the Luciferian doctrine or the satanic secret.

In 2001, a reporter named Ron Rosenbaum from the *New York Observer* used a night vision camera to videotape the initiation ritual from the ledge of an adjacent building that overlooked the courtyard of the Skull & Bones clubhouse. The footage shows initiates kneeling down and kissing a skull, and then appearing to take a knife and slit the throat of a naked woman who was being held down by other members.[147]

People were also heard chanting a strange mantra, "The hangman equals death, the Devil equals death, death equals death!" The hangman likely refers to Jesus hanging on the cross and the mantra appears to convey the same meaning as the riddle of the four human skulls when they are asked which one is the wise man, the beggar, the king, and the fool. The answer given is that it doesn't matter to them because "all is the same in death."

Rosenbaum was not sure what to make of this behavior and asked, "Is that the secret they've been covering up ever since the society was founded in 1832, the offshoot of a German secret society: devil worship? A fulfillment of the paranoid fantasies of the fundamentalist right, who believe the Eastern establishment *is* a front for satanic conspiracy."[148]

---

[147] *New York Observer* "At Skull and Bones, Bush's Secret Club Initiates Ream Gore" by Ron Rosenbaum (April 23rd 2001)

[148] Ibid.

Scroll and Key Society

The Scroll & Key society is a another secret society at Yale University, created in 1842, ten years after Skull & Bones, and was the second secret society at the school composed of seniors. Just like Skull & Bones, Scroll & Key recruits fifteen new students at the end of their junior year who they see as having the potential and willingness to further the organization's goals. Scroll & Key is considered one of the "Big Three" senior societies at Yale —the other two being, of course, Skull & Bones, along with Wolf's Head.

Fareed Zakaria, a CNN commentator on foreign affairs, was initiated as a member of Scroll & Key when he attended the university in 1986. Fareed went onto to attend Bilderberg meetings (in 1993 and 2009), and became a member of the Council on Foreign Relations as well. He didn't just join the CFR, he actually was the managing editor of their publication *Foreign Affairs* which serves up their political propaganda on a platter for the members.

Fareed once argued that the Constitution is outdated and should be "fixed" to remove the Second Amendment in order to "modernize the Constitution for the 21st Century."[149]

Other notable members include Ari Shapiro (class of 2000) who became the White House Correspondent for National Public Radio (NPR); James Stillman Rockefeller

---

[149] *CNN* "Fareed Zakaria GPS: Is it Time To Correct the Constitution?" (June 20th 2011)

(class of 1924) who was the President and Chairman of the First National City Bank of New York; Cornelius Vanderbilt III of the wealthy Vanderbilt dynasty (class of 1895); and Huntington D. Sheldon (class of 1925) worked for the CIA as the Director of the Office of Current Intelligence.

The Scroll & Key society operate under the legal entity called the Kingsley Trust Association which creates a shield of privacy to protect them from people searching for information using the name "Scroll & Key" and according to their 2012 IRS filings, which must be made available for public inspection, they have over $9 million dollars in assets and spent $650,000 dollars that year.[150]

Wolfs Head

Wolf's Head is the third of the "Big Three" senior secret societies at Yale and was founded in 1884, partly to counter the dominance of Skull & Bones over student affairs. They too recruit fifteen new upcoming seniors for membership and are now part of the larger network consisting of Skull & Bones and Scroll & Key.

The club's logo is a wolf's head on an inverted Egyptian hieroglyph called an ankh, which is often called the Egyptian Cross and said to symbolize "the key of life." Wolf's Head built its own Egyptian themed "tomb" headquarters in 1924 thanks to a donation from one of their members, Edward Harkness, who went on to become

---

[150] IRS Form 990 2012 EIN: 06-0706508 Kingsley Trust Association, Line 18: Total Expenses and Line 22: Net Assets

John D. Rockefeller's right hand man. Harkness himself was listed by Forbes magazine as the 6th richest man in the world during his life.

The club holds meetings every Thursday and Sunday night where the men (and since 1992 some women) prepare themselves for life after college, when their real work begins.

One of their most well-known members was Erastus Corning, who went on to become the Mayor of Albany, New York for more than 40 years! Another prominent members was Paul Moore Jr. who later became a bishop of the New York Episcopal Church and one of the best known clergy. After his death his daughter revealed that Moore was bisexual and had a history of homosexual affairs.[151] She detailed her father's double life in her book *The Bishop's Daughter: A Memoir*. While the Bush crime family has been active in Skull & Bones for generations, they also have a hand in Wolf's Head. President George H. W. Bush's younger brother William Henry Trotter "Bucky" Bush (born July 14, 1938) was inducted in 1960.

The business name of Wolf's Head is the Phelps Association, and according to their 2013 IRS filings, which must be made public since they are registered as a 501c3 tax exempt foundation, the organization holds over $6 million dollars in assets and spent over $373,000 dollars on their members that year alone.[152] Wolf's Head

---

[151] *The New Yorker* "The Bishop's Daughter" by Honor Moore (March 3, 2008 Issue)

[152] IRS Form 990 2012 EIN: 06-6069051 Phelps Association, Line 18: Total Expenses and Line 20: Net Assets

members were responsible for the formation of the Yale
Political Union which is the center for politically minded
students at the University.

Communism

Communism is most often promoted as a political
philosophy to allegedly help the average worker
(proletariat) fight against the "oppressive" business
owners (bourgeoisie), but it's actually a conspiracy
controlled by the elite who have used Communism as a
mechanism to encourage the creation of an all-powerful
super state that they themselves are in control of.

As Gary Allen puts it, author of *None Dare Call it
Conspiracy*, "Communism is not a movement of the
downtrodden masses but is a movement created,
manipulated and used by power-seeking billionaires in
order to gain control over the world...first by establishing
socialist governments in the various nations and then
consolidating them all through a 'Great Merger,' into an
all-powerful world, socialist super-state probably under
the auspices of the United Nations."[153]

The Communist Manifesto, written by Karl Marx and
his often overlooked coauthor Frederich Engles, was first
published in 1848, and is widely believed to have sparked
the Communist Revolution in Russia in 1917 and
spreading to other countries such as North Korea in 1948,
China in 1949, and a few years later moving to Cuba in
1953—but what most people overlook is that Karl Marx

---

[153] Allan, Gary – *None Dare Call It Conspiracy* page 35

was really just a secretary who wrote the book outlining the Communist philosophy for a secret society called the Communist League.

The manifesto itself reads, "The Communist League (formerly called the League of Just Men)...which could of course only be a secret one...commissioned the undersigned [Karl Marx and Friedrich Engels], at the Congress held in London in November 1847, to draw up for publication a detailed theoretical and practical program of the Party.   Such was the origin of the following Manifesto, the manuscript of which traveled to London to be printed, a few weeks before the February Revolution."[154]

The California Senate Investigating Committee on Education in 1953 stated, "So-called modern Communism is apparently the same hypocritical and deadly world conspiracy to destroy civilization that was founded by the secret order of the Illuminati in Bavaria on May 1, 1776, and that raised its hoary head in our colonies here at critical periods before the adoption of our Federal Constitution."[155]

The report goes on to say, "The recognition of May 1, 1776, as the founding date of this world revolution conspiracy is not difficult to understand, when it is realized that May Day is frequently celebrated, even in

---

[154] *The Communist Manifesto* - Preface to the German Edition of 1872

[155] Eleventh Report Senate Investigating Committee On Education published by the Senate of California page 169

recent times, by rioting and bloodshed on a world-wide scale."[156]

"It was not until 1847 or 1848, that the Communist conspirators, who had theretofore operated in secret, came out in the open with the Manifesto of the Communist Party, by Karl Marx and Friedrich Engels, boldly proclaiming against practically everything upon which civilization is based—God, religion, the family, individual liberty, and so forth—the concluding paragraph of the manifesto reading: 'Communists scorn to hide their views and aims. They openly declare that their purpose can only be achieved by the forcible overthrow of the whole extant social order. Let the ruling classes tremble at the prospect of a Communist revolution. Proletarians have nothing to lose but their chains. They have a world to win.'"[157]

"In issuing this manifesto the Communist conspirators evidently believe the time had arrived when, with the aid of ignorant victims, a world-wide take-over could be accomplished; but there were not enough ignorant victims then, and the expected coup failed."[158]

"The Communist conspirators thereupon conceived the plan, for the future, of supplementing the long-established secret conspiracy, in existence since May 1,

---

[156] Eleventh Report Senate Investigating Committee On Education published by the Senate of California page 170

[157] Eleventh Report Senate Investigating Committee On Education published by the Senate of California page 170

[158] Eleventh Report Senate Investigating Committee On Education published by the Senate of California page 170

1776, with an unremitting publish campaign for victims among the ignorant of all nations. And, in an attempt to hide from view the underlying hypocritical conspiracy existing since May 1, 1776, it was decided that, in such public campaign, the manifesto of 1848 should be heralded as the founding date of communism, and Karl Marx falsely proclaimed as its author."[159]

New Age guru Benjamin Crème, who is looking forward to the arrival of the Antichrist, thinking he will turn earth into a heavenly paradise, admitted, "Marx was indeed a member of the Hierarchy, of a certain degree. Looking at the effect of his work over the years—that could only have been the work of a disciple of some degree, an initiate of some level—first to have the vision, and secondly to have the capacity to embody that vision so that the work could spread."[160]

While Christians are often said to have killed the most number of people in the name of God, the reality is that Communists have been responsible for the greatest genocides in the world, killing in the name of the State (their government), in countries like China and North Korea. Over 30 million were killed in the Chinese Communist Revolution lead by Mao Zedong, and Joseph Stalin killed over 3 million in Russia in the name of

---

[159] Ibid.

[160] Crème, Benjamin – *The Reappearance of the Christ and the Masters of Wisdom* p. 190-191

Communism.[161]   Massive numbers have also been killed in Vietnam and North Korea by Communist revolutionaries.   Belief in any God other than the government is forbidden, because it reduces people's allegiance to the State.   The government is God in Communist countries.

At the heart of Communism is an enormous all-powerful government that controls every aspect of people's lives—from the schools, to their jobs, to healthcare and banking; with a small group of elite bureaucrats living lives of luxury at the expense of the working class.   This is, of course, one of the primary goals of the Illuminati, who are promoting the idea as a utopian paradise.

Bohemian Grove

Because the Bohemian Grove has become fairly well-known in terms of the Illuminati conspiracy, many people may think they know all about it, but in most cases their knowledge is limited to only a few basic facts.   Because of its extraordinarily bizarre rituals and elite membership list causing widespread rumors, most people who have done a brief investigation into the Illuminati are probably familiar with the basics of the Bohemian Grove, but for

---

[161]Stephen G. Wheatcroft, "Victims of Stalinism and the Soviet Secret Police: The Comparability and Reliability of the Archival Data. Not the Last Word", Source: Europe-Asia Studies, Vol. 51, No. 2 (Mar. 1999), pp. 315–345

those who wish to scratch beyond the surface of this subject, there is certainly a lot to be learned.

As you may have heard, it's a 2700 acre privately owned redwood forest in Northern California located about an hour north of San Francisco in a small town named Monte Rio and serves as a vacation spot for elite men every summer in mid-July, where around 1000 of the world's most powerful men gather for a "men's retreat" inside the Grove which is kicked off by the infamous Cremation of Care ritual, the human sacrifice-depicting ceremony, where a life-size effigy of a person is burned on an altar at the base of a 40-foot tall demon-looking statue. It's sort of the Camp David of California (with some Satanism mixed in) and was created back in 1872.

The term *Bohemian* refers to people who live non-traditional lifestyles and people who are adventurers, or vagabonds. The club's annual mid-summer encampment is called the "greatest men's party on earth" by members, who include many former presidents, military leaders, famous journalists, and top businessmen.

The Bohemian Grove's mascot (and logo) is the Owl of Minerva, the same symbol that Adam Weishaupt used as his emblem.[162] Within the original Illuminati there was a level in the hierarchy called the Minervals and the owl symbolizes wisdom because it can "see in the dark" which is analogous to being enlightened.

Out of curiosity, in the past, occasionally a reporter would try to sneak inside the now highly guarded

---

[162] Barruel, Abbe- *Memoirs Illustrating the History of Jacobinism* page 582

compound, and some have been successful, yet little has been reported in major publications. Membership lists and program guides have sometimes been stolen and published by employees, and in the 1980s a group called the Bohemian Grove Action Network dedicated themselves to doing just that.

The "patron saint" of the Bohemian Grove is Saint John of Nepomuk and a large statue of him stands inside the grounds with him holding his index finger over his mouth, signifying secrecy and reminding members to keep their mouths shut. A patron saint is someone who embodies a group's philosophies or goals. John of Nepomuk received the confessionals of the queen of Bohemia in the 1300s and when pressured by the king to reveal her confessions after he suspected her of cheating on him, Saint John refused and was killed by the king. Paralleling Robert De Niro's gangster gospel in *Goodfellas* that you "never rat on your friends, and always keep your mouth shut," the Illuminati cherish the power of secrecy and remind all Bohos (the name members are often referred to) of this with the statue of John of Nepomuk standing prominently in their forest.

A presidential advisor to Presidents Ford, Nixon, Reagan, and Clinton, named David Gergen, who also worked as a CNN contributor, was confronted on camera by Alex Jones from Infowars.com on the streets of New York during the 2004 Republican National Convention when Jones stuck a microphone in his face and asked if he'd ever seen the Cremation of Care ritual.

Gergen, looking visibly uncomfortable, responded, "Frankly I don't think that's something I need to talk to you about."[163]   When Jones asked him again about the ritual, Gergen snapped, "That's none of your damn business!" and walked away.[164]   The clip can be seen on YouTube.

One of their popular sayings is that "weaving spiders come not here," which is said to mean that the Grove is not a place for conducting business or working, hence "weaving," but this explanation is just a cover story for the saying's true meaning. It actually means "don't dare challenge the members," (or really, the "Gods," as they see themselves) and comes from the ancient story in Greek mythology of Arachne, a woman weaver who disrespected Athena, the Goddess of weaving, by failing to acknowledge that the woman's skills came from the Goddess and not from her own power.   Athena then turned her into a spider as punishment, dooming her and her descendants to weave webs forever, since out of her own ignorance she thought she was better than the "Gods."

The club is divided into about 124 different camps inside the grounds, each one having anywhere from a dozen to 125 men.   Each individual camp has its own sleeping quarters, kitchen and bar, and each one has a captain who is responsible for managing their territory.[165] Each camp has a different name and tends to contain

---

[163] Jones, Alex - *The Order of Death* (2005)

[164] Ibid.

[165] Phillips, Peter - *A Relative Advantage: Sociology of the San Francisco Bohemian Club. A Doctoral Dissertation* (1994) Page 67

members who work in the same field. For example, the Hill Billies camp is comprised of mainly men in big business, bankers, politicians, and media moguls from Texas. The sign for Hill Billies' camp, which the Bush family belongs to, consists of a cloven hoofed horned Devil figure.

The Mandalay camp is made of mainly political figures such as former presidents and defense contractors. Owls Nest is another elite camp of former presidents, high ranking military personnel and defense contractors. Other camp names include the Lost Angels (banking and media), Stowaway (Rockefeller family members and other big oil men), and Hillside (military men including Joint Chiefs of Staff members), just to name a few. No seated president ever attends because his schedule and location is so closely monitored that his visitation would bring too much unwanted attention to the club, but once they are out of office (and before they are even elected) many are fixtures at the encampment.

Sociologist Peter Phillips, who earned his Ph. D. by writing his doctoral dissertation on the Grove in 1994, wrote, "Sharing a camp together at the Grove gives Bohemian directors of major U.S. policy councils ample opportunity to discuss current affairs and socio-economic policy issues. Watching and listening to reactions to Lakeside Chats by various other Bohemians also gives policy directors an opportunity to evaluate policy concerns from the broad sampling of the American corporate business community encamped at the Grove. In this sense, the Grove serves as an informal evaluatory feedback process to the top socio-economic domestic and foreign policy councils in the United States."[166]

The midsummer encampment, as their annual gathering is called, lasts for two weeks from mid-July to the end of the month, with some members and guests coming for a weekend, and others staying for several days or even an entire week or longer. Every afternoon during the two weeks a "Lakeside Chat" is given at 12:30pm, just after lunch, where a political insider or industry leader gives a 30-minute talk on his area of expertise.

It has been rumored that Alan Greenspan was chosen to be nominated as Chairman of the Federal Reserve after a meeting in the Grove, and Arnold Schwarzenegger's successful bid for governor of California was allegedly given the green light by insiders at the Grove as well. There's even a famous picture taken in 1967 showing Ronald Reagan (then Governor of California) and Richard Nixon, who would be elected president the following year, sitting next to each other, where they are said to have been coordinating their political careers.[167]

Despite claiming the Grove is just a vacation spot and no work is conducted during the encampment, the Manhattan Project (the plan for the atomic bomb) was

---

[166] Phillips, Peter - *A Relative Advantage: Sociology of the San Francisco Bohemian Club. A Doctoral Dissertation* (1994) page 127

[167] Phillips, Peter - *A Relative Advantage: Sociology of the San Francisco Bohemian Club. A Doctoral Dissertation* (1994) page 95

actually hatched inside the club.[168] Aside from the atomic bomb being born in the Bohemian Grove, the United Nations was hatched from the club as well.[169] Peter Phillips reveals, "One of the foremost political events in which the Bohemian political network played a significant role was the United Nations Conference of International Organization (UNCIO), April 25th to June 26, 1945, in San Francisco. This was the original formation meeting for the United Nations, with delegates from fifty nations. Receptions for UNCIO delegates and key dignitaries were held at the Bohemian Club on May 17, May 29, June 4, and June 5. Towards the end of the U.N. conference the Club invited all delegates to a program at the Grove."[170]

The club has limited number of rare yearbooks that are occasionally printed for members, called the *Annals of the Bohemian Grove,* that contain photos of attendees dressed in drag, along with pictures of the Cremation of Care ritual so men can reminisce about their time there. I have been able to obtain several copies of these books since every once in a while they'll find their way into the public after older members die and their book collections are sold at estate sales or donated to charity. In one Annal

---

[168] Phillips, Peter - *A Relative Advantage: Sociology of the San Francisco Bohemian Club. A Doctoral Dissertation* (1994) page 92

[169] Phillips, Peter - *A Relative Advantage: Sociology of the San Francisco Bohemian Club. A Doctoral Dissertation* (1994) page 93

[170] Phillips, Peter - *A Relative Advantage: Sociology of the San Francisco Bohemian Club. A Doctoral Dissertation* (1994) page 111

there is a photo of George Bush Senior and George W. Bush standing at the podium giving a Lakeside talk in 1995 where Bush Senior reportedly told the audience that his son would make a great president one day.[171]

The first book dedicated to exposing the Bohemian Grove was published in 1974 titled *The Bohemian Grove and other Retreats*, written by William Domhoff, a sociologist and professor who taught at the University of California, Santa Cruz.

The preface to his book explains that upper-class retreats are of a major sociological relevance, because "they increase the social cohesiveness of America's rulers and provide private settings in which business and political problems can be discussed informally and off the record."[172]

The book continues on page one saying, "You are one of fifteen hundred men gathered together from all over the country for the annual encampment of the rich and famous at the Bohemian Grove. And you are about to take part in a strange ceremony that has marked every Bohemian Grove gathering since 1880."[173] He goes on to include a transcript and detailed description of the Cremation of Care, which was a historic revelation,

[171] Rothkopf, David - *Superclass: The Global Power Elite and the World They are Making* page 284

[172] Domhoff, William - *The Bohemian Grove and Other Retreats: A Study in Ruing-Class Cohesiveness* Preface

[173] Domhoff, William - *The Bohemian Grove and Other Retreats: A Study in Ruing-Class Cohesiveness* Page 1

especially considering this was back in the 1970s before the Information Age.

Twenty-five years later, in the year 2000, Alex Jones from Infowars would sneak inside and capture the first ever video footage of the ritual. While it's one thing to read about the ceremony, actually seeing it leaves you with your head shaking and confirms many of the supposed "rumors" are true. Jones' footage is authentic, and after his infiltration they beefed up security and began using thermal imaging scanners and K-9 police tracker dogs to identify anyone lurking around the grounds who doesn't belong there.

The most disturbing allegations about the Bohemian Grove don't just lurk in the dark depths of the Internet, but actually come largely from a former U.S. Senator named John DeCamp. The allegations are so horrific and graphic, I don't even like to talk about them because they involve claims of sadistic child abuse, human sacrifice, and snuff films, said to have occurred there in the 1980s. If you are interested in learning about John DeCamp's allegations, you can check out his book *The Franklin Cover-up*, but I warn you, it is extremely disturbing and you may wish you had never heard of them.

Belizean Grove

When talking about secret societies or the Illuminati, most people often think of a group of men, since they have been the dominant sex throughout history, but powerful female secret societies, although rare, do exist. The Belizean Grove is a group of around 100 influential women from politics, media, and high ranking women in the military, that was created as a female version of the Bohemian Grove! It was founded on Super Bowl Weekend in 2001 by Susan Stautberg while her husband and most men were preoccupied with football, since she obviously had something else in mind.

The Belizean Grove, while inspired by the Bohemian Grove, is named after the country of Belize in Central America where the women meet every year for three days of private off-the-record talks, which is said to be "a balance of fun, substantive programs and bonding."[174] It certainly is strange that some of the world's most powerful women would fly down to Central America for a weekend when they could simply meet locally at one of their lavish private residences. Perhaps this is so they can go out to the bars without the risk of being recognized by the locals so they can engage in extramarital affairs with younger men willing to bed a cougar. Since such behavior would run them the risk of getting caught or recognized if they did it in a major American city, perhaps the long distance ladies night was designed to facilitate such activities.

While high level female executives from major banks, public relations firms, and even the U.S. Military, all belong to the Belezian Grove, perhaps the group's most famous member is Supreme Court Justice Sonia Sotomayor, who was nominated by Barack Obama to sit as a justice on the court. During the vetting process it was

---

[174] *New York Times* "Sotomayor Defends Ties to Association" by Savage, Charlie and Kirkpatrick, David D (June 15th 2009)

uncovered that she was a member of this strange girls group, causing her to resign since the American Bar Association forbids a judge to be a member of any organization that "discriminates" against anyone based on sex, race, religion or national origin.

If it had not been for Republicans digging for dirt on Sonia Sotomayor hoping to derail her appointment to the Supreme Court, we likely would still be unaware of the Belizean Grove's existence. Founder Susan Stautberg was not happy about the new publicity, and said, "we like to be under the radar screen."

The group says they are "a constellation of influential women who are key decision makers in the profit, nonprofit and social sectors; who build long-term, mutually beneficial relationships in order to both take charge of their own destinies and help others to do the same."

One member, Mary Pearl, dean of New York's Stony Brook University, said, "It's hard if you're someone who's a type 'A' personality, who's achieved a lot and who may be in the public eye—it's hard to make friends, so it's just a mutually supportive wonderful experience. We get together just for socializing and also just for intelligent conversation."[175]

In order to join, a member must recommend a woman to the Belizean Grove "advisory board" that then decide whether or not to admit them to the club. A few known members are Army General Ann E. Dunwoody, former

---

[175] *Politico* "Sonia Sotomayor found friends in elite group" by Keneth Vogel (June 4th 2009)

Goldman Sachs executive Ann Kaplan, and General Services Administration Director Lurita Doan. Facebook's Chief Operating Officer Sheryl Sandberg is a likely member as well.

A New York Times article written in 2011 said, "Belizean Grove has connected the top women in technology to the top women in finance, to the top women in media, to the top women in law, to the top women in retail, and so on."[176] It is currently unknown if the group conducts any bizarre rituals like their male counterpart at the Bohemian Grove, and at the time of this writing little else is known about the Belizean Grove.

Seraphic Society

Would you believe there's a secret society of elite *secretaries*? I'm not kidding. Known as the Seraphic Society, this strange group was founded in 1940 in New York to supply, "leaders in industry, and social, civic, philanthropic, professional and other important enterprises" with trustworthy secretaries."[177] The most powerful CEOs in America get their secretaries from the Seraphic Society, which is named after the Seraphim, the highest order of angels in Heaven, because the society considers their secretaries angels who protect Gods.

---

[176] *The New York Times* "A Club for the Women Atop the Ladder" by Pamela Rychman (April 2, 2011)

[177] *New York Times* "Status is ... for C.E.O.'s; Having a Networked Secretary" by John Glassie (November 15th 1998)

David Rockefeller, Steve Forbes, CEOs from Meryl Lynch, Goldman Sachs, Chase Manhattan Bank, Sony, and many other Fortune 500 companies all use the Seraphic Society to provide them with "trustworthy" secretaries. A *Fortune* magazine article in 2009 even admitted that the Federal Reserve Bank of New York and the Council on Foreign Relations use this "secretarial Skull and Bones" society.[178]

When journalist John Glassie of the New York Times was working on an article about the group in 1998, he was told by the Seraphic president at the time, who asked not to be identified, that "We're very quiet, very low-key," and "It's very touchy."[179]

One "Angel" who was willing to speak with the reporter on the condition of anonymity told him, "Some people would love to be members but they just don't fit the qualifications, and that's what keeps this organization so special...You can't just say you want to join."[180]

With many high-powered CEOs of international banks being essentially organized crime bosses, they can't just hire any secretary to deal with their shady affairs. The Seraphic Society can provide them with women they know will not have any second thoughts or misgivings

---

[178] *Fortune Magazine* "Corner Office Confidential" by Jennifer Reingold (August 31st 2009)

[179] *New York Times* "Status is ... for C.E.O.'s; Having a Networked Secretary" by John Glassie (November 15th 1998)

[180] *New York Times* "Status is ... for C.E.O.'s; Having a Networked Secretary" By John Glassie (November 15, 1998)

about the kind of work their boss is involved in, and who will be compensated very well for their cooperation. The saying goes that behind every great man is a great woman, and the same is true that behind every *corrupt* man, is a woman who's willing to look the other way.

Secretaries for rich and powerful, or "administrative assistants," as they are often called, don't just deal with their boss's work schedule, but are also closely intertwined with their personal lives as well. Personal assistants often get to know the intimate details of their boss's lives and are trusted to manage what are called P & C's or personal and confidentials, which may range from doing their personal shopping, to even arranging the delivery of drugs or hookers.

The Ordo Templi Orientis

Ordo Templi Orientis (Latin for Order of the Temple of the East or Order of Oriental Templars, often abbreviated to O.T.O.) is a secret society (or "fraternal order" as they say) founded between 1895 and 1906 in Germany or Austria (their exact origin is unverified) whose spiritual teachings are based on the philosophy of Aleister Crowley and uses his *Book of the Law* as it's Bible. The O.T.O. was inspired by Freemasonry and its founders concocted nine different levels (or degrees) for initiates that each supposedly reveal new spiritual teachings. These degrees were later expanded to thirteen.

Aleister Crowley claimed a demon who possessed his wife while they were in Egypt dictated his *Book of the Law* to him in 1904, commanding him to obey the entity's ruthless social darwinistic rules such as, "Compassion is the vice of kings: stamp down the wretched and the weak: this is the law of the strong, this is our law and the joy of the world."[181] The demon, whose words Crowley wrote down in what would later be published as *The Book of the Law*, also commands readers to "Worship me with fire & blood; worship me with swords and with spears, is the command...let blood flow to my name. Trample down the Heathen; be upon them, o warrior, I will give you of their flesh to eat! Sacrifice cattle, little and big, after a child."[182]

It continues, "Damn them who pity! Kill and torture; spare not; be upon them! The best blood is of the moon, monthly, then the fresh blood of a child."[183] The demonic entity voicing its instructions finally said, "I am in a secret fourfold word, the blasphemy against all gods of men. Curse them! Curse them! Curse them! With my Hawk's head I peck at the eyes of Jesus as he hangs upon the cross."[184]

While anyone can pick up a copy of Crowley's book and read his teachings which make up the core of the O.T.O., many believe the organization's best kept secrets are only communicated orally, and involve what is called

---

[181] Crowley, Aleister – *The Book of The Law* page 31

[182] Crowley, Aleister – *The Book of The Law* page 40

[183] Crowley, Aleister – *The Book of The Law* page 41

[184] Crowley, Aleister – *The Book of The Law* page 47

sex magic (often spelled sex magick, with a "k" on the end), which is the belief that through certain sexual practices, one can reach a level of enlightenment that is unattainable by any other means.

"Dr. Israel Regardie [Crowley's personal secretary] believed that certain sex magick techniques could be used by advanced students to incarnate 'spiritual' energies on the physical place, as well as making important shifts in the orientation of the Psyche and the Universe. In other words, if these methods were used properly, couples could bring into the world 'divine' forces in the children they generated, who could influence the future of the race."[185]

"The realization that man's emotional, physical and sexual energies are food for the 'gods' can create great personal turmoil at first, however when one begins to joyously participate in the spiritual feeding frenzy, one is 'elevated perpendicularly to infinity.'"[186]

Crowley revealed in his autobiography that, "the O.T.O. is in possession of one supreme secret. The whole of its system at the time when I became an initiate of the Sanctuary of the Gnosis was directed towards communicating to its members, by progressively plain hints, this all-important instruction. I personally believe that if this secret, which is a scientific secret, were perfectly understood, as it is not even by me after more than twelve years' [of] almost constant study and experiment, there would be nothing which the human

---

[185] Crowley, Duquette, & Hyatt - *Enochian Sex Magick* page 116

[186] Crowley, Duquette, & Hyatt - *Enockian Sex Magick* page 117

imagination can conceive that could not be realized in practice…I make these remarks with absolute confidence, for even the insignificant approaches that I have been able to make towards the sanctuaries of this secret have shown me that the relations between phenomena are infinitely more complex than the wildest philosophers have ever imagined, and that the old proverb 'where there's a will there's a way' needs no caveat."[187]

What he's talking about is his belief that through various sexual practices, heterosexual and homosexual, he believed one could "super charge" in a sense, his ability to "manifest" things into his life that he wanted. Crowley was a bisexual, heroin addict, who ate human feces and reportedly had sex with animals in his quest for enlightenment, yet he is still seen as an idol by rebellious teenagers and many mainstream musicians have paid homage to him.

The fact that the Ordo Templi Orientis bases its teachings on such a perverted and wicked man casts a dark cloud of suspicion over the entire organization. Little is known about the membership and current activities of the OTO but many suspect their secret sex magic rituals have attracted some very powerful men from Hollywood's elite. Others believe that high level Illuminati members engage in homosexual Enochian sex magic rituals inside the Bohemian Grove every summer in attempts to activate latent metaphysical power allegedly hidden deep inside the brain.

---

[187] Crowley, Aleister - *Confessions of Aleister Crowley* page 702

Jekyll Island Meeting

The infamous Federal Reserve, the privately owned banking cartel that is in control of America's currency and financial system, was born out of a secret meeting held by a handful of banking elite on a secluded island off the coast of Georgia in 1910. Under the cover story of going on a hunting trip, a small group of men met on Jekyll Island for a week and a half to draft what would later be passed into law through a clever and sneaky tactic of voting on their plan on December 23rd 1913, the eve of Christmas Eve, while almost every congressman was at home with their families for Christmas, thus slipping the Federal Reserve Act into law.

While the Federal Reserve sounds like a department of the United States government, it is actually a conglomerate of privately owned banks who dictate America's monetary policy, and as the saying goes, "those with the gold make the rules." Just as the elite Illuminati have secretly maneuvered themselves to control both major political parties in the American government, along with the world's resources, infrastructure, and media though their business monopolies; of course they planned (and successfully accomplished) to take over the financial system as well, and are now in charge of printing the money.

The Jekyll Island meeting included executives from the major banks, such as Rockefeller family associate Frank A. Vanderlip, who was president of the National City Bank of New York; Henry Davison of J.P. Morgan Company; Charles D. Norton, president of the First

136

National Bank of New York; Paul Warburg of Kuhn, Loeb, & Co; and Colonel Edward House, one of the founding members of the Council on Foreign Relations. The plan they put together would then be presented to Senator Nelson Aldrich, whose daughter was married to John D. Rockefeller Jr., who then presented it to Congress where it became known as the Aldrich Plan.

Paul Warburg later admitted, "The matter of a uniform discount rate [interest rate] was discussed and settled at Jekyll Island."[188]   Frank Vanderlip, who worked for the Rockefellers and attended the Jekyll Island meeting, would later admit in his autobiography that, "Discovery, we knew, simply must not happen, or else all our time and effort would be wasted. If it were to be exposed publicly that our particular group had gotten together and written a banking bill, that bill would have no chance whatever of passage by Congress."[189]

Congressman Ron Paul wrote in his book *End the Fed*, "A secret meeting was convened at the coastal Georgia resort called the Jekyll Island Club, co-owned by J. P. Morgan himself.   The press said it was a duck-hunting expedition.   Those who attended took elaborate steps to preserve their secrecy, but history recorded precisely who was there: John D. Rockefeller's man in the senate, Nelson Aldrich, Morgan senior partner Henry Davison, German émigré and central banking advocate

---

[188] Stephenson, Nathaniel Wright - *Nelson W. Aldrich: A Leader in American Politics* (1930) page 485

[189] Vanderlip, James - *From Farmboy to Financier, autobiography* (1935)

Paul Warburg, National City Bank vice president Frank Vanderlip, and NMC staffer A. Piatt Andrew, who was also Assistant Secretary of the Treasury to President Taft."[190]

William Greider, author of the New York Times bestseller *Secrets of the Temple: How the Federal Reserve Runs the Country*, mostly dismisses what he calls "conspiracy-minded" accusations, but does admit that, "their suspicions were poetically accurate—the bankers met secretly because they knew that any proposal identified as Wall Street's bill would be doomed in the Democratic House of Representatives."[191]

Those who own the banking system have a tremendous amount of power in their hands because those who control the issuance of currency have the ability to create money out of nothing, declare it's legal tender, and then loan it out to people (or the government) and then collect interest on the money they lend out. It's the perfect scam because instead of earning their money by building something, delivering packages, raising livestock, or any number of other ways people earn a living, the banksters have cleverly positioned themselves into the place where they take in a massive amount of money for basically doing nothing other than acting as the self-proclaimed sole authority on money itself. Once you can wrap your mind around what it means to "create

---

[190] Paul, Ron – *End the Fed* page 22

[191] Greider, William - *Secrets of the Temple* page 276

money out of nothing and loan it out at interest," you can realize just how monumental their scam is.

The President of the Bank of England and the second richest man in Britain in the 1920s, Sir Josiah Stamp, is reported to have revealed that, "The modern banking system manufactures money out of nothing. The process is perhaps the most astounding piece of sleight of hand that was ever invented. Banking was conceived in iniquity and born in sin...Bankers own the Earth. Take it away from them but leave them the power to create money, and with a flick of a pen, they will create enough money to buy it back again...Take this great power away from them and all great fortunes like mine will disappear, for then this would be a better and happier world to live in....But if you want to continue to be the slaves of bankers and pay the cost of your own slavery, then let bankers continue to create money and control credit."[192]

In 1816 Thomas Jefferson wrote to his longtime friend John Taylor thanking him for sending copy of his book *An Inquiry into the Principles and Policy of the Government of the United States* (1814). Jefferson concluded his letter saying, "And I sincerely believe, with you, that banking establishments are more dangerous than standing armies; and that the principle of spending money to be paid by posterity [future generations], under the name of funding, is but swindling futurity [the future] on a large scale."[193]

---

[192] Reportedly from a speech at the University of Texas in the 1920s but the source of this quote is unverified.

[193] Memoirs, Correspondence, and Private Papers of Thomas Jefferson, vol. 4, Thomas Jefferson Randolph, ed., 1829, pp. 285-288.

Abraham Lincoln reported believed that instead of private banks having this power, "The government should create, issue and circulate all the currency and credit needed to satisfy the spending power of the government and the buying power of consumers.....The privilege of creating and issuing money is not only the supreme prerogative of Government, but it is the Government's greatest creative opportunity."[194]

He goes on to say, "By the adoption of these principles, the long-felt want for a uniform medium will be satisfied. The taxpayers will be saved immense sums of interest, discounts and exchanges. The financing of all public enterprises, the maintenance of stable government and ordered progress, and the conduct of the Treasury will become matters of practical administration. The people can and will be furnished with a currency as safe as their own government. Money will cease to be the master and become the servant of humanity."

The Federal Reserve Bank is working with other central banks around the world to incrementally introduce regional currencies in different areas of the world by merging several currencies into one. Taking America off the gold standard in 1972, and continuing to run up the national debt is the bankers plan to inflate the United States Dollar to the point of worthlessness, forcing it to be replaced with a new regional currency or even bypassing that step and moving right to a global currency. The saying goes that the love of money is the root of all evil,

---

[194] McGeer, Gerald Grattan - *The Conquest of Poverty Chapter 5 - Lincoln, Practical Economist* page 186 (Gardenvale, Quebec: Garden City Press 1935)

and that root leads directly to the Federal Reserve banksters and the global financial mafia.

World-renowned economist John Maynard Keynes (whose philosophies are known as Keynesian economics) wrote in his book *The Economic Consequences of the Peace*, that, "Lenin is said to have declared that the best way to destroy the capitalist system was to debauch the currency. By a continuing process of inflation, governments can confiscate, secretly and unobserved, an important part of wealth of their citizens. There is no subtler, no surer means of overturning the existing basis of society than to debauch the currency. The process engages all the hidden forces of economic law on the side of destruction, and does it in a manner which not one man in a million is able to diagnose."[195]

In the Bible it is written in John 2:15 that Jesus not only denounced the money changers at the Temple, but he actually tipped over their tables and used a whip to chase them away. "So he made a whip out of cords, and drove all from the temple courts, both sheep and cattle; he scattered the coins of the money changers and overturned their tables."

In the 2000 years since then, the corrupt money changers and tax collectors have only grown more powerful through their sneaky tactics, and have continued to systematically turn most people into peasants or debt slaves. "The rich ruleth over the poor, and the borrower is servant to the lender," reads Proverbs 22:7.

---

[195] Keynes, John Maynard - *The Economic Consequence of the Peace* page 235-236

The Zodiac Club

J.P. Morgan Jr., the infamous Illuminati money master (and one of the men instrumental in the creation of the Federal Reserve Bank which was conceived during the secret meeting on Jekyll Island), was also a major figure in another financial secret society called the Zodiac Club.[196] Not much is known about this intimate secret society, but a few details were uncovered in the archives of the Morgan library in New York.[197]

What is known about the Zodiac Club is that it was created in 1868 and is made up of twelve men, no more and no less, who each represent one of the twelve signs of the Zodiac and meet about a half dozen times every year for dinner to discuss their financial interests and cultural issues.

Their dinners are black tie events that are held in New York City on the last Saturday of every month between November and May at homes of the members. Dinner is provided by a fancy catering service and unlike the enormous undertaking to organize the Bilderberg Group meeting or the annual Bohemian Grove retreat; the Zodiac Club's small gathering has largely stayed under the radar and has received little press attention.

One interesting factoid reported is that during prohibition, when alcohol was illegal to produce or

---

[196] No relation to the Zodiac Club music venue in Oxford, England

[197]J. P. Morgan Jr Papers "Archives of The Pierpont Morgan Library" New York 401 The Zodiac Club Dinners 1913–41

AFFILIATED SECRET SOCIETIES

consume, the Zodiac Club continued to enjoy drinking by either brewing their own alcohol or using their connections to obtain it. Of course, when do the elite ever follow the law anyway?

A member usually only leaves the club when they die or resign due to old age or health problems. Once someone steps down then a replacement is chosen only after they are unanimously approved by rest of the current group.

What little information that's known about the Zodiac Club was only discovered in 2013 after a reporter for *The Gothamist,* a blog focusing on events and culture in New York City, took a tour of the Morgan Library where she noticed a strange arrangement of astrological signs painted on the ceiling. After asking about them, the curator admitted that he thought it was some kind of "Morgan Code" and then searched the library for any books or documents containing the word "Zodiac."[198] It was only then that the Zodiac Club's minutes and several menus from some of their past dinners were discovered.

"I made an appointment to see the material myself. Expecting to find handwritten notes, I was instead handed a striking seafoam green book with an intricate monogram embossed in gold," wrote art historian Danielle Oteri on *The Gothamist* blog.[199]

---

[198] *The Gothamist* "Inside The Zodiac Club: NYC's 145 Year Old Secret Dinner Society" by Danielle Oteri (May 16, 2013)

[199] Ibid.

143

Oteri's article explains, "The volumes were richly illustrated with photographs of the members and the special menus from their dinners. Only a hundred copies were printed (by Charles Scribner & Sons, the letters designed by Tiffany & Co.) and they were distributed among Zodiac Club members and their heirs for a sum of $4,800 (the equivalent of around $100,000 today). The two volumes cover the club from its genesis in 1868 up until 1928."[200]

Of the few who have heard of the Zodiac Club, some believe that J.P. Morgan founded it, but apparently it was created by Edward Elmer Potter, a Major General for the Union Army during the Civil War. A book titled *America's Secret Aristocracy* was published in 1987 by historian Stephen Birmingham that discussed the group and even mentioned the names of several men who he reported as being members, including real estate mogul Robert G. Goelet, who's related to Astors and Vanderbilts; Robert S. Pirie, who was president of Rothschild Inc.; and Pittsburgh steel magnate Howard Phipps Jr. were among those identified.

Other than this little known book, and Danielle Oteri's article in *The Gothamist*, virtually nothing has been printed about this intimate group of the Eastern Establishment.

---

[200] Ibid.

Council on Foreign Relations

While not exactly a secret society, the Council on Foreign Relations is a society with secrets, and while sounding like an ordinary committee in Congress, the CFR is actually a private organization whose foreign policy recommendations are practically marching orders for the many elite politicians who belong to it. The "council" was founded in 1921 in Manhattan by Colonel Edward Mandell House, who was Woodrow Wilson's chief advisor, along with Paul Warburg, who was at the Jekyll Island meeting held to create the Federal Reserve Bank, Elihu Root, who was the Secretary of War under both President McKinley and Roosevelt, and a handful of other insiders who then received funding for their venture from the Rockefeller family.

The Council on Foreign Relations was a major force behind the push to launch the War in Iraq which was based on the fraud (a conspiracy theory really) that Saddam Hussein was close to building nuclear weapons so he could supposedly attack the United States and our allies—claims that the world would come to learn were completely false.

At a press conference celebrating their newly opened Washington D.C. office, Hillary Clinton said, "I am delighted to be here in these new headquarters. I have been often to, I guess, the 'mother ship' in New York City, but it's good to have an outpost of the Council right here down the street from the State Department. We get a lot of advice from the Council, so this will mean I won't have as far to go to be told what we should be doing."[201]

Aside from most high-powered politicians being members of the council, many mainstream journalists are members as well, and use their positions to promote the agenda of the CFR. Antony Sutton, author of *America's Secret Establishment* points out, "Most CFR members are not involved in a conspiracy and have no knowledge of any conspiracy...however, there is a group within the Council of Foreign Relations which belongs to a secret society, sworn to secrecy, and which more or less controls the CFR. CFR meetings are used for their own purposes, ie., to push out their own ideas, to weigh up people who might be useful, to use meetings as a forum for discussion."[202]

The CFR has been the driving force and inspiration behind much of America's foreign policy and operates as a consensus building and lobbying firm to persuade politicians to carry out their directives. The prominent politicians and journalists then pass the propaganda they are fed into the mainstream.

Richard Haas, who has been the president of the CFR for over ten years, appeared on Bill Maher's HBO show *Real Time* in 2010 to promote his book, *War of Necessity, War of Choice*, and as soon as the interview began Maher started off by joking, "OK, as we discussed last time, you

---

[201] *YouTube* "Hillary Clinton addresses the Council on Foreign Relations, admits CFR runs the government"

[202] Sutton, Antony – *America's Secret Establishment* p. 3-4

are the president of the Council on Foreign Relations, which secretly controls the world I believe."[203]   Haas sat there grinning ear to ear and nodded his head in agreement as the audience laughed.

Robert Pastor, who was once the Chairman of the Council on Foreign Relations, wrote a book in 2001 titled *Toward a North American Community*, where he said, "In the long term, the amero is in the best interests of all three countries,"[204] referring to the United States, Canada, and Mexico, which the Illuminati want to merge into a regional union modeled after the European Union that they plan to call the American Union. The "amero" he mentioned is the proposed new regional currency the Illuminati would like the North American Union to Implement.

The Illuminati's ultimate plan regarding currency is to first establish regional unions and currencies around the world and then merge all of them into one unified global currency (potentially called the Phoenix) which will be a digital electronic currency. Once physical currency like cash and coins have been eliminated or made nearly impossible to use, the unified electronic currency will be the global standard controlled by the World Bank and its affiliates.

This is the fulfillment of the mysterious "Mark of the Beast" prophecy written about over 2000 years ago in the

[203] *HBO* "Realtime with Bill Maher" - Richard Hass Interview (April 29th 2010)

[204] Pastor, Robert - *Toward a North American Community: Lessons from the Old World for the New* page 115

Bible's Book of Revelation, which warned "And he causeth all, both small and great, rich and poor, free and bond, to receive a mark in their right hand, or in their foreheads: And that no man might buy or sell, save he that had the mark, or the name of the beast, or the number of his name...and his number is Six hundred & sixty-six." (Revelation 13:15-18)

As I'm sure you are aware, cash is slowly being phased out and even using it is now seen as suspicious because it can't be easily traced, and keeps one's purchasing history private. The "convenience" of a cashless society is one of the top goals of the Illuminati, and the Council on Foreign Relations is one of the front groups working to make that happen.

The Jasons

We think of most secret societies as political or spiritual associations, but one founded in 1960 is comprised of elite scientists. They are called *The Jasons*, a name that refers to Jason and the Argonauts from Greek mythology who ventured out to obtain the "golden fleece" (a piece of fabric woven from golden hair) which is symbolic of authority and kingship.

The Jasons, or sometimes referred to as JASON, is a small group of 30 to 60 of the world's top physicists, biologists, mathematicians, and computer scientists who advise the U.S. Government in their area of expertise. These men are from academia and private business who do not work directly for the government, but instead serve as advisors who are reportedly paid $850 a day from a budget of $3.5 million a year.[205]   Many members are university professors who work a full time job during the school year, but in the summer months spend their time working on classified projects for the Department of Defense, the Department of Energy, and other government agencies.

The Jasons were responsible for a 1982 report that served as the foundation for the growing barrage of global warming propaganda titled *The Long Term Impact of Atmospheric Carbon Dioxide on Climate.*   They are believed to have been involved with various missile defense programs (Star Wars or HAARP), and gave their analysis contemplating America's possible use of tactical nuclear weapons against the Vietcong during the Vietnam war.[206]

The JASONS are technically a 501C3 tax exempt nonprofit organization run through the MITRE Corporation in McLean, Virginia, and were only discovered when the Pentagon Papers were published by Daniel Elsberg in 1971 after Elsberg, a military analyst working for the RAND Corporation, photocopied seven thousand pages of government documents and leaked them to the press after discovering the extent that the Johnson administration lied to Congress and the public about the Vietnam War.   Very little has been reported on them, and at the time I'm writing this there is currently

---

[205] Finkbeiner, Ann - *The Jasons: The Secret History of Science's Postwar Elite* (2006) page (xxiv)

[206] The Nautilus Institute "Tactical Nuclear Weapons in 1966"

only *one* book published dedicated to the group—*The Jasons: The Secret History of Science's Postwar Elite* (2006) by Ann Finkbeiner.

When researching her book, Finkbeiner reached out to members asking for interviews, including the director, who responded with an e-mail saying, "Frankly, we could not identify an up-side for our organization, but could identify potential downsides to such a book."[207]

The reason they are paid as part time contractors and kept outside the bureaucracy of the Department of Defense is because the government feels if they were actual full time employees, their advice would be biased because they would have a vested interest in pushing for certain programs or for advising against others. After all, what government employee is going to actually report to their boss that their own job is unnecessary?

Ann Finkbeiner explains in her book, "A government wanting scientists' advice on, say the feasibility of a particular system of missile defense could ask scientists who are nearest—that is, who are in the defense industry or on the Defense Department's various advisory committees. But those scientists like the national lab scientists, would have something political or financial to gain or lose and might hedge their advice accordingly. Disinterested advice comes best from independent scientists, like those on PSAC, outside the government and outside industry—that is from scientists employed in

[207] Finkbeiner, Ann - *The Jasons: The Secret History of Science's Postwar Elite* (2006) page xxvi.

academia whose livelihoods will not depend on the advice they give."[208]

The original JASONS were former Manhattan Project physicists who just so happened to hold a major meeting in the Bohemian Grove! Peter Philips, who earned his Ph.D. in sociology after writing his dissertation on the Bohemian Grove, had this to say about the subject: "The atom bomb made this particular meeting at the Grove world famous, but it was not an isolated case of business and government planning through Bohemian club facilities. This was but one in a long series of historical business-related activities done in the context of a Bohemian corporate family network. The Club takes pride in this event, and members often tell new guests this story while at the Grove."[209]

"[Ernest] Lawrence's use of the Grove's river clubhouse for a Manhattan Project planning meeting in September of 1942 is well documented."[210] Lawrence would later join the board of directors of Monsanto and worked as a consultant to General Electric.[211] The JASONS continue to receive funding from the

---

[208] Finkbeiner, Ann - *The Jasons: The Secret History of Science's Postwar Elite* (2006) page 33

[209] Phillips, Peter - *A Relative Advantage: Sociology of the San Francisco Bohemian Club. A Doctoral Dissertation* (1994) page 93

[210] Phillips, Peter - *A Relative Advantage: Sociology of the San Francisco Bohemian Club. A Doctoral Dissertation* (1994) page 92

[211] Phillips, Peter - *A Relative Advantage: Sociology of the San Francisco Bohemian Club. A Doctoral Dissertation* (1994) page 91

Department of Defense through DARPA [the Defense Advanced Research Projects Agency] as well as money from other agencies who sometimes attempt to hide the paper trail through various means. DARPA is responsible for building neural interface systems they plan to wire directly into people's brains, and they're behind a whole list of some of the creepiest high tech Orwellian cybernetic devices you could imagine.

The Bilderberg Group

Every Spring since 1954 a group of around one hundred of the world's most powerful politicians, businessmen, bankers, media executives, and international royalty have been holding a secret three-day long meeting in an evacuated hotel that's surrounded by armed guards. Once inside the members and invited guests engage in intense off-the-record talks about the top issues facing the world. It's called the Bilderberg Group, or the Bilderberg meeting, named after the Bilderberg Hotel in Oosterbeck, Holland, the site of their first gathering organized by Prince Bernhard of the Netherlands. Attendees agree not to discuss publicly who was in attendance or what specifically was discussed, and most of them have denied any knowledge of the Bilderberg Group at all.

For over sixty years there has been an almost complete blackout in the mainstream media about the meetings, yielding to the Bilderberg Group's wishes that they keep them out of the press. For decades, news of the infamous Bilderberg Group spread in Patriot circles, in underground newsletters and websites, until the advent of YouTube and social media finally forced *some* major mainstream media outlets to admit that Bilderberg is real and some very powerful people attend. Here's a brief history of how the meetings were first discovered and how news of the group began to spread.

In 1957 a Pulitzer Prize winning columnist named Westbrook Pegler who wrote for Scripps Howard News Service, the Chicago Tribune, and other papers, published the first article on the Bilderberg Group—although he did not know their name at the time—his report marked the beginning of the unraveling of one of the most interesting conspiracies of all time.

In his 1957 article, Westbrook Pegler wrote, "Something very mysterious is going on when a strange assortment of 67 self-qualified, polyglot designers and arbiters of the economic and political fate of our western world go into a secret huddle on an island of Brunswick, GA and not a word gets into the popular press beyond a little routine AP story. These gumshoe super state architects and monetary schemers were drawn from all NATO countries. The fact of this weird conclave as spooky as any midnight meeting of the Klux in a piney wood, was bound to get known to the world eventually."[212]

He continues to explain how he first learned of this meeting, saying, "I got my first word of it from a reader who happened onto St. Simon Island, Brunswick, [Georgia] on her way to West Palm Beach. She wrote that

---

[212] Tucker, Jim – *Jim Tucker's Bilderberg Diary* page 231

the hotel on St. Simon was almost deserted, but that when she commented on this, the clerk said the place had been alive with mysterious characters a few days earlier and with Secret Service and FBI too."

While not yet having the group's name, Westbrook did connect them with the same gang who met on Jekyll Island to formulate the plans for the Federal Reserve. He said, "Senator Aldrich of Rhode Island, called this one into being. He was the father of Winthrop Aldrich. There have been many excited versions of that ancient hoedown on Jekyll Island, but relatively few have ever heard of it at all."

After Westbrook Pegler began criticizing executives of the powerful Hearst Corporation that owned and controlled almost 30 different newspapers in America, he was fired. Hearst newspapers literally created "yellow journalism" which refers to sensationalistic headlines and careless reporting with a disregard for the facts in order to sell more newspapers.

A man named Willis Carto read Westbrook Pegler's article and it motivated him to begin investigating and tracking the Bilderberg Group himself. In June of 1958 Willis Carto founded Liberty Lobby that published a newsletter titled *Liberty Lowdown* that included articles exposing the Bilderberg Group. He would later begin publishing a newspaper called *The Spotlight*.

Over two decades later, Jim Tucker learned of this elusive group from Carto and would become the world's foremost expert on them. Tucker explained, "Had it not been for Willis A. Carto, who hired me as editor of *The Spotlight* and then put me on the tack of Bilderberg, I would probably—almost assuredly—never heard of the word 'Bilderberg.' Having had the opportunity, through Carto's good offices as founder of Liberty Lobby, publisher of *The Spotlight*, to begin what ultimately proved to be a generation of world-wide Bilderberg-hunting, I was able to bring news about Bilderberg to literally millions of folks who would like myself have otherwise remained in the dark about these globalist schemers."[213]

Tucker tracked the Bilderberg Group from 1975 until his death in 2013 at the age of 78. His book, titled *Jim Tucker's Bilderberg Diary* contains decades of information about where the Bilderbergers met, who was in attendance and what was discussed. Tucker had somehow gained the support of an insider who would leak information to him every year about the location and date of the meeting, as well as attendee lists and other information.

It's foolish to claim there hasn't been a secret arrangement between the Bilderberg Group and the American mainstream media to keep them out of the press. When over 100 of the world's most influential politicians, media owners, banking executives, and business elite fly half way around the world to meet for three days in a closed down five star hotel that's surrounded by armed guards, you can't say it's not newsworthy. And you certainly can't say it's not interesting. For years, if anyone called into any of the major talk shows like Rush Limbauh, Sean Hannity,

---

[213] Tucker, Jim – *Jim Tucker's Bilderberg Diary* page 218

Glenn Beck and others, and told the call screener they wanted to ask about the Bilderberg Group, the call would never be put through. "We're not taking calls on that right now, sorry. Click." If the person calling gave the call screener a bogus question and happened to be put on air and then asked about the Bilderbergers, they would be ridiculed and the call would be dropped immediately (something that's happened to me many times).

After decades of news blackouts, more recently because social media has helped expose Bilderberg, some outlets have reluctantly (and briefly) mentioned the event in attempts to avoid looking like they were covering it up.

In 1991 an Arkansas newspaper published an article reporting that Bill Clinton was attending the Bilderberg meeting. This of course was before people were using the Internet to spread news and at a time when one local newspaper's report would rarely be seen by anyone outside its limited circulation area. The article stated, "Private sponsors picked up the tab for Gov. Bill Clinton's recent trips to Germany and the Soviet Union—a journey he made without staff aids, spokesman said Thursday. Mike Gauldin, the governor's spokesman, said the Bilderberg Conference paid for Clinton's trip to Germany and a Washington DC philanthropist paid for the Soviet Union visit."[214]

In the 1970s a Democratic U.S. representative from Louisiana named John R. Rarick caught wind of the meetings and became suspicious and wanted to know if

---

[214] "Governor's Visits abroad Paid with Private Money" by Rachel O'neal and Larry Rhodes

taxpayers were paying for American officials to attend the secret meeting. Rarick typed up a ten-page statement and actually entered it into the official Congressional Record. "Mr. Speaker, on several occasions during recent months, I called the attention of our colleagues to activities of the Bilderbergers—an elite international group comprised of high government officials, international financiers, businessmen, and opinion-makers..." the statement begins.

"This exclusive international aristocracy holds highly secret meetings annually or more often in various countries. The limited information available about what transpires at these meetings reveals that they discuss matters of vital importance which affect the lives of all citizens. Presidential Advisor Henry Kissinger, who made a secret visit to Peking from July 9 to July 11, 1971, and arranged for a presidential visit to Red China, was reported to be in attendance at the most recent Bilderberg meeting held in Woodstock, Vermont, April 23 to April 25, 1971. The two points reportedly discussed at the Woodstock meeting were, 'the contribution of business in dealing with current problems of social instability' and 'the possibility of a change of the American role in the world and its consequences.'"

"Following these secret discussions, which are certainly not in keeping with the Western political tradition of 'open covenants openly arrived at,' the participants returned to their respective countries with the general public left uninformed, notwithstanding the attendance of some news media representatives, of any of the recommendations and plans agreed upon as a result of the discussions—or for that matter even the occurrence of the meeting itself."[215]

President Dwight D. Eisenhower, best known for warning the world about the Military Industrial Complex in his 1961 farewell address, wrote a memo to his assistant in 1955 about that year's Bilderberg meeting which took place in Barbizon, France. While Eisenhower didn't mention them by name, it's pretty obvious who he's talking about in the memo when he says, "I understand next week Prince Bernhard is having a meeting at Barbizon, continuing his exploration looking toward improving European and American relations. If personally you can fit such a trip into your schedule, I suggest you find the money and go to France."[216]

I have been able to obtain several recent years of Bilderberg's IRS filings since they are registered as a 501c3 "charitable foundation," certain financial information must be made available for public inspection, if you know where to look.[217] I discovered they operate under the business entity "American Friends of Bilderberg" and the documents show that in 2008 they received $645,000 in contributions to fund their annual meeting, with money coming from Goldman Sachs ($25,000), Microsoft ($75,000), Henry Kissinger

---

[215] John R. Rarick, *Congressional Record*, 92nd Congress, 1st Session, Wednesday, Volume 117, No. 133, 15 September 1971, pp. E9615-E9624

[216] Eisenhower memo from March 11th 1955

[217] 2008 IRS Form 990-PF OMD No 1545-0052

($20,000), David Rockefeller ($50,000) and others. The 2009 returns show the Washington Post newspaper donated $25,000.[218]

Under the "Summary of Direct Charitable Activities," the forms list the organization's goals as "Organizing & sponsoring conferences which study & discuss significant problems of the western alliance [and] collaborating on the Bilderberg meetings held in Europe & North America."

The expenses on the 2008 and 2012 documents are listed as approximately $900,000 per year, which covers renting out the entire hotel for three days, paying the private security forces and compensating local police for the extra man-hours, and for paying the travel expenses of members and attendees.

The documents list James Johnson as the treasurer, who is also the chairman of Perseus LLC, a merchant bank and private equity fund management company based in Washington D.C. with offices in New York and an associated advisory firm in Munich, Germany. Perseus is a leading figure in Greek Mythology and is the one who beheaded Medusa.

Johnson was once the Chairman of the Executive Committee at Fannie Mae; and before that he was a managing director at Lehman Brothers. He's also on the Board of Directors for Goldman Sachs and a member of the Council on Foreign Relations.

I have personally been to the offices of Perseus in Washington D.C. seeking a comment on the documents,

---

[218] 2009 IRS Form 990-PF OMD No 1545-0052

and as soon as I mentioned "Bilderberg," James Johnson's secretary said they have no comment and slammed the door. The person listed on the forms as the accountant is Robert T. Foldes of Leon D. Alpern & Company and when I called them, the secretary confirmed they handle the taxes for American Friends of Bilderberg but declined to give me any further information.

Documents leaked from the 1955 Bilderberg meeting show they were planning the European Union and a central currency back in the 1950s, decades before the EU was formed and their new Euro currency introduced. The documents are marked "Personal and strictly confidential," and "Not for publication either in whole or in part." Two years later, in 1957, the European Union started to take shape with the creation of the European Economic Community (EEC), which merged the markets of six European countries: France, Germany, Italy, Belgium, the Netherlands and Luxembourg. This later grew into the European Union in 1993 containing 28 nation states: Austria, Belgium, Bulgaria, Croatia, Cyprus, Czech Republic, Denmark, Estonia, Finland, France, Germany, Greece, Hungary, Ireland, Italy, Latvia, Lithuania, Luxembourg, Malta, Netherlands, Poland, Portugal, Romania, Slovakia, Slovenia, Spain, Sweden, and the United Kingdom.

Most of their plan has been accomplished, and while they will continue to play themselves off as just an ordinary business conference, the decades of denials and media blackouts prove the Bilderberg Group has been deceptive from their inception and the inside sources who have leaked their plans over the years prove the power they wield. Most often, what's talked about or agreed upon inside Bilderberg soon mysteriously finds its way into becoming law. It clearly appears that wars, economic booms and busts, and controversial new legislation are often traced back to this small group of around 100 men.

While politicians love to point the finger at their rivals and place all the country's ills on the opposing party, most politicians (at least at the time I'm writing this) haven't even uttered the word Bilderberg. Congressman Ron Paul, one of the rare honest politicians, was once asked about the Bilderberg Group by a fan at a book signing who videotaped the interaction and posted it on YouTube. "Did you hear about that recent Bilderberg Group meeting in Chantilly, Virginia?" the person asked. Ron Paul responded, "Yeah, recently there was one and there were some reports on it—I didn't read a whole lot about it but they certainly were there."[219]

The cameraman then asked what he thought they were doing there, and Paul responded, "Well, they probably get together and talk about how they're going to control the banking systems of the world and natural resources—and we get together and talk about how we're going to get our freedom back. So we have our own things to talk about too."

Ron Paul didn't play dumb and didn't ridicule the man's question—instead he answered it quite frankly, which is surprising for a politician, particularly when it comes to talking about the Bilderberg Group. Ron Paul

---

[219] YouTube: "Ron Paul talks about the Bilderberg Group" (posted August 16th 2008)

was (and still may be, depending on what happens after this book is published) the only politician (at the time) to have ever even uttered the word "Bilderberg."

When Hillary Clinton was campaigning for president hoping to secure the election in 2008, someone asked her about the Bilderberg Group at an event in New Hampshire and posted the video on YouTube. "What's going on at the Bilderberg meeting and what are you guys talking about up there?" She cackled, "Ha ha ha, I have no idea what you're talking about." The man responded, "Why are they such top secret meetings?" To which she answered (looking like a kid with their hand caught in the cookie jar), "Sir, I have no idea what you're talking about."[220]

She has no idea what he's talking about? How could one of the most powerful and politically connected women in the world possibly not know about them? It's ridiculous to claim that she isn't intimately aware of the Bilderberg Group and obviously she was playing dumb to uphold their secrecy policy. Hilary wrote her college thesis on Saul Alinsky, the leftist extremist who dedicated his book *Rules for Radicals* to Lucifer, and adored his subversive tactics to further the Big Government agenda.

Because of social media and independent blogs and YouTube channels gaining so much popularity in the early 2000's, Bilderberg's secrecy has been blown, and they, (along with their accessories to the cover-up in the mainstream media) have been forced to break their silence

---

[220] YouTube: "Did Hillary Clinton Attend the 2006 Bilderberg Conference?"

on the group and finally, beginning in around the year 2012, *some* mainstream outlets began to *briefly* touch on the meeting to try to give the impression they weren't obviously blacking them out in a desperate attempt to maintain their fading facade of credibility.

Almost every article or brief TV news segment mentions how "conspiracy theorists" think the group is up to no good, while glossing over the fact that for over a half century they conveniently ignored the meetings or how the top radio hosts like Sean Hannity, Glenn Beck and others actually ridiculed any caller who even brought it up.

When hosting his popular show on the Fox News Channel, Glenn Beck once claimed that talking about the Bilderberg Group was going down a "tin foil hat road," and said he didn't care about the Bilderberg Group, and then compared them to a toy company. "The Bilderbergers had their meeting, I don't really know much about these people, and I don't really care. I know probably more about the Build a Bear people in the malls, and I know those people are brainwashing our kids with teddy bears. I don't know what kind of secret meetings they have to get our kids into the bear industry, but I don't like it. If the Bilderberg's are half as evil as the teddy bear people, look out."[221]

Beck then went on to say that those inside the Bilderberg meeting were probably talking about how to help the world.

---

[221] *Fox News Channel* "Glenn Beck Program" (June 2010)

Spiritual Beliefs

It is often said that the Illuminati are "satanic" or Luciferian, which seems unbelievable to someone new to this material because it's so far outside of most people's realm of understanding that such claims are often met with skepticism, disbelief, or outright ridicule. But when one takes a closer look and understands just what Satanism and Luciferianism is, such claims not only seem reasonable, but they are undeniable. First we must look at the story of Adam and Eve to begin to understand this.

While Christians, Jews, and many others believe that the first humans disobeyed God in the Garden of Eden by following the advice of Satan, the Illuminati (and every occult association, fraternity, or secret society) believes that Satan actually saved Adam and Eve from enslavement to God, who they say was holding back Mankind's true potential and keeping Adam and Eve imprisoned in ignorance.

Many religions have an esoteric and an exoteric doctrine, one interpretation for the masses, and another doctrine with deeper or different interpretations for the scholars or religious insiders, often called "adepts" or "the elect." In Judaism this "second" doctrine is called the Midrash, which goes "beyond" the "simple" and "legal" interpretations of the Torah (the Old Testament) and gives an "expanded view" of the Bible's stories.

Remember that Albert Pike said, "Masonry, like all the Religions, all the Mysteries, Hermeticism and

Alchemy, *conceals* [emphasis in original] its secrets from all except the Adepts and Sages, or the Elect, and uses false explanations and misinterpretations of its symbols to mislead those who deserve only to be misled; to conceal the Truth, which it [the Mason] calls Light, from them, and to draw them away from it."[222]

In his book, *The Wisdom of the Knowing Ones*, Manly P. Hall explains, "all of these religions had been divided into two sections, one of which was for the public and the other essentially an esoteric or mystical tradition for a few who were willing to consecrate their lives through a process of internal enlightenment. For the many there was obedience to the forms and letters of religious law. For the few there was an insight into the deeper meanings of these things by means of which orthodoxies were transformed into great spiritual systems."[223]

Lucifer and Satan

The biggest secret of the Illuminati is that they believe Satan is good, because in their view he is the "superior God," and this secret has endowed them with tremendous power. Helena Blavatsky in her 1888 book *The Secret Doctrine*, explains, "Thus Lucifer—the spirit of Intellectual Enlightenment and Freedom of Thought—is metaphorically the guiding beacon, which helps man to

---

[222] Pike, Albert - *Morals and Dogma* p. 104-105

[223] Hall, Manly P. - *The Wisdom of the Knowing Ones* page 127-128

find his way through the rocks and sand banks of Life, for Lucifer is the Logos in his highest."[224]

She continues, "Lucifer is divine and terrestrial light, the 'Holy Ghost' and 'Satan,' at one and the same time, visible space being truly filled with differentiated breath invisibly; and the Astral Light, the manifested efforts of two who are one, guided and attracted by ourselves, is the karma of humanity, both a personal and impersonal entity...The Fall was the result of man's knowledge, for his 'eyes were opened.' Indeed, he was taught wisdom and the hidden knowledge by the 'Fallen Angel'...And now it stand proven that Satan, or the Red Fiery Dragon, the "lord of Phosphorus" (brimstone was a theological improvement), and Lucifer, or 'Light-Bearer,' is in us: it is our Mind—our tempter and Redeemer, our intelligent liberator and Savior from pure animalism...Without this quickening spirit, or human Mind or soul, there would be no difference between man and beast."[225]

Satanist Aleister Crowley said, "This serpent, Satan, is not the enemy of Man, be He who made Gods of our race, knowing Good and Evil; He bade 'Know Thyself' and taught initiation. He is 'the Devil' of the book of Thoth, and His emblem is Baphomet, and Androgyne who is the hieroglyph of arcane perfection."[226]

---

[224] Blavatsky, H.P. - *The Secret Doctrine v. II* p. 162

[225] Blavatsky, *H.P. - The Secret Doctrine v. II* page 513

[226] Crowley, Aleister - *Magick: In Theory and Practice* p. 193

The Secret Doctrine states, "For no one, not even the greatest living adept, would be permitted to, or could—even if he would—give out promiscuously, to a mocking, unbelieving world, that which has been so effectually concealed from it for long aeons and ages."[227]

Such views can also be considered Gnosticism, which is a philosophical belief that a lower level evil god called the Demiurge created humans as slaves and in order to be free from the enslavement they must be given the secret knowledge (gnosis) from a higher level God (Satan). Manly P. Hall explains, "Gnostics never looked to salvation from sin (original or other), but rather they desired release from unconsciousness and incomprehension, whereby they meant primarily ignorance of spiritual realities. Salvation, (or liberation) is a potential present in every man and woman, and it is not vicarious but individual. The great Messengers of the Light come to stimulate this potential and they do not by their death but by their lives."[228]

Those who believe they have discovered this "secret to life" often keep it contained within occult fraternities, hoping to keep the vast majority of people ignorant of their supposed "truth" so they can keep others from becoming "enlightened" so they can more easily take advantage of them. This sort of spiritual supremacism often leads to Social Darwinism, which is the philosophy of the survival of the fittest. These people have no

---

[227] Blavatsky, Helena - *The Secret Doctrine* v. I page xvii

[228] Hall, Manly P. - *The Wisdom of the Knowing Ones* page 19

concern for their fellow man, but are narcissistic, megalomaniacs who view themselves as Gods as a result of Satan's secret. This superiority complex is conveyed by the "do what thou wilt" philosophy that Aleister Crowley and Church of Satan founder Anton LaVey preached, which means "do whatever you want" because you are your own God.

In his authorized biography *The Secret Life of a Satanist*, it was revealed that Anton LaVey wasn't concerned if Satanism inspired people to commit mass murder. It reads, "Anton LaVey maintains that he isn't really concerned about accusations of people killing other people in the name of Satan. He swears that each time he reads of a new killing spree, his only reaction is, 'What, 22 people? Is that all?...There will undoubtedly be more Satanically-motivated murders and crimes in the sense that *The Satanic Bible* tells you 'You don't have to take any more shit.'"[229]

LaVey also admired a homosexual serial killer from the early 1900s named Carl Panzram, who killed at least twenty-two people, and who claimed to have raped one thousand men. "The only way I would like to 'help' the great majority of people is the same way Carl Panzram 'reformed' people who tried to reform him. It would be most merciful to help them by relieving them of the life they seem to hate so much. People should be happy I'm not a humanitarian—or I'd probably be the most

---

[229] Barton, Blanche - *The Authorized Biography of Anton LaVey* page 218-219

diabolical mass murderer the world has ever known,"
LaVey said.[230]

Richard Ramirez, the "Night Stalker" serial killer
from Los Angeles, and Charles Manson were both
interested in Satanism. Ramirez famously drew a satanic
pentagram on the palm of his hand during his trial and
would shout "Hail Satan!" to television cameras and
reporters.

Because Satanists do not believe in an afterlife or an
all-knowing, all-powerful God, they are not concerned
with any kind of divine retribution for their actions, and
are thus motivated even more to ruthlessly take advantage
of others since they believe in the "survival of the fittest"
and that "might is right" and that they themselves are
Gods.

This "royal secret" of Satanism will likely one day
soon be revealed to the world after having been practiced
in secret for thousands of years. The Illuminati and the
counterfeit (anti)Christ will likely openly reveal Satanism
as the new World Religion and claim it had to be kept a
secret all these years until the New World Order was
complete. Anyone who denounces this antichrist or the
new World Religion will be targeted for termination and
will be blamed for trying to stop the completion of
"heaven on earth."

---

[230] Barton, Blanche – *The Authorized Biography of Anton LaVey*
page 133

Double Speak

The Illuminati often use "double speak" to conceal their real agenda and present powerful propaganda to the masses who often blindly accept it as the truth without a second thought. The general public have been so dumbed down, they will believe anything their favorite political party tells them and are easily mislead by language and rhetoric that is meant to disguise the speaker's true intentions. For example, the Department of Defense is really the Department of War, and that's what it used to be called until the government changed its name in 1949.

The Patriot Act, the bill signed into law shortly after the September 11ᵗʰ attacks on the World Trade Center in 2001, was actually an assault on the Bill of Rights and anything but patriotic, but the term Patriot Act was designed to make the new laws sound as American as the Fourth of July. President Bush declared a "War *on* Terror" when really it was a "War *of* Terror." President Obama said that raising the debt ceiling wouldn't increase our country's debt, when that's clearly exactly what it does, but because the masses have become zombies who react to keywords or neuro linguistic programming language patterns, most people accept statements from presidents as truth without thinking twice.

In some of my viral YouTube videos I've asked people to sign petitions supporting legislation that nobody in their right mind would even consider agreeing to, but because I prefaced the question with "would you support Obama..." countless people signed the fake petitions because their blind support for the president caused them to shut off their brain and not even listen to what I was actually asking them to support.

The Hegelian Dialectic

Because the elite Illuminati are social Darwinist Satanists, they often employ what's called the Hegelian Dialectic, which allows them to roll out their diabolical plans with little opposition. What this entails is creating a problem on purpose through covert means so the government can then present their solution, which is a plan they had waiting in the wings but were unable to implement without the proper crisis which was needed to justify their desired actions.

The Hegelian Dialectic consists of a thesis, an antithesis, and a synthesis, or a problem, a reaction, and a solution. This is the basic structure of a false flag operation which is a military strategy where a government commits a terrorist act while making it appear as if it came from their political enemy—or they allow a terrorist attack to occur when they could have easily stopped it—because the success of the event serves as a pretext (a reason) to carry out actions that previously would have been widely unacceptable by the public, but after the attack occurs, much of the public actually demands that a reaction occur, all the while unaware that behind the scenes the entire operation was planned to get that exact support which was lacking before the attack occurred.

Just three days after the 9/11 attacks, the co-chair of the Council on Foreign Relations stated, "There is a chance for the President of the United States to use the

172

SPIRITUAL BELIEFS

disaster to carry out what his father—a phrase his father used I think only once, and it hasn't been used since—and that is a New World Order."[231]

This attack was precisely the "New Pearl Harbor" event discussed in the Project for the New American Century think tank's own *Rebuilding America's Defenses* report published in September of 2000. From this Illuminati front group came the very plan explaining their need for a "catalyzing event—a new Pearl Harbor"[232] which would be used to set the stage for America to carry out the Illuminati's agenda by invading the Middle East to complete the New World Order.

In 1962, a false flag attack plan was drawn up by top U.S. military officials who wanted to commit various acts of terror *in Washington* D.C. and in Miami that would be made to appear as if Cuba had done them, in order to generate public support for an invasion of Cuba. Operation Northwoods, as it was called, plainly stated, "We could develop a Communist Cuban terror campaign in the Miami area, in other Florida cities, and even in Washington…The terror campaign could be pointed at Cuban refugees seeking haven in the United States… Hijacking attempts against civil aircraft surface craft should appear to continue as harassing measures condoned by the government of Cuba."

---

[231] *C-Span* - September 14th 2001

[232] *The Project for the New American Century* "Rebuilding America's Defenses" page 51

173

When confronted with such damning evidence, most people immediately dismiss it as a "conspiracy theory" but the Operation Northwoods documents have been declassified and are 100% authentic. The plan was even reported on ABC News in 2001 on their website where the article reads, "In the early 1960s, America's top military leaders reportedly drafted plans to kill innocent people and commit acts of terrorism in U.S. cities to create public support for a war against Cuba."[233]

For people still skeptical about the September 11th inside job, all they need to do is read the Northwoods documents and understand that plans like this have actually been put on paper, and approved by the Joint Chiefs of Staff (the heads of all U.S. military branches). Similar attacks have been carried out in the past by governments throughout history such as Operation Gladio throughout Europe, the Gleiwitz incident and the Reichstag fire in Germany, the Gulf of Tonkin incident in Vietnam, and others.

Henry Kissinger has been intimately involved with nearly every major organization or front group that is behind the push for a New World Order and was originally named the Chairman of the 9/11 Commission by President Bush, which was set up to (pretend to) investigate the terrorist attacks on September 11th 2001. Kissinger resigned from the commission after family members of 9/11 victims discovered his business ties with

---

[233] *ABC News* "US Military wanted to provoke war with Cuba" by David Ruppe (5-01-2001)

the Bin Ladens.[234] In an interview on CNBC in February 2009, Kissinger was asked about the problems the Obama administration was facing regarding the ongoing "War on Terror" and the economic meltdown, where he responded that Obama, "can give new impetus to American foreign policy partly because the reception of him is so extraordinary around the world. His task will be to develop an overall strategy for America in this period when, really, a New World Order can be created. It's a great opportunity, it isn't just a crisis."

President Obama's Chief of Staff Rahm Emanuel made a startling statement after the economic crash of 2008, when he said, "You never let a serious crisis go to waste. And what I mean by that it's an opportunity to do things you think you could not do before."[235]

Since we're talking about power-mad megalomaniac Satanists here, it shouldn't come as a surprise that these men would orchestrate terror attacks in order to gain more power and further their political agendas. And it's certainly not a surprise that most of these men have ties to occult cabals like Skull & Bones, Freemasonry, or the Bohemian Grove—all of which are incubators for corruption and keepers of the great "secret of secrets."

---

[234] *CNN* "Kissinger Resigns as Head of 9/11 Commission" (December 13, 2002)

[235] *Wall Street Journal* "In Crisis, Opportunity for Obama" by Gerald Seib (November 21 2008)

Sex Magic

As I mentioned in a previous section of this book, sex magic (sometimes stylized *sex magick* with a "k" on the end) is the belief that through secret sexual intercourse rituals one can achieve altered states of consciousness which activate dormant metaphysical powers locked inside the mind, supposedly enabling the practitioners to harness God-like manifestation abilities in what has been described as a conscious, living lucid dream. As strange as this idea may be, it isn't necessarily a crime for two consenting adults to engage in bizarre sex acts, but unfortunately there are some very disgusting and horrific types of sex magic that are beyond evil, and I caution you —what you are about to read is extremely disturbing.

In parts of Africa many men believe if they rape an albino woman it will give them magical power.[236] "There is a belief that if you have [sexual] relations with a girl with albinism, you will cure AIDS. So there are many girls with albinism who are being raped in [Africa] because of this belief," warned Peter Ash, founder of human rights group Under The Same Sun.[237]

The London *Telegraph* reported in 2001 that some South African men rape babies believing it is a 'cure' for

---

[236] *Reuters* "Albinos in Tanzania murdered or raped as AIDS 'cure' by Fumbuka Ng'Wanakilala (May 5th 2011)

[237] Ibid.

AIDS.[238]   More than 67,000 cases of rape and sexual assault against children were reported in the year 2000 in South Africa alone.[239]

In 2013 the singer of a popular heavy metal band in the United Kingdom called Lost Prophets was sentenced to thirty-five years in prison for thirteen child sex offenses including sexually abusing babies in black magic rituals.[240]   Several women were also sent to prison for willingly giving him their small children so he could use them for this exact purpose.

The singer, Ian Watkins, was apparently a fan of Aleister Crowley, as many musicians are—who wrote in his book *Magick: In Theory and Practice* that people can obtain satanic power by murdering children.   In the chapter on blood sacrifices Crowley wrote, "For the highest spiritual working one must accordingly choose that victim which contains the greatest and purest force. A male child of perfect innocence and high intelligence is the most satisfactory and suitable victim."[241]

In 2014 it was revealed that a group of Aleister Crowley fans were abusing children in an England suburb

---

[238] *Telegraph* "South African men rape babies as 'cure' for Aids" by Jane Flanagan (November 11th 2001)

[239] Ibid.

[240] *BBC* "Lostprophets' Ian Watkins sentenced to 35 years over child sex offences"

[241] Crowley, Aleister - *Magick: In Theory and Practice* page 95

by doing Satanic sex rituals.[242]   A woman named Jacqueline Marling even turned her daughter over to the cult and forced her to participate in sex magic rituals beginning when she was just seven years old.[243]

Such insane and evil sex magic practices aren't just contained to primitive tribes in Africa or twisted rock stars or Aleister Crowley fans. It appears to be one of the deepest and darkest secrets of the Illuminati as well. Apparently in some sects within the Illuminati, initiates believe this kind of child abuse can "super charge" their "metaphysical powers" enabling them to conjure into their life whatever they wish, in a perverted version of the "Law of Attraction," the philosophy popularized by the DVD *The Secret* in 2006.

In the 1990s a Republican Nebraska State Senator named John DeCamp published a book titled *The Franklin Cover-Up* where he alleged children were taken into the Bohemian Grove and ritualistically raped and murdered in black magic rituals at the hands of some of the members in the 1980s.[244]   DeCamp, who was an attorney, said he personally interviewed several children from orphanages who allegedly identified the Bohemian Grove as the location of this supposed abuse.[245]

---

[242] *Daily Mail* "House of horrors: Daughter tells how she was forced to sleep with 1,800 men by the time she was 18 as part of Satanic sex cult" by Jennifer Smith (September 21, 2014)

[243] Ibid

[244] DeCamp, John - *The Franklin Cover-Up* page 326-327

[245] DeCamp, John - *The Franklin Cover-Up* page 326-327

Former CIA director Bill Colby is said to have warned DeCamp that he was looking into something so dark he should walk away and "Get as far away from this thing as you can. Forget you ever saw it or know it, heard it or anything else."[246] Colby later died in what was called a canoeing accident, but many suspect he was murdered because of the strange circumstances surrounding his death and his conversations with DeCamp about sex magic. There were no witnesses to his death and he drowned after mysteriously going canoeing by himself.

In 1989 the *Washington Times* printed a front-page headline reading, "Homosexual Prostitution Inquiry Ensnares VIPs with Reagan and Bush," after it was discovered that a high-powered lobbyist named Craig Spence was operating a pedophile prostitution ring in the Washington D.C. area that catered to elite clients.[247] Spence turned up dead a few months after the article was published from an alleged suicide. Whispers of elite pedophile rings have alleged for decades that high-powered politicians and businessmen engage in child abuse for fun or part of secret society rituals. This same dark cloud has hung over the heads of Catholic priests for many decades.

A major star at the BBC in England [the British Broadcasting Corporation] named Jimmy Savile reportedly abused hundreds of children, some as young as

[246] *The Alex Jones Show* - Alex Jones Interviews John DeCamp, Author of The Franklin Cover-up (July 21, 2004)

[247] *Washington Times* "Homosexual Prostitution Inquiry Ensnares VIPs with Reagan, Bush" by Paul Rodriguez and George Archibald (June 29th 1989)

two-years-old, and even had sex with dead bodies, according the *Washington Post* and other mainstream media outlets.[248] Such news leads many to believe this kind of activity is part of an organized network of powerful perpetrators, not just separate incidences.

It's unknown how common these kinds of sex magic rituals are within the Illuminati or other Aleister Crowley-inspired groups, and when one tries to understand why anyone would even consider doing such a thing it challenges the mind to come up with an answer. These perpetrators obviously aren't just sick psychopaths living in an abandoned cabin in the woods. These are successful men (and possibly women) who are addicted to power and wealth and fuel their ego with all of the finest pleasures of this world, often becoming so jaded and desensitized they are eventually unable to find excitement or pleasure in anything normal.

Since these acts of sexual abuse are the worst thing anyone could possibly do to another human being, these acts of ultimate evil are believed to cause some kind of hormones to be released into the blood which give the perpetrators a kind of satanic adrenaline rush that magnifies their supposed ability to alter reality metaphysically by their thoughts, thus being the most potent "supernatural steroid" in the world. There is no doubt why sex magic is considered the deepest and darkest secret of the Illuminati, and any human being with

---

[248] *Washington Post* "How BBC star Jimmy Savile got away with allegedly abusing 500 children and sex with dead bodies" by Terrence McCoy (June 27th 2014)

a soul can agree that sex offenders of all kinds must be eradicated from the earth.

Transhumanism

One of the ultimate goals of the Illuminati is to become Gods themselves in what they believe is the final stage of their evolution or "transcendence." This branch of science is called *Transhumanism*—meaning supporters hope to transition from a human into a totally new species or transcend into a "God."[249] This isn't just a lofty science fiction pipe dream of a few megalomaniacs with God complexes, this is a very real plan being pursued by some very wealthy and powerful people. Billionaire Peter Thiel, the cofounder of PayPal and early investor in Facebook, believes scientists will soon "cure death" enabling him and other billionaires to live forever. "You can accept [death], you can deny it or you can fight it. I think our society is dominated by people who are into denial or acceptance, and I prefer to fight it."[250]

The most popular "guru" of Transhumanism (sometimes symbolized as H+) is Google engineer Ray Kurzweil who believes by the year 2045 he and other elite will achieve immortality through cybernetic enhancements that transform them into literal

---

[249] *Daily Mail* "Are we evolving into a NEW type of human? 'Different' species will have evolved by 2050, scientist claims" by Ellie Zolfagharifard (September 11th 2014)

[250] *Telegraph* "Peter Thiel: the billionaire tech entrepreneur on a mission to cheat death" by Mick Brown (September 19th 2014)

supercomputing cyborgs who are physically wired into the Internet at all times—or even replacing their biological brains and bodies entirely with "more efficient" silicone computers and mechanical bodies in order to "transcend." Kurzweil predicts, "As you go out to the 2040s, now the bulk of our thinking is out in the cloud. The biological portion of our brain didn't go away but the nonbiological portion will be much more powerful. And it will be uploaded automatically the way we back up everything now that's digital."[251]

In 2013 Google created Calico, a life extension and anti-aging biotech company to help them pursue Kurzweil's dream of beating death, and many other companies are pouring billions of dollars into transhumanist technology and working non-stop hoping to soon unlock immortality.

Transhumanist philosopher Zoltan Istvan, who believes that teaching children about the Bible should be banned and that the government should regulate who is allowed to have children, writes, "The transhumanist age —where radical science and technology will revolutionize the human being and experience—will eventually bring us indefinite lifespans, cyborgization, cloning, and even ectogenesis, where people use artificial wombs outside of their bodies to raise fetuses...Breeding controls and measures make more sense when you consider that some

---

[251] *The Wall Street Journal* "Will Google's Ray Kurzweil Live Forever?" by Holman W. Jenkins Jr. (April 12th 2013)

leading life extensionist scientists believe we will conquer human mortality in the next 20 years."[252]

These "breeding controls" also seem to align with the Georgia Guidestones, the 19-foot-tall granite monument calling for a world population reduction down to 500 million people in order to preserve the earth's natural resources. The idea is, if the life extension technology will extend people's lives by hundreds of years or more, the elite feel they need to save the planet's resources for themselves, because as CNN founder Ted Turner says, "There's too many people...too many people are using too much stuff, if there were less people, they'd be using less stuff."[253]

The mysterious man behind the strange structure made a reference to transhumanism in a little known book he published shortly after the stones were erected in 1980. "We suggest that scholars throughout the world begin now to establish new bases upon which later generations can develop a totally new universal language for men and machines. It will be adapted to our speech mechanism and to the language faculties and patterns impressed in our nervous systems. Its spoken and printed forms will be capable of accurate interchange by electromechanical means," wrote R.C. Christian, an admitted pseudonym.[254]

---

[252] *Wired* "It's Time To Consider Restricting Human Breeding" by Zoltan Istvan (August 14th 2014)

[253] PBS "Charlie Rose" - Guest Ted Turner (April 1st 2008)

[254] Christian, Robert – *Common Sense Renewed* p. 14-15

On the inside cover of the book, titled *Common Sense Renewed*, it says the first two printings were sent to several thousand political leaders and "shapers of public opinion" around the world. Aside from admitting he represented the unnamed group responsible for the creation of the Georgia Guidestones, the author says part of their purpose is that, "The hearts of our human family must be touched and warmed to welcome a global rule by reason."[255]

May I remind you that several of the "guides," or commandments as many people call them, aside from reducing to human population down to 500 million (which is more than a 90% reduction from 2014 levels) suggest creating a global government, a global universal language, and the last of the ten "guides," engraved in eight different languages on the faces of the stones, warns people to not be a "cancer on the earth."

The elite's insane dreams of becoming God get even more horrifying the closer you look into them. Richard Seed, a leading geneticist and Transhumanist promoter, said, "God made man in his own image. God intended for man to become one with God. We are going to become one with God. We are going to have almost as much knowledge and almost as much power as God. Cloning and the reprogramming of DNA is the first serious step in becoming one with God."[256]

---

[255] Christian, Robert – *Common Sense Renewed* page 6

[256] *National Public Radio* NPR (July 1st 1998)

Regarding the resistance to such plans, he ominously responded, "We are going to become Gods, period. If you don't like it, get off. You don't have to contribute, you don't have to participate, but if you are going to interfere with *me* becoming a God, you're going to have trouble. There'll be warfare."[257]

Illuminati Transhumanists believe what Satan told Adam and Eve in the Garden of Eden will soon come to pass—that they will become all-knowing, all-powerful, immortal Gods who will rule planet earth forever and ever. This New Age philosophy falls in line with their Social Darwinist "survival of the fittest" mentality, and while history is filled with a long list of men who have believed they themselves were Gods—from the ancient pharaohs in Ancient Egypt to Adolf Hitler—today the elite, and much of the general public, anxiously await the Singularity and believe they will soon achieve their Luciferian transition into a God, just as Satan promised mankind so long ago.

[Author's Note: Please take a moment to rate and review this book on Amazon.com or wherever you purchased it from to let others know what you think. This also helps to offset the trolls who keep giving my books fake one-star reviews when they haven't even read them. Almost all of the one-star reviews on my books are from NON-verified purchases which is a clear indication they are fraudulent, hence me adding this note. It's a major

---

[257] *TechnoCalyps - Part II - Preparing for the Singularity* (2008) Documentary by Frank Theys

problem for many authors, and at the time I'm writing this Amazon (and all the major e-book stores) haven't done much of anything to stop it, so I really need your help ASAP if this book has helped open your eyes! Thank you!]

Symbolism

A picture is worth a thousand words, as the cliché goes, because pictures contain so much information someone could speak for hours trying to describe every detail but still couldn't convey everything one encapsulated. Symbols reach deep into the psyche and the soul, and consciously and unconsciously convey meanings and evoke emotional responses. We live in a world full of symbols. A red light at an intersection means stop; a wedding ring symbolizes a man and woman's commitment to each other. The American flag represents the values, principles, and hard work that built America. The true power of symbols comes from their ability to evoke certain thoughts and feelings.

A souvenir you bought on a trip reminds you of all the fun you had there and just the sight of the object stimulates memories and feelings about the trip. A framed photo of your favorite car hanging on the wall in your office subconsciously reminds you of the freedom you feel on the weekends driving down a country road, briefly leaving your worries behind. Family photos invoke feelings of joy and fond memories just from glancing at them for a moment as they sit on our desk or hang on our refrigerator.

While we can all agree and articulate what many symbols mean, what makes them so mysterious is that the same symbol may have completely different meanings to different people. Let us now decode some popular

Illuminati symbols and uncover their occult "hidden" meanings and see why they are used and what they mean to insiders. Most of these symbols themselves aren't "evil" in and of themselves, they've just been adopted by groups or people who are evil, so various symbols have taken on a negative connotation. The swastika was a popular Hindu symbol of health and well-being before the Nazis incorporated it as the logo of the Nazi party, and so now we have a negative association to what was originally a positive symbol. The symbol itself is certainly not evil, but we have come to associate it with evil, when in reality it was hijacked and perverted, so for most people its meaning has been tainted from what it originally meant to convey.

The Sun

To the ancient Mystery Schools in the past, as well as numerous modern mystical or enlightenment groups, (including the Illuminati), the sun is their primary symbol and is often incorporated into their logos and artwork. The sun represents power and light. The word *Illuminati* means *enlightened ones*, and the word *enlighten* contains the word *light*, which comes from the sun. Someone is said to be *bright* if they are intelligent and are also called *brilliant*, which, if you look that word up in the dictionary, you will also find that it means "shining brightly."

The sun rises and brings life to the world by chasing away the cold and scary darkness of the night. It is an awesome, enormous, and mysterious power that affects all life on planet earth. We tell time based on the sun, it affects the seasons, and it even has an immense effect on our psyche and our health. The 28th degree in Freemasonry is called the Knight of the Sun, and is just one example of how Masons pay homage to this massive star at the center of our solar system.

The Pyramid

The pyramid represents the social hierarchy of society, symbolically depicting a small enlightened few at the top, and the masses of ignorant "worker bees" on the bottom. A sun on top of a pyramid symbolically represents the small number of Illuminati "enlightened leaders" at the top of the social hierarchy ruling over the masses of ignorant slaves below who make up the base of the pyramid.

The Dictionary of Symbols explains, "The base is square and represents the earth. The apex is the starting-point and the finishing-point of all things—the mystic 'center.' Joining the apex to the base are the triangular-shaped faces of the pyramid, symbolizing fire, divine revelation and the threefold principle of creation. In consequence the pyramid is seen as a symbol expressing the whole of the work of creation in its three essential aspects."[258]

The ancient Egyptian pyramids, built over four thousand years ago, are still one of the seven wonders of the world and have been an endless source of mystery still

---

[258] Cirlot, J.E - *Dictionary of symbols* page 255.

to this day. While mainstream historians believe the pyramids were built as tombs for the Pharaohs, the belief in the Illuminati is that they were actually temples where the Mystery Schools taught their secrets.

33rd degree Freemason Manly P. Hall explains, "The Great Pyramid was not a lighthouse, an observatory, or a tomb, but the first temple of the Mysteries, the first structure erected as a repository for those secret truths which are the certain foundation of all the arts and sciences...Through the mystic passageways and chambers of the Great Pyramid passed the illumined of antiquity. They entered its portals as men; they came forth as gods. It was the place of the 'second birth,' the womb of the Mysteries, and wisdom dwelt in it as God dwells in the hearts of men."259

As I'm sure you are aware, a pyramid with an all-seeing eye can be found on the back of the one-dollar bill, which many people believe is basically a stamp of ownership by the Illuminati. The man who designed this Great Seal was a Freemason named Charles Thomson, confirming many peoples' suspicions that a hidden hand strategically placed the symbol on the currency as a secret sign of their power.

The phrase *Novus Ordo Seclorum* (Latin for New Order for the Ages) has appeared on the bottom of the pyramid on the back of the one dollar bill since 1935. At the opening of the 110th Congress on January 4th 2007, Speaker of the House Nancy Pelosi made a cryptic reference to the Great Seal, announcing, "Our Founders

259 Hall, Manly P. - *Secret Teachings of All Ages* page 118

envisioned a new America driven by optimism, opportunity, and courage. So confident were they in the new America they were advancing, they put on the Great Seal of the United States, 'Novus ordo seclorum'—a new order for the ages...This vision has sustained us for more than 200 years, and it accounts for what is best in our great nation: liberty, opportunity, and justice. Now it is our responsibility to carry forth that vision of a new America."

The All-Seeing Eye

The symbol of one eye, often with rays of light emanating from it, represents God's omniscient power and dates back to ancient Egypt where it represented the sun God Horus who could see all. It's sometimes called the Eye of Providence, and as you know, sits on top of the pyramid on the back of the one dollar bill. This all-seeing eye symbol also represents Big Brother and the Orwellian power of the intelligence agencies watching what everyone does, what they buy, and cataloging their online activities.

Not only are there all-seeing eyes watching people in shopping malls and walking down the streets of major cities, but most people have willingly installed an all-seeing eye in their living rooms—and even their bedrooms—and with the click of a few keys these eyes can be activated by crafty hackers or government agencies. Of course I'm talking about webcams that are built into tablets, laptops, and televisions, not to mention, perhaps even more disturbing, listening to people as well through the microphones that accompany them.

Check out my previous book, *Big Brother: The Orwellian Nightmare Come True* to learn about actual high-tech spy gadgets, mind-reading machines, government projects, and emerging artificial intelligence systems that seem as if they came right out of George Orwell's novel *Nineteen Eighty-Four* and how our own world is unfortunately eerily paralleling the dystopia in his classic book.

While much of this has become fairly well known by now, one interesting point few people ponder is that the all-seeing eye—aside from representing the Illuminati—may actually become a symbol of the Antichrist himself. One Bible prophecy about the Antichrist is that an attempt will be made on his life that will take out or damage one of his eyes.[260] Since the symbol often represents a "God," it's possible that the coming counterfeit Christ may literally embody this symbol as a tactic to convince the masses that he himself is God. In Islam, Muslims have a prophecy almost identical saying that the Antichrist, who they call the Dejjal, will be symbolized by one eye.

Snakes and Serpents

The symbol of the serpent is perhaps best known as the creature in the Garden of Eden who tempted Adam and Eve into disobeying God by eating from the Tree of Knowledge of Good and Evil. The very word *snake* has

---

[260] Zechariah 11:17

negative connotations, meaning someone is a liar or deceptive. While the typical connotation of a snake is negative, and the Biblical story of Adam and Eve depicts Satan as the enemy of God and mankind, the occult interpretation is quite different. Occultists and Satanists praise the serpent and believe it brought wisdom to Mankind, enabling humans to become gods.

Again we look to the revelations of 33rd degree Freemason Manly P. Hall who explains, "The serpent is true to the principle of wisdom, for it tempts man to the knowledge of himself. Therefore the knowledge of self resulted from man's disobedience to the Demiurges, Jehovah [God]."[261] Hall continues, saying "The serpent is the symbol and prototype of the Universal savior, who redeems the worlds by giving creation the knowledge of itself and the realization of good and evil."[262]

The Secret Doctrine says, "The Serpent of Eternity and all Knowledge, that Manasic spirit [the rational faculty of the mind], which made him learn the secret of creation on the Kriyasaktic, and of procreation on the earthly planes—led him as naturally to discover his way to immortality, notwithstanding the jealously of the Gods."[263]

The evil scumbag Aleister Crowley had this to say: "This serpent, Satan, is not the enemy of Man, [because it

---

[261] Hall, Manly P. - *The Secret Teachings of All Ages* p. 272

[262] Hall, Manly P – *The Secret Teachings of All Ages* p. 272

[263] Blavatsky, H.P. – *The Secret Doctrine* v. II p. 283

is he] who made Gods of our race, knowing Good and Evil."[264]

Like Satanists and occultists, Freemasons adore the serpent as a savior and worship its wisdom. Here is a quote from Albert Pike's *Morals and Dogma* about the serpent, reading, "It is the body of the Holy Spirit, the Universal Agent, the Serpent devouring its own tail."[265]

Complicating the meaning of the serpent symbol are several cryptic statements in the Bible, the first of which is when Jesus advised people to be as wise as serpents yet as gentle as doves in Mathew 10:16. This statement seems to acknowledge that serpents contain wisdom or represent a power that may be used for either good or evil. Another interesting and hard to reconcile story about serpents is when Moses made a brazen (brass) serpent and attached it to the top of his staff in order to heal the Israelites who had been bitten by snakes in the desert. The American Medical Association's logo is a snake coiled around on a staff and the same symbol is often found on ambulances as a symbol of health and healing. When someone reaches the 25th degree of Freemasonry, they are called a Knight of the Brazen Serpent.

One of the reasons serpents have come to symbolize wisdom and enlightenment is because their eyes are always open since they don't have any eyelids. Snakes are very unique creatures because they have no legs yet move around shooting across the ground like a bolt of

---

[264] Crowley, Aleister - *Magick: In Theory and Practice* p. 193

[265] Pike, Albert – *Morals and Dogma* p. 734

lightning. To early Man, they may have seemed magical because they can appear out of nowhere and then disappear into the grass or into the earth itself. The shedding of their skin has come to symbolize a rebirth or immortality, possibly because primitive man thought that snakes were immortal and would give birth to a new self, when a snake "died" it would rise again leaving behind its old "carcass" in the form of its shed skin and continue to live on.

It's possible that the serpent does not necessarily represent evil in and of itself, but may represent a force that may be used for either good or evil.

The Phoenix

A phoenix is a large mythical bird that symbolizes cyclical renewal, immortality, or resurrection. The creature is depicted similar to an eagle and is often associated with the sun, and many myths talk about the phoenix dying, decomposing, and then rising again out of its own ashes. Some believe that many of the eagle symbols we see today are actually secretly symbols of a phoenix, including the double-headed "eagle" that is a symbol of the 33rd degree of Freemasonry.

The eagle that has come to be a popular symbol of America, and found on the back of the one dollar bill, is also believed by some to occultly signify a phoenix. *The Secret Teachings of All Ages* states that "The hand of the mysteries controlled in the establishment of the new government for the signature of the mysteries may still be seen on the Great Seal of the United states of America.

Careful analysis of the seal discloses a mass of occult and masonic symbols chief among them, the so-called American Eagle...only the student of symbolism can see through the subterfuge and realize that the American eagle upon the Great Seal is but a conventionalized phoenix."[266]

The book, published in 1928, also states that, "Not only were many of the founders of the United States government Masons, but they received aid from a secret and august body existing in Europe which helped them to establish this country for a peculiar and particular purpose known only to the initiated few. The Great Seal is the signature of this exalted body—unseen and for the most part unknown—and the unfinished pyramid upon its reverse side is a teeterboard setting forth symbolically the task to the accomplishment of which the United States Government was dedicated from the day of its in conception."[267]

The phoenix has been proposed to be the name of the new unified global currency that international banksters have long awaited. The cover of the January 1988 edition of *The Economist* magazine read "Are you ready for a world currency" and contained an article that explained, "Thirty years from now, Americans, Japanese, Europeans, and people in many other rich countries, and some relatively poor ones will probably be paying for their shopping with the same currency. Prices will be quoted not in dollars, yen or D-marks but in, let's say, the

---

[266] Hall, Manly P. - *The Secret Teachings of All Ages* p. 282

[267] Hall, Manly P. - *The Secret Teachings of All Ages* p. 283

phoenix. The phoenix will be favored by companies and shoppers because it will be more convenient than today's national currencies."[268]

The metaphor of "rising from the ashes like a phoenix" refers to a rebirth, or something being killed or destroyed in order to give birth to something new, and so by killing off the U.S. Dollar and other currencies around the world through inflation, the banksters are symbolically giving birth to their new currency, which many plan to call the "phoenix."

The Owl

When discussing Illuminati symbolism, the owl is most known for its connections to the Bohemian Grove, the Illuminati's summer retreat in northern California. Esoterically, the owl represents wisdom because it sees in the dark, and the Owl of Athena was chosen by Adam Weishaupt as one of the symbols of the Bavarian Illuminati. Early civilizations saw the owl as mysterious because it is only seen at night since they are nocturnal animals.

The Dictionary of Symbols explains, "In the Egyptian system of hieroglyphs, the owl symbolizes death, night, cold and passivity. It also pertains to the realm of the dead sun, that is, it is of the sun which has set below the

---

[268] *The Economist* "Get Ready for the Phoenix" (01/9/88) Vol. 306, pp 9-10

horizon and which is crossing the lake or sea of darkness."[269]

A tiny owl can also be found hidden on the one dollar bill, perched on the upper left corner of the frame that surrounds the "1" located in the upper right hand corner of the bill. Many people see an owl designed into the street layout of Washington D.C., right on top of the U.S. Capitol building when viewing the location from overheard or looking at it on a map.

Pictures of owls are often seen in classrooms standing on a small stack of books in order to symbolize knowledge. The National Press Club's logo also contains an owl standing on a book. Owls are also seen as guardians and often owl statues are put on the top of buildings to scare away other birds.

The Skull and Crossbones

The skull and crossbones symbol has a sinister look to it, which is why it has been used by nefarious groups for centuries—from pirates and biker gangs, to the Nazis. It represents death, or the power over life and death, which is why it appeals to megalomaniacs and psychopaths. The Nazi SS officers in charge of concentration camps where over six million people were exterminated wore a skull and crossbones symbol on their uniforms, the same emblem used by the Skull & Bones secret society as their logo. The Nazis called it the *Totenkopf* (German for *skull* or *dead man's head*) and it was a blatant statement of their

---

[269] Cirlot, J.E.– *Dictionary of Symbol* 235-236

intention and purpose. Hitler personally handed out a Death's Head ring to elite SS soldiers.

The Knights Templar incorporated the symbol into their lives because they were dedicated to fight to the death and vowed never to be taken alive as a prisoner. Many Freemasons have a human skull (or a replica) sitting on their desk to remind them of their own mortality and that their life is quickly ticking away. It is meant to urge them to work towards the achievement of their goals before it's too late.

As you may recall from earlier, both the Bavarian Illuminati and Skull & Bones society at Yale use the object in their induction ceremony with their four different skulls and the question about which one is the fool, the wise man, the beggar or the king. The answer to this induction riddle, "Whether poor or rich, all's the same in death," is meant to reinforce their mortality to them and remind them that the clock of life is ticking so they had better do all they can to become kings here in this life because when you're dead—to them—nothing matters. The riddle is obviously meant to convey that they don't believe in an afterlife or a final judgment from God.

Baphomet

Baphomet is an occult idol that is depicted as an androgynous man with female breasts that has the head of a goat. The torch of Prometheus is often sticking out of its head and intertwining serpents are rising from its crotch. It's a mysterious and hideous looking figure that dates back to the 1300s when the inner circle of Knights

Templar allegedly incorporated it into their rituals and secret doctrine.

An early depiction of the figure comes from an 1854 book titled *Transcendental Magic* that was written by a French occultist Eliphas Levi.[270] Accompanying his illustration, Eliphas Levi wrote, "According to some, the Baphomet was a monstrous head, but according to others, a demon in the form of a goat. A sculptured coffer [chest] was disinterred [dug up] recently in the ruins of an old Commandery of the Temple, and antiquaries observed upon it a Baphometic figure, corresponding by its attributes to the goat of Mendes and the androgyne of Khunrath."[271]

Many Satanists have proudly incorporated the Baphomet figure into their symbols and rituals. Aleister Crowley wrote that the serpent or the "devil's emblem" was Baphomet, who he also called the "hieroglyph of arcane perfection."[272]

One version of the figure is the Church of Satan's logo, which is printed on the cover of *The Satanic Bible*. While many people claim that the Catholic Church fabricated the claims that the Knights Templar were using it in secret rituals as an excuse to arrest them and confiscate their wealth during the Inquisition, most

---

[270] Levi, Eliphas - *Transcendental Magic*

[271] Levi, Eliphas - *Transcendental Magic* page 316

[272] Crowley, Aleister – *Magick: In Theory and Practice* page 193

Satanists and occults hold the belief that the Catholic Church's claims were actually true.[273]

Again, Eliphas Levi boldly proclaimed in his book *Transcendental Magic*, "Yes, in our profane conviction, the Grand Masters of the Order of the Templars worshipped the Baphomet, and caused it to be worshipped by their initiates."[274]

The Pentagram

An upside down pentagram drawn inside of a circle is one of the most obvious and familiar satanic symbols that is used by occult organizations, rebellious teenagers, and rock stars today. It is a lower level occult symbol often used to represent dark powers or sinister forces. Because it's so widely known, it's never really used by high-level occultist or the Illuminati, who instead use much less familiar symbols like pyramids, all-seeing eyes, owls, black and white checkerboards, and other, less polarizing images.

A pentagram differs from an ordinary five-pointed star in a few ways. First, a pentagram is drawn using five straight lines making up the points and also forming a pentagon in the center. The Satanic pentagram is drawn upside down, and often encompassed by a circle. The reason Satanists use it is because Christians originally used the five points of a (right-side up) pentagram (called

---

[273] Levi, Eliphas - *Transcendental Magic* p. 7-8

[274] Levi, Eliphas – *Transcendental Magic* p. 307

the pentalpha) to symbolize the five wounds of Jesus (the two spikes through his hands, two through his feet, and the spear that pierced his side). Satanists like to pervert things and flip Christian symbols upside down or backwards to signify their opposing views and beliefs, and this is how their use of upside down pentagrams came into being.

The Dictionary of Symbols entry on the star reads, "As far back as in the days of Egyptian hieroglyphics a star pointing upwards signified 'rising upwards towards the point of origin' and formed part of such words as 'to bring up,' 'to educate,' and 'the teacher.' The inverted five-pointed star is a symbol of the infernal and used in black magic."[275]

In Freemasonry, the pentagram is called the Blazing Star and represents the sun, Lucifer, carnal knowledge and power. To Wiccans and Pagans, the five points of the star represent air, fire, water, Earth, and spirit. The female branch of Freemasonry, called Eastern Star, actually uses an upside down pentagram as their emblem.

Square and Compass

A square (the tool used by carpenters to lay out a right angle or a "square" angle) overlaid on top of a compass (the tool used for drawing circles and arches—not the navigation tool for identifying direction) is a popular symbol in Freemasonry and is often seen with the letter G in the center. The square and compass signify the

---

[275] Cerlot, J. E - *The Dictionary of Symbols* page 295

alchemical doctrine of "as above, so below" or the joining of heaven and earth by forming two opposite facing pyramids with one pointing up and the other one pointing downward. The letter G in the center stands for God or Gnosis [the Greek word for knowledge.] It is also often said to stand for the "Great Architect of the Universe," a term many masons use to refer to God.

The Statue of Liberty

If you asked the average American what the Statue of Liberty represented, they'll probably tell you it has to do with "America," "freedom," or "democracy." Some may know that it was given to America by the French, but few know its very design and creation was orchestrated by Freemasons, the secret society, not the government of France, who then gave it to America as a "gift" and placed it in New York Harbor.

Frederic Bartholdi, the designer of the Statue of Liberty, was, of course, a Freemason, and very familiar with occult and Illuminati symbolism and philosophies. In fact, the three major figures involved with the Statue— Frederic Bartholdi, who designed the statue itself; Gustave Eiffel, who designed the inner support structure; and Richard Hunt, who designed the pedestal—were all Freemasons.

Bartholdi's original plan for a giant statue of this type was actually that it be placed in a harbor in Egypt. After his proposal was turned down by the Egyptian government, he changed his design a little bit and approached America to see if he could erect his newly designed statue in the United States. The point is, he originally wanted to build a bizarre "God-like" statue and have it stand somewhere other than America. Bartholdi's first choice for his mystical statue was Egypt, not the United States.

The original name of the statue was "Liberty Enlightening the World," not the "Statue of Liberty." Again, the word *Enlightening* fits in with the Illuminati theme—Enlightening, enlightenment, light, the sun, intelligence, bright, brilliance, Lucifer. You get the picture by now.

A near mirror image of the Statue of Liberty stands in France, also on an island, in the Seine River in Paris, that was set up in 1889, just three years after the one in America was completed. If it's an "American" symbol then why is there an almost identical one in France? There are actually hundreds of nearly identical "Statue of Liberty" figures all around the world, including Leicester, England; Lviv, Ukraine; Carinthia, Austria; Cenicero, Spain; Arraba in Israel, and many, many other places.

The Statue of Liberty is essentially a modern version of the Colossus of Rhodes, which was a 100-foot-tall statue depicting the Greek sun god Helios (Helios being Greek for *sun*) that once stood in ancient Greece. The Colossus was created in the 3rd century B.C. and depicted Helios (the Sun God) holding a torch high in one hand and stood on the island of Rhodes facing the water. "This gigantic gilded figure, with its crown of solar rays and its upraised torch, signified occultly the glorious Sun Man of the Mysteries, the Universal Savior," says *The Secret Teachings of All Ages*.[276]

There is a poem printed on a plaque that sits prominently near the base of the Statue of Liberty titled *The New Colossus*, clearly signaling that it was modeled after the Greek sun god. There was a Masonic cornerstone ceremony conducted when construction began, and a Masonic plaque was placed on the site as well. The statue also symbolizes a composite of a variety of ancient goddesses who represent the feminine principle.

The torch that the Statue of Liberty is holding represents the torch of Prometheus, who occultly signifies Lucifer. The Greek mythological story of Prometheus is the same allegory of stealing fire (i.e. knowledge) from God or the Gods, and giving it to humans, thus angering God.

Here is Manly P. Hall again, one of Freemasonry's greatest philosophers, explaining in *Lectures on Ancient Philosophy*, that, "Man wandered hopelessly in the gloom of mortality, living and dying without light or understanding in his servitude to the Demiurgus [the creator God] and his host of spirits. At last the spirit of rebellion entered the creation in the form of Lucifer, who in the guise of a serpent tempted man to revolt against the mandates of Jehovah (the Demiurgus). In Greece this character was known as Prometheus, who brought from

[276] Hall, Manly P. – *The Secret Teachings of All Ages* p. 189

the gods the impregnating flame that would release the life latent in this multitude of germlike potentialities."[277]

The seven horn-looking spikes coming out of the Statue of Liberty's head represent rays of the sun, and symbolically represents the spirit radiating from the mind as knowledge or "enlightenment." There are seven of them because the rays represent the seven liberal arts and sciences, thus comprising an essential knowledge base. The statue is also holding a book, obviously, symbolic of knowledge and information—again fitting in with the theme of knowledge and enlightenment, because knowledge is power, and that is what the Illuminati has.

Rockefeller Center's Prometheus

Rockefeller Center in New York City is a huge 22-acre complex made up of nineteen different buildings and the home of Bank of America, NBC, General Electric and other major international Illuminati-controlled corporations. Standing prominently within the property is a huge gold colored statue of Prometheus holding a ball of fire in one hand as he flies through the air. The mythological Greek story of Prometheus stealing fire from the Gods and giving it to mankind despite the punishment he will face is seen by occultists as identical to the story of Lucifer giving mankind the knowledge of good and evil that God had forbid us to have.

So essentially this statue that stands outside of Rockefeller Center is a tribute to Lucifer, which goes

---

[277] Hall, Manly P. - *Lectures on Ancient Philosophy* page 163

unnoticed by the average person not familiar with Illuminati symbolism. Most people are probably not even familiar with the Prometheus myth, or have long since forgotten about it since studying Greek mythology in high school and simply think the statue is just another random piece of art with little to no significance.

Helena Blavatsky explains in her classic occult work, *The Secret Doctrine,* that, "The allegory of Prometheus, who steals the divine fire as to allow men to proceed consciously on the path of spiritual evolution, thus transforming the most perfect of animals on Earth into a potential god, and making him free to take the kingdom of heaven by violence. Hence also, the curse pronounced by Zeus against Prometheus, and by Jehovah [God] against his 'rebellious son,' Satan."[278]

So as you can see, it's not just me making the connection between Prometheus and Lucifer—It's occultist insiders themselves, and of course it's no coincidence this stands on a Rockefeller property, a family with generational ties to the Illuminati establishment.

The Washington Monument

The Washington Monument, which is located directly west of the United States Capitol building in Washington DC, standing approximately 555 feet high, dominates the sky throughout the city and can be seen from miles around, especially at night with the red light shining from

[278] Blavatsky, H.P. – *The Secret Doctrine* v. II p. 244

the top looking like the evil Eye of Sauron in the *Lord of the Rings* movies. The monument is an Egyptian obelisk with a pyramid capstone on the top and was completed in 1884.

The structure is one of the most important symbols in America to the Illuminati, although most people are clearly unaware of it having any hidden meaning. Occultists see the monument as an enormous phallic symbol—a big penis—representing masculine energy and dominance. One would expect the "Washington" Monument to be a statue of George Washington himself, much like the Lincoln Memorial houses a huge statue of Abraham Lincoln, but instead it's a giant erect penis of the Egyptian god Baal. Of course, it too was designed and built by Freemasons, who even had a ceremony to lay the cornerstone when construction began.

Fritz Springmeier, author of *Bloodlines of the Illuminati*, wrote, "Every morning when the United States President wakes up he can look out the window, see the Masonic obelisk and be reminded of who controls America. If the president has any training in the Mystery Religion of Egypt, he will also know what body part is symbolically erected in the Washington Memorial."[279] Springmeier goes so far as to say, "If the U.S. were ever to return to serving God, that monument would be a good one to destroy. God asked the Israelites not just simply to avoid worshiping such abominations, He asked His

---

[279] Springmeier, Fritz – *Bloodlines of the Illuminati* page 191

people to destroy them, for their very creation was an abomination."[280]

Cleopatra's Needle

While the Washington Monument may be the most well-known Egyptian obelisk in America, it isn't the only one. Another one stands in Central Park in New York City—called Cleopatra's Needle, and this one is actually an authentic Egyptian obelisk that dates back to around 1500 B.C. and was transported to New York in 1881.

Similar "Cleopatra's Needles" actually stand in London and Paris, signifying the Illuminati's rule in those countries as well. Not surprising, there is also one in Vatican City as well. The one in New York's Central Park stands 70-feet tall and weighs 220 tons. Why and how it was brought to America all the way from Egypt is an interesting story.

For some reason Henry G. Stebbins, who was the Commissioner of the Department of Public Parks in New York in the 1880s, announced he was looking for help financing a plan to bring the statue to America. William H. Vanderbilt, who was one of the wealthiest men in the world, was asked to help make it happen and donated over $100,000 (over $2 million in 2014 dollars) to help. Interestingly, the shipping costs for the one sent to London were paid for by Dr. Erasmus Wilson, a Freemason.

---

[280] Ibid

Once the obelisk arrived in America, thousands of Freemasons took part in a parade as it was rolled up Fifth Avenue from 14th Street to 82nd Street. When it was erected at its final destination in the park, the Grand Master of Masons in New York performed a cornerstone laying ritual as a celebration. When it first arrived in New York in 1881, Cleopatra's Needle was covered with clearly visible hieroglyphics about the sun god Horus, but most of the carvings have since been warn away from acid rain. While they survived 3000 years in Egypt, it seems the ancient relic was no match for the pollution of New York City.

Movies and Music

For hundreds of years, knowledge of the Illuminati and their symbols was largely contained within the Mystery Schools that taught the esoteric tradition. Outsiders didn't even think twice about most occult symbols because they were seen as ordinary art and few people paid much attention to them. But with the birth of the information age, things started to change. In the 1990s and early 2000s, a growing number of websites and forums were dedicated to investigating secret societies, and began to expose these once little known issues to a larger number of people.

For decades, those interested in such material were considered a fringe minority of patriots and "conspiracy theorists," but with the emergence of social media becoming a standard feature in most people's lives, and with video sharing websites like YouTube changing the nature of media and information exchange, an interesting phenomenon began to occur early in the twenty-first century. Illuminati and occult symbolism spilled over from what was once primarily the topic of fringe websites, and "computer geeks" on Internet forums, to became part of pop culture finding its way into various mainstream music videos and blockbuster movies.

While a sizable portion of the population has become familiar with the use of Illuminati symbolism in rap videos and supposed "Illuminati hand signs" being flashed by celebrities, most people who pay attention to this aspect of the symbolism barely have a basic understanding of the history of the symbols or their meanings. Many people who have heard the oftentimes farfetched claims about "Illuminati celebrities" have dismissed the existence of the Illuminati all together as a conspiracy theory or believe it's simply a secret society in Hollywood that top celebrities are part of.

Checkout my previous book *Illuminati in the Music Industry* to read about this fascinating history since it is a very lengthy analysis in and of itself. While there certainly have been countless allegations made against a variety of celebrities like Jay-Z, Beyoncé, Lady Gaga, Kanye West and others, when you take a critical analysis of celebrity as a whole and the power their music and personas have over the culture, it becomes very clear that music is not always "just entertainment."

As the Illuminati prepare to announce the "royal secret," as they call it, by declaring that Satan is the King of the Earth and the "savior of mankind," hoping to finally overthrow the "inferior" and "evil" Creator God to complete the New World Order "utopia," celebrities have recently played a major part in paving the path to the apocalypse.

The vast majority of the public literally worship celebrities who function as modern day Gods that shape our cultural attitudes and beliefs since their every action is mimicked, and every opinion they voice is seen as profound.

The general public is growing to see the Illuminati—not as a threat to their freedoms or a corrupt mafia of politicians, bankers and businessmen—but as a "cool" group of powerful men they wish they could be a part of. The moral decay and erosion of the work ethic have resulted in the average person willing to do almost anything for just a taste of the Illuminati's "success." Pop culture has begun portraying the Illuminati as holding the secret to success or a secret society of the rich and famous.

Occasionally films have portrayed the Illuminati or an affiliated group as the antagonist in a plot to convey a warning to the audience, and some celebrities have publicly denounced them as the shadowy puppet masters pulling the strings in global affairs, but the overwhelming majority of mainstream media content and celebrity idols paint the Illuminati as holding the master key to success and as a result countless people would practically kill their own mother to join them in order to have a bigger piece of the pie.

Insiders' Hints

If you want to truly understand what the Illuminati is, what they are doing, what they are planning, and what they believe, there's no better place to go than to elite insiders themselves who can't always keep their mouths shut, and occasionally can't help but brag about their "great work." While there's a long list of people who claim to be Illuminati defectors that speak about their alleged activities while supposedly being a "member of the Illuminati," most of these people are hoaxers and fraudsters with no credibility who are just trying to make a few bucks from selling books, or just looking for attention, and many of them have been easily debunked.

Of course if you do an Internet search for "the Illuminati," you'll find countless websites making claims about what they are, what they do, who's supposedly involved, etc. There's even a Wikipedia page giving a few details about them, although it's largely incomplete and inaccurate. While it's not difficult at all to find Illuminati conspiracy theories online, what is difficult; however, is finding accurate and reliable information that is properly sourced and verified, and this is my primary goal with this book.

While everyone seems to have an opinion about the Illuminati these days, most people think "research" consists of watching a few YouTube videos or glancing over a Wikipedia article. There are, however, some very well connected and powerful men who have either

213

dropped hints about the Illuminati and their secret agenda, or those who have gotten close enough to the power structure to see for themselves that a powerful secret society does exist and has tremendous influence over the world.

David Rockefeller

The Rockefeller family is often mentioned as one of the families that has been involved with the Illuminati for generations and have accumulated a vast amount of wealth and influence because of this. The Rockefeller family made most of their money in oil and banking, and using their wealth they have wrapped their tentacles around some of the most infamous groups and conspiracies connected to the Illuminati.

For example, Rockefeller money was instrumental in the early growth of the Council on Foreign Relations, the Trilateral Commission, and the Bilderberg Group. They were a major funder of Eugenics and the CIA's MK-ULTRA mind control experiments at over 30 American Universities, hospitals, and government facilities. The Rockefellers bought seventeen acres of land for the United Nations headquarters to be built in Manhattan; and even financed the development of facial recognition systems through their Rockefeller University that recruited and funded a man named Joseph Atick in the early 1990s who was given use of the Computational Neuroscience Laboratory where he developed his facial recognition systems.

In his 2002 book, *Memoirs*, Illuminati kingpin David Rockefeller arrogantly admitted, "For more than a century ideological extremists at either end of the political spectrum have seized upon well-publicized incidents such as my encounter with Castro to attack the Rockefeller family for the inordinate influence they claim we wield over American political and economic institutions. Some even believe we are part of a secret cabal working against the interests of the United States, characterizing my family and me as "internationalists" and conspiring with others around the world to build a more integrated global political and economic structure—one world, if you will. If that's the charge, I stand guilty, and I am proud of it."[281]

In a 1980 PBS documentary titled *The World of David Rockefeller*, host Bill Moyer said that "David Rockefeller is the most conspicuous representative today of the ruling class, a multinational fraternity of men who shape the global economy and manage the flow of its capital. Rockefeller was born to it, and he has made the most of it. But what some critics see as a vast international conspiracy, he considers a circumstance of life and just another day's work... In the world of David Rockefeller it's hard to tell where business ends and politics begins."[282]

---

[281] Rockefeller, David - *Memoirs* page 405.

[282] PBS *The World of David Rockefeller* (1980) hosted by Bill Moyers

Carroll Quigley

In 1966 an Establishment insider and mentor of President Bill Clinton published a book for fellow Establishment insiders titled *Tragedy & Hope* to help them understand how the Illuminati empire works. Carroll Quigley, a professor at Georgetown University, knew that most of the public doesn't read books or newspapers and are more interested in sports entertainment and celebrity news than business or politics.

Quigley openly revealed, "There does exist, and has existed for a generation, an international Anglophile network which operates, to some extent, in the way the radical Right believes the Communists act. In fact, this network, which we may identify as the Round Table Groups, has no aversion to cooperating with the Communists, or any other groups, and frequently does so. I know of the operations of this network because I have studied it for twenty years and was permitted for two years, in the early 1960's, to examine its papers and secret records. I have no aversion to it or to most of its aims and have, for much of my life, been close to it and to many of its instruments. I have objected, both in the past and recently, to a few of its policies (notably to its belief that England was an Atlantic rather than a European Power and must be allied, or even federated, with the United States and must remain isolated from Europe), but in general my chief difference of opinion is that it wishes to remain unknown, and I believe its role in history is significant enough to be known."[283]

He described how the financial elite created front groups to influence governments around the world, writing, "...in New York it was known as the Council on Foreign Relations, and was a front for J. P. Morgan and Company in association with the very small American Round Table Group. The American organizers were dominated by the large number of Morgan 'experts'... The Round Table for years (until 1961) was edited from the back door of Chatham House grounds in Ormond Yard, and its telephone came through the Chatham House switchboard."[284]

Quigley also explained how it was to the elite's advantage to have only two political parties for people to choose from. The reason being, "The two parties should be almost identical, so that the American people can 'throw the rascals out' at any election without leading to any profound or extensive shifts in policy."[285]

Regarding the Federal Reserve and the financial takeover of governments by private banks he said, "The powers of financial capitalism had a far-reaching aim, nothing less than to create a world system of financial control in private hands able to dominate the political system of each country and the economy of the world as a

---

[283] Quigley, Carroll – *Tragedy and Hope* page 950

[284] Quigley, Carroll – *Tragedy and Hope* pages 951-952

[285] Quigley, Carroll – *Tragedy and Hope* pages 1247-1248

whole. This system was to be controlled in a feudalist fashion by the central banks of the world acting in concert, by secret agreements arrived at in frequent meetings and conferences. The apex of the systems was to be the Bank for International Settlements in Basel, Switzerland, a private bank owned and controlled by the world's central banks which were themselves private corporations. Each central bank...sought to dominate its government by its ability to control Treasury loans, to manipulate foreign exchanges, to influence the level of economic activity in the country, and to influence cooperative politicians by subsequent economic rewards in the business world."[286]

Basically in his lengthy and dry book, *Tragedy & Hope,* he quietly confirmed what many "conspiracy theorists" had been saying for decades, but unlike most outsiders, he was in a position to learn directly from the perpetrators.

Cecil Rhodes

The most notorious diamond monopoly man in history, and the person behind the elite Rhodes Scholarships, which awards young men and women who the Establishment feel will be willing and useful servants with a free ride to Oxford University and basically an invitation to the Illuminati, was a man named Cecil Rhodes, who didn't just talk about his plans to further the

---

[286] Quigley, Carroll – *Tragedy and Hope* page 324

Invisible Empire, he actually wrote in his will that after he died his fortune would go to finance this.

Rhodes is the man behind the DeBeers diamond cartel who became extremely wealthy by monopolizing diamond mines in Africa and then launching a brilliant propaganda campaign with the help of Edward Bernays designed to brainwash women around the world into thinking that when a man proposes marriage he must do so with a diamond ring.

Rhodes, who died in 1902, wrote in his will that his fortune was to be used, "To and for the establishment, promotion and development of a Secret Society, the true aim and object whereof shall be for the extension of British rule throughout the world, the perfecting of a system of emigration from the United Kingdom, and of colonization by British subjects of all lands where the means of livelihood are attainable by energy, labor and enterprise, and especially the occupation by British settlers of the entire Continent of Africa, the Holy Land, the Valley of the Euphrates, the Islands of Cyprus and Candia, the whole of South America, the Islands of the Pacific not heretofore possessed by Great Britain, the whole of the Malay Archipelago, the seaboard of China and Japan, the ultimate recovery of the United States of America as an integral part of the British Empire, the inauguration of a system of Colonial representation in the Imperial Parliament which may tend to weld together the disjointed members of the Empire and, finally, the foundation of so great a Power as to render wars impossible, and promote the best interests of humanity."[287]

To help carry out his plan, certain money from his estate is designated to what's called the Rhodes Scholarship, which is a student fund that awards carefully chosen individuals who don't necessarily come from wealthy families but who are seen as likely assets of the Illuminati with a free ride post graduate education at England's Oxford University, where they are groomed to later become pawns of the global elite. President Bill Clinton was awarded a Rhodes Scholarship to bring him into the fold, as was the liberal lesbian Rachel Maddow of MSNBC who uses her national mainstream media platform to promote bigger government and the radical liberal agenda on a continual basis.

Edward Bernays

In 1928 Edward Bernays, the man considered to be the father of public relations, revealed in his book *Propaganda* that, "Those who manipulate the unseen mechanism of society constitute an invisible government which is the true ruling power of our country. We are governed, our minds are molded, our tastes formed, our ideas suggested, largely by men we have never heard of...in almost every act of our lives whether in the sphere of politics or business in our social conduct or our ethical thinking, we are dominated by the relatively small

---

[287] Rotberg, Robert - *The Founder: Cecil Rhodes and the Pursuit of Power* (1988) page 101-102

number of persons who understand the mental processes and social patterns of the masses. It is they who pull the wires that control the public mind, who harness old social forces and contrive new ways to bind and guide the world."[288]

He went on to admit, "Whatever of social importance is done today, whether in politics, finance, manufacture, agriculture, charity, education, or other fields, must be done with the help of propaganda. Propaganda is the executive arm of the invisible government."[289]

Bernays also stated plainly that, "The invisible government tends to be concentrated in the hands of the few because of the expense of manipulating the social machinery which controls the opinions and habits of the masses."[290]

The Department of Defense (previously called the Department of War) actually hired Bernays to help influence public opinion to support America's involvement in World War I. The tobacco industry also paid him to use his methods to encourage women to smoke cigarettes since at the time it was seen as unattractive.[291] Bernays is also the person all men can thank for having to cough up thousands of dollars for a

---

[288] Bernays, Edward – *Propaganda* page 37-38

[289] Bernays, Edward – *Propaganda* page 47-48

[290] Bernays, Edward – *Propaganda* page 63

[291] *New York Times* - "Group of Girls Puff at Cigarettes as a Gesture of Freedom" (April 1st 1929)

diamond ring when we propose marriage since that tradition was started as a clever marketing ploy he crafted for the DeBeers diamond monopoly.

Woodrow Wilson

The 28th President of the United States, Woodrow Wilson, was the man responsible for signing the Federal Reserve Act into law and handing America's banking system over to the money manipulating mafia in 1913. Wilson later admitted, "Since I entered politics, I have chiefly had men's views confided to me privately. Some of the biggest men in the United States, in the field of commerce and manufacturing, are afraid of something. They know that there is a power somewhere so organized, so subtle, so watchful, so interlocked, so complete, so pervasive, that they better not speak above their breath when they speak in condemnation of it."[292]

After he was out of office, Woodrow Wilson allegedly voiced regret for cooperating with the banking cartel's plan for the Federal Reserve Banking system, reportedly saying, "I am a most unhappy man. I have unwittingly ruined my country. A great industrial nation is now controlled by its system of credit. We are no longer a government by free opinion, no longer a government by conviction and the vote of the majority, but a government

---

[292] Wilson, Woodrow -*The New Freedom, Chapter I: The Old Order Changeth*

by the opinion and duress of a small group of dominant men."[293]

John F. Kennedy

When speaking to the American Newspaper Publishers Association in 1961, President Kennedy actually condemned secret societies, saying, "The very word 'secrecy' is repugnant in a free and open society; and we are as a people inherently and historically opposed to secret societies, to secret oaths and to secret proceedings."[294]

He continued, "We decided long ago that the dangers of excessive and unwarranted concealment of pertinent facts far outweighed the dangers which are cited to justify it...For we are opposed around the world by a monolithic and ruthless conspiracy that relies primarily on covered means for expanding its sphere of influence, on infiltration instead of invasion, on subversion instead of elections, on intimidation instead of free choice, on guerrillas by night instead of armies by day. It is a system which has conscripted vast human and material resources into the building of a tightly knit highly efficient machine that combines military, diplomatic, intelligence, economic, scientific and political operations, its

[293] This quote is disputed and various sources purporting to be its origin are debated.

[294] President Kennedy's address before the American Newspaper Publishers Association (April 27th 1961)

preparations concealed, not published, its mistakes are buried not headlined, it's dissenters are silenced not praised, no expenditure is questioned, no rumor is printed, no secret is revealed."

Kennedy issued an interesting Executive Order (number 11110) in 1963 that many interpret as directing the Secretary of the Treasury to start once again issuing silver certificates (which looked similar to dollar bills) that would be redeemable for their face value in silver coins or bullion, in what many saw as an attempt to remove power from the Federal Reserve Bank and give it back to the Treasury department.

Silver certificates [called United States Notes] were originally put in circulation in 1878 by the Treasury department and used as money, but Federal Reserve Notes (commonly known as U.S. dollars) replaced them after the creation of the Federal Reserve banking system in 1913.

Kennedy's Executive Order 11110 was soon reversed by President Lyndon B. Johnson after he was sworn in as JFK's replacement after his assassination. Many people cite Kennedy's supposed opposition to the Federal Reserve cartel as a major factor in the reason he was assassinated, believing the CIA orchestrated the event and blamed "patsy" Lee Harvey Oswald. Others believe Kennedy planned to pull out of the Vietnam War, in opposition to secret Establishment, which was another motive for wanting him dead.

A Gallup poll was published in 2013 as the 50th anniversary of his death approached showed that 61% of Americans believed someone other than Lee Harvey

Oswald was involved in the assassination.[295]   The poll notes that at one time 81% of Americans thought there was more than one person involved in the shooting, despite the official story of Oswald acting alone, and the "JFK conspiracy" is one of the most popular conspiracy theories in history.

President Dwight Eisenhower

President Dwight Eisenhower, who was a five-star general during World War II, gave his Farewell Address to the Nation on January 17, 1961 where he popularized the term "Military Industrial Complex" after he warned about the dangers of weapon manufacturers influencing the government to go to war primarily for profit.

"This conjunction of an immense military establishment and a large arms industry is new in the American experience.   The total influence—economic, political, even spiritual—is felt in every city, every statehouse, every office of the federal government.   We recognize the imperative need for this development.   Yet we must not fail to comprehend its grave implications. Our toil, resources and livelihood are all involved; so is the very structure of our society."[296]

---

[295] *Gallup* "Majority in U.S. Still Believe JFK Killed in a Conspiracy" by Art Swift (November 15, 2013)

[296] President Dwight Eisenhower's Farewell Address to the Nation (January 17, 1961)

One part of the speech that still resonates today is when he said, "In the councils of government, we must guard against the acquisition of unwarranted influence, whether sought or unsought, by the military–industrial complex. The potential for the disastrous rise of misplaced power exists, and will persist. We must never let the weight of this combination endanger our liberties or democratic processes. We should take nothing for granted. Only an alert and knowledgeable citizenry can compel the proper meshing of the huge industrial and military machinery of defense with our peaceful methods and goals so that security and liberty may prosper together."

This Military Industrial Complex can be seen functioning today when major defense companies receive no-bid contracts handed to them by their politician friends to hire ex-soldiers as private security guards in war torn countries, or when the Bilderberg Group meeting includes CEOs from private defense companies who meet with current U.S. military heads to come to a consensus about a current or future military action.

President George Bush Senior

Two hours after bombing in Iraq and Kuwait began in 1991 (Operation Desert Storm) kicking off the first Gulf War, President Bush addressed the nation from the Oval Office explaining his goal, saying, "We have before us the opportunity to forge for ourselves and for future generations a New World Order, a world where the rule of law, not the law of the jungle, governs the conduct of nations. When we are successful, and we will be, we have a real chance at this new world order, an order in which a credible United Nations can use its peacekeeping role to fulfill the promise and vision of the U.N.'s founders."[297]

A few weeks later at his State of the Union Address in 1991, President Bush was talking about America's military action in the Gulf when he doubled down, saying, "What is at stake is more than one small country, it is a big idea—a New World Order."[298]

Before becoming Ronald Reagan's vice president, and then president himself after that, George Bush Senior was the head of the Central Intelligence Agency in the late 1970s, not to mention a member of Skull & Bones *and* the Bohemian Grove, where he and his son George W. Bush were photographed giving a Lakeside talk in 1995 where Bush Senior reportedly told the audience his son would make a fine president one day.[299]

President George W. Bush

Shortly after the September 11th terrorist attacks on the World Trade Center and the Pentagon in 2001,

---

[297] *The New York Times* "NYT transcript of Bush speech from the Oval office January 16, 1991" (January 17, 1991)

[298] George H. W. Bush *State of the Union Speech* (January 29th 1991)

[299] Rothkopf, David - *Superclass: The Global Power Elite and the World They are Making* page 284

sparking the never-ending "War on Terror," President George W. Bush addressed the growing "conspiracy theories" from people thinking the U.S. government was behind the attacks—or at the bare minimum—allowed them to happen on purpose as a pretext to launch the pre-planned wars in the Middle East. While speaking at a United Nations conference Bush announced, "Let us never tolerate outrageous conspiracy theories concerning the attacks of September the 11th; malicious lies that attempt to shift the blame away from the terrorists themselves, away from the guilty."[300]

The fact that the president even addressed the "conspiracy theories" shows just how far they were spreading, and what would come to be known as the 9/11 Truth Movement started making headlines in the years to come and gained a sizable number of supporters who were suspicious of the "official story" of 9/11.[301]

A leaked memo from a 2003 meeting between President Bush and British Prime Minister Tony Blair later revealed that Bush once proposed luring Saddam Hussein into the War on Terror by flying an unmanned drone disguised as a United Nations airplane into Iraqi airspace hoping it would get shot down so the United States could then use the event as a justification for

[300] White House Press Release "President Bush Speaks to United Nations" (11/10/2001)

[301] *The Washington Post* "The Disbelievers" by Michael Powell (September 8th 2006)

expanding the War on Terror into Iraq.[302] As we all know, he later did invade Iraq after fabricating "evidence" claiming Saddam Hussein was working with Al Qaeda to soon nuke the United States. Many people still weren't convinced there was any proof of this, but the administration's mantra was, "We don't want the smoking gun to be a mushroom cloud."

In 2004 when Bush was campaigning for reelection he appeared on NBC's *Meet the Press* where host Tim Russert surprisingly asked him about being a Bonesman. "You were both in Skull & Bones, the secret society," Russert stated, referring to both Bush and his Democrat opponent John Kerry.

"It's so secret we can't talk about it," Bush responded.

"What does that mean for America? The conspiracy theorists are going to go wild," Russert pressed.

"I'm sure they are. I don't know. I haven't seen the web pages yet." (Laughs)[303]

Of course, George W. Bush was not the mastermind behind the 9/11 attacks or the War on Terror, but rather a willing servant and asset of the Illuminati whose strings were being pulled by the powers that be from behind the scenes. Having sworn allegiance to Skull & Bones and being part of a Bones family, he undoubtedly felt obligated to carry out the Order's directives.

---

[302] *The Independent* "Bush plotted to lure Saddam into war with fake UN plane" By Andy McSmith (February 3rd 2006)

[303] *NBC* "Meet the Press" (2/08/2004)

Vice President Dick Cheney

When giving a speech at a Council on Foreign Relations meeting in 2002, Vice President Dick Cheney cracked an inside joke about his affiliation with the organization, saying, "I want to thank you all for the warm welcome today. I see a lot of old friends in the room. And it's good to be back at the Council on Foreign Relations. As Pete mentioned, I've been a member for a long time, and was actually a director for some period of time. I never mentioned that when I was campaigning for reelection back home in Wyoming (laughter) but it stood me in good stead. I value very much my experience, exposure to the tremendous people involved and the involvement and the ideas and the debates on the great policy issues of the day."[304]

The reason everyone laughed when he said he never mentioned he was a member when he was campaigning is because they all know the sinister reputation their group has. Anyone unfamiliar with the history and activities of the CFR would have no idea why everyone laughed, but those "in the know" surely "got" what he said.

A Pulitzer Prize winning journalist for The New Yorker named Seymour Hersh reported that his sources revealed to him that Cheney once proposed creating a false flag "Gulf of Tonkin" type of scenario in the Middle East to expand the War on Terror into Iran by having

---

[304] CFR.org "Launch of the Maurice R. Greenberg Center for Geoeconomic Studies with Vice President Dick Cheney" (February 15th 2002)

some U.S. Navy SEALS attack American ships in the Straits of Hormuz in order to make it appear as if Iranian PT boats had done it.[305] Cheney is seen by many as one of the evil Neocon architects behind the 9/11 attacks and the ensuing War on Terror. Of course, he publicly advocated torture and refused to testify under oath at the 9/11 Commission hearings.[306]

Smedley Butler

A United States Marine Corps Major General, the highest rank at that time, came forward in 1934 revealing a conspiracy that was organized by Wall Street bankers who wanted to overthrow President Roosevelt and replace him with a fascist dictator to serve the will of the financial elite. A congressional committee named the McCormick Dickstein Committee was formed to investigate General Butler's allegations.

Butler testified that a Wall Street insider named Gerald P. MacGuire approached him on behalf of a secret organization hoping he would lead a coup against the United States government that was to be backed by three million dollars (over 35 million in 2014 dollars) coming

---

[305] *Think Progress* "To Provoke War, Cheney Considered Proposal To Dress Up Navy Seals As Iranians And Shoot At Them" by Faiz Shakir (July 31, 2008)

[306] *New York Times* "Bush-Cheney 9/11 Interview Won't Be Formally Recorded" by Elizabeth Bumiller and Philip Shenon (April 28 2004)

from the Wall Street elite. The conspiracy was dubbed the Business Plot.

While no one was indicted, the congressional committee concluded that some of Butler's claims were true, and that such a plan was discussed and contemplated, but the committee questioned whether an actual coup by the group was actually an immediate threat or just some wild scheme the bankers had fanaticized about.

The Congressional committee's final report stated, "In the last few weeks of the committee's official life it received evidence showing that certain persons had made an attempt to establish a fascist organization in this country...There is no question that these attempts were discussed, were planned, and might have been placed in execution when and if the financial backers deemed it expedient."[307]

Butler would later go on to write his famous book *War is a Racket* that denounced most major wars and military actions as money-making schemes hatched by corrupt politicians intertwined with the weapons industry.

Zbigniew Brzezinski

The national security adviser for President Jimmy Carter, founding member of the Trilateral Commission,

---

[307] 74th Congress House of Representatives Report, pursuant to House Resolution No. 198, 73d Congress, February 15, 1935. Quoted in: George Seldes, 1000 Americans (1947), pp. 290–292. See also Schmidt, p. 245

and protégé of David Rockefeller, Zbigniew Brzezinski has made some startling admissions about the secret establishment. Brzezinski was in charge of covertly funding Osama Bin Laden and the Mujahedeen army in Afghanistan in the 1980s so they could fight off the Soviet Union who were trying to move into that area. This radical group of Muslims who America funded with several billion dollars, coordinated by Brzezinski, would later morph into Al Qaeda.

Back in 1970 he published a book called *Between Two Ages: America's Role in the Technetronic Era*, where he wrote, "The technocratic era involves the gradual appearance of a more controlled society. Such a society would be dominated by an elite, unrestrained by traditional values...The capacity to assert social and political control over the individual will vastly increase. It will soon be possible to assert almost continuous surveillance over every citizen and to maintain up-to-date, complete files, containing even most personal information about the health or personal behavior of the citizen in addition to more customary data. These files will be subject to instantaneous retrieval by the authorities."[308]

In his 1997 book, *The Grand Chessboard*, he lamented, "...as America becomes an increasingly multicultural society, it may find it more difficult to fashion a consensus on foreign policy issues, except in the

---

[308] Brzenzinski, Zbigniew - *Between Two Ages: America's Role in the Technetronic Era* (1970 Viking Press)

circumstances of a truly massive and widely perceived direct external threat."[309]

He seems to suggest a false flag attack as a pretext to carry out his plans, saying, "The public supported America's engagement in World War II largely because of the shock effect of the Japanese attack on Pearl Harbor."[310]

In a speech which can be seen on You Tube, he openly admitted, "I am deeply troubled that a very vague emotionally stated semi-theologically defined diagnosis of the central global menace is obscuring our national ability to comprehend the historically unprecedented challenge which is being posed in our time by a massive global political awakening and thus is obstructing our ability to deal effectively with the global political turmoil that this awakening is generating."[311]

At a Council on Foreign Relations meeting in Montreal, Canada, Brzezinski again lamented to his fellow elitists that a "global political awakening," was occurring and that the world had become more difficult to manage because it was "lacking internal unity with many of its members in bilateral antagonisms" and that "For the first time in all of human history mankind is politically awakened—that's a total new reality—it has not been so for most of human history…[and the] "politically

---

[309] Brzenzinski, Zbigniew *The Grand Chessboard* page 211

[310] Brzenzinski, Zbigniew - *The Grand Chessboard* page 25

[311] YouTube: Zbigniew Brzenzinzki Deeply Troubled

awakened masses makes it a much more difficult context for any major power, including, currently, the leading world power, the United States."[312]

John Hylan

A former mayor of New York City made a detailed denouncement against "the interests" in 1922, in a speech that is often incorrectly attributed to President Theodore Roosevelt. John Hylan, who was mayor from 1918 to 1925, revealed, "The real menace of our Republic is the invisible government, which like a giant octopus sprawls its slimy legs over our cities, states and nation. To depart from mere generalizations, let me say that at the head of this octopus are the Rockefeller–Standard Oil interests and a small group of powerful banking houses generally referred to as the international bankers. The little coterie of powerful international bankers virtually run the United States government for their own selfish purposes."[313]

He continued, "They practically control both parties, write political platforms, make cats paws of party leaders, use the leading men of private organizations, and resort to every device to place in nomination for high public office

---

[312] YouTube: CFR Meeting - Zbigniew Brzenzski Fears Global Awakening

[313] *New York Times* "Hylan Adds Pinchot to Presidency List; Foresees a Revolt" (December 10, 1922)

only such candidates as will be amenable to the dictates of corrupt big business."[314]

"These international bankers and Rockefeller–Standard Oil interests control the majority of the newspapers and magazines in this country. They use the columns of these papers to club into submission or drive out of office public officials who refuse to do the bidding of the powerful corrupt cliques which compose the invisible government. It operates under cover of a self-created screen [and] seizes our executive officers, legislative bodies, schools, courts, newspapers and every agency created for the public protection."[315]

Winston Churchill

One of the most well-known prime ministers of England, Winston Churchill, once made a statement warning about what he called a "world conspiracy" and even named Illuminati founder Adam Weishaupt as the perpetrator.

"From the days of 'Sparticus' Adam Weishaupt, Karl Marx, Trotsky, Belacoon, Rosa Luxenberg and Ema Goldman, this world conspiracy has been steadily growing. This conspiracy played a definite recognizable role in the French Revolution. It has been the mainspring of every subversive movement during the 19th century. And now at last, this band of extraordinary personalities

[314] Ibid

[315] Ibid

from the under-world of the great cities of Europe and America have gripped the Russian people by the hair of their head and have become the undisputed masters of that enormous empire."[316]

The Rothschilds

The patriarch of the Rothschild international banking dynasty was Mayer Amschel Rothschild, whose family fortune would become the largest fortune in the history of the world in the 1760s. He is seen as the "founding father of international finance," and *Forbes* magazine listed him as one of the "Twenty Most Influential Businessmen of All Time."[317] Mayer arranged marriages for his five sons so they married their first or second cousins in order to keep his massive wealth within the family. He also assigned each of his sons to different countries to each run those regions' economy.

A quote often attributed to Mayer Rothschild, although unverified, alleges that he once stated, "Let me issue and control a nation's money and I care not who writes the laws." Whether he actually said this or not is uncertain, but what is certain, however, is that one of his sons, Nathan, made an almost identical statement that *has* been confirmed by the well-respected historian Niall Ferguson, whose book *The House of Rothschild* reports

---

[316] *The London Press* (1922)

[317] *Forbes* "The Twenty Most Influential Business Men of All Time" by Michael Noel (7-29-2005)

that in 1815 Nathan stated, "I care not what puppet is placed upon the throne of England to rule the Empire on which the sun never sets. The man who controls the British money supply controls the British Empire, and I control the British money supply."[318]

Nathan multiplied the family fortune many fold partly due to his advanced knowledge of the British victory at the Battle of Waterloo over the French in 1815, which enabled him to rake in a fortune on the London Stock Exchange. A Rothschild courier was able to get word of Duke Wellington's victory over Napoleon's French Army to Nathan hours before anyone else in London learned of the outcome which gave him an enormous advantage over other investors whose financial future largely hinged on the outcome of this event. Rothschild also allegedly put out the false rumor that Duke Wellington and the British had *lost*, thus enabling him to further capitalize on the market since he knew the opposite was true.

The Rothschild family downplays the significance of this event and the amount of money they made from it, but historians do agree that a courier did in fact reach Rothschild informing him about the outcome of the battle before anyone else.[319] Sometimes people are accused of "anti-Semitism" for pointing out the Rothschild influence in the world of international banking, a claim that is often

---

[318] Ferguson, Niall - *The House of Rothschild (vol. 2) : The World's Banker: 1849-1999* Diane Publishing Co. (1999)

[319] Ferguson, Niall - *The House of Rothschild (vol.1): Money's Prophets, 1798-1848* Penguin Publishing (1999)

thrown at people who are critical of someone who happens to be Jewish.

Heir Nathaniel Rothschild lost a libel lawsuit he filed against London's *Daily Mail* after the paper claimed he was the billionaire "puppet master" behind convincing the European Union Trade Commissioner Lord Mandelson to lift some trade barriers involving importing aluminum from Russia.[320] So in a sense, by losing the libel suit, the court confirmed that he was indeed a "puppet master" pulling the strings of back-room big business and political dealings.

Many people point the finger at the Rothschild family as being one of the primary sources of the Illuminati's finances, and the family helped fund the initial Jewish occupation of Israel and have been a major financial supporter of Zionism.

James Paul Warburg

James Paul Warburg (August 18, 1896 – June 3, 1969) was the son of Paul Warburg, the "father" of the Federal Reserve Bank, and the man who organized the secret Jekyll Island meeting to formulate their plan. The apple didn't fall too far from the tree in this case, because his son James went on to become the financial adviser for President Roosevelt, and a member of the Council on Foreign Relations—of which he was a founding member. At an appearance before the U.S. Senate Committee on

---

[320] *The Independent* "Rothschild loses libel case, and reveals secret world of money and politics" (April 29th 2014)

Foreign Relations he once flatly stated, "We shall have world government, whether or not we like it. The question is only whether world government will be achieved by consent or by conquest."[321]

Henry Kissinger

One of the most infamous political figures in American history is Henry Kissinger, a man who is seen by many as a treacherous war criminal for helping the CIA organize various covert operations designed to overthrow democratically elected leaders in several countries (Chili, and Argentina, for example) in order to install a leader who was more in tune with American foreign policy.[322]   Award winning journalist Bob Woodward and Carl Bernstein, the guys who blew open the Watergate scandal, revealed that Kissinger once referred to our military men and women as "dumb, stupid animals" to be used as pawns for America's foreign policy.[323]

---

[321] Senate Report (Senate Foreign Relations Committee) (February 17th 1950). Revision of the United Nations Charter: Hearings Before a Subcommittee of the Committee on Foreign Relations, Eighty-First Congress. United States Government Printing Office. p. 494.

[322] *SMH.com.au* "Why the law wants a word with Kissinger" by Christopher Hitchens (April 30th 2002)

[323] Bob Woodward & Carl Bernstein *The Final Days* second Touchstone paperback edition (1994) Chapter 14, pp. 194-195

Kissinger once remarked that power was the greatest aphrodisiac. Back in 2001 President George W. Bush chose him to be the Chairman of the 9/11 Commission to investigate the September 11th attacks, but shortly after it was revealed he was Bush's choice outraged victims' family members who had learned of his financial ties to the Bin Laden family forced the commission to drop him. His sole purpose as head commissioner would have been, of course, to prevent the truth about what really happened from seeing the light of day. The 9/11 attacks are seen by many as another false flag attack, or an incident that was purposefully allowed to happen in order to spark the endless War on Terror and justify the reduction of American liberties.

David Rothkopf, the managing director of Kissinger and Associates, an international advising firm founded by the infamous Henry Kissinger, wrote a very interesting book in 2009 titled *Superclass: The Global Power Elite and the World They are Making,* where he openly discussed the ruling elite and the various organizations that largely influence the political and economic landscape of the world. While not revealing any earth-shattering insider secrets, his book serves to confirm many of the allegations made against the ruling elite by so called "conspiracy theorists."

Rothkopf wrote that, "A global elite has emerged over the past several decades that has vastly more power than any other group on the planet. Each of the members of the superclass has the ability to regularly influence the lives of millions of people in multiple countries worldwide. Each actively exercises this power, and they often amplify it through the development of relationships with others in this class."[324]

He goes on to say, "That such a group exists is indisputable. Heads of state, CEOs of the world's largest companies, media barons, billionaires who are actively involved in their investments, technology, entrepreneur, oil potentates, hedge fund managers, private equity investors, top military commanders, a select few religious leaders, a handful of renowned writers, scientists, and artists, even terrorist leaders and master criminals, meet the above criteria for membership."[325]

He proposes that this ruling elite, or "superclass" as he calls them, consists of roughly 6,000 people.[326] The Occupy Wall Street protesters often spoke out against what they called the "1%" who they saw as being the ruling elite, but this equates to approximately 70 million people. (1% of the earth's 7 billion people is 70 million.) Of course Occupy's assessment of who is the problem is wildly inaccurate. Using Rothkopf's figure, it wouldn't be the 1%, but more like the .0001%. In reality, it's probably more like the .00001% which is around 700 people who are the Illuminati or their associates.

---

[324] Rothkopf, David - *Superclass: The Global Power Elite and the World They are Making* Preface page xiv

[325] Rothkopf, David - *Superclass: The Global Power Elite and the World They are Making* Preface page xiv

[326] Rothkopf, David - *Superclass: The Global Power Elite and the World They are Making* Preface page xiv

Another interesting admission is when Rothkopf says, "From behind the scenes, it was clear that these individuals influenced everything from the way currencies were priced worldwide to which political candidates would have sufficient funding for their presidential campaigns."[327]

Perhaps Rothkopf started to grow a conscience after being so close to the superclass and seeing exactly what they're doing to the planet. He even admitted that in the post-9/11 era and with the War on Terror being waged to fight al Qaeda, that much of the information coming from the government was basically fear mongering to achieve a political goal. "While the United states was in a real struggle with Communist Russia, the assertion that Communists were everywhere and intent on undermining the United States was vastly exaggerated in much the same way that the terror threat is exaggerated today."[328]

He even said the Bilderberger Group meetings reveal the "informal mechanisms of power" that shape the world[329] and was well aware of the allegations made about the Bohemian Grove, writing, "Critics on the left worry about political conspiracy and global policies plotted at the Grove, while critics on the right cite stories

---

[327] Rothkopf, David- *Superclass: The Global Power Elite and the World They are Making* Preface page xviii

[328] Rothkopf, David - *Superclass: The Global Power Elite and the World They are Making* page 257

[329] Rothkopf, David- *Superclass: The Global Power Elite and the World They are Making* Page 265

of homosexual rituals, devil worship, and child sacrifice."[330]

President Richard Nixon

In his memoirs, published in 1978, President Richard Nixon wrote, "If I were to choose the speech that gave me the most pleasure and satisfaction in my political career, it would be my Lakeside Speech at the Bohemian Grove in July 1967. Because this speech traditionally was off the record it received no publicity at the time. But in many important ways it marked the first milestone on my road to the presidency."[331]

The University of California, Berkeley, located on the San Francisco Bay, has a photograph in their archives of Nixon sitting at a table with Ronald Reagan inside the Bohemian Grove during this same visit. The two were said to have sat down to "work a political deal wherein Reagan was to run only if Nixon faltered."[332]

While Nixon publicly praised the Bohemian Grove to the small group of politically minded people who would read his memoirs, privately he had something quite different to say. In one of the now publicly available

---

[330] Rothkopf, David- *Superclass: The Global Power Elite and the World They are Making* Page 283

[331] Nixon, Richard - *Memoirs* (1978)

[332] Phillips, Peter - *A Relative Advantage: Sociology of the San Francisco Bohemian Club. A Doctoral Dissertation* (1994) page 95 citing Domhoff 1974 p.42

Watergate tapes released by the National Archives, Nixon can clearly be heard expressing disgust for the Grove when speaking in the Oval Office with his Chief of Staff H. R. Haldeman and aide John D. Ehrlichman. "The Bohemian Grove—which I attend, from time to time—it is the most faggy goddamned thing you could ever imagine, with that San Francisco crowd. I can't shake hands with anybody from San Francisco."[333]

The Bohemian Grove yearbooks show members dressed in drag and rumors of homosexual activities by members have persisted for decades.

George Washington

President George Washington acknowledged the Illuminati's presence in America in his personal correspondence in one particular letter dated October 24th 1798, that's been preserved at the Library of Congress. This was thirteen years after the Illuminati was discovered and eleven years after they were banned and allegedly stamped out according to "sources" like Wikipedia.

Washington acknowledged, "It was not my intention to doubt that the Doctrines of the Illuminati and principles of Jacobinism had not spread in the United States. On the

---

[333] President Richard M. Nixon on the Watergate tapes in 1971 conversation with John D. Ehrlichman, and H. R. Haldeman made public in 1999 by the National Archives

contrary, no one is more truly satisfied of this fact than I am."[334]

In the letter George Washington clarifies that he did not believe that Freemasonry as a whole was involved in the conspiracy, but that certain individuals within certain lodges did in fact have these aims. If you look up the letter on the Library of Congress website, it can be difficult to read his handwriting, but it is accompanied by an official transcript.

Part of the letter reads, "The idea that I meant to convey, was, that I did not believe that the Lodges of Freemasons in this country had, as Societies, endeavored to propagate the diabolical tenets of the first, or pernicious principles of the latter (if they are susceptible of separation). That individuals of them may have done it, or that the founder, or instrument employed to found, the Democratic Societies in the United States, may have had these objects; and actually had a separation of the people from their government in view, is too evident to be questioned."

So there you have it—George Washington was concerned that the "doctrines of the Illuminati" had spread to the United States and were using certain Masonic lodges to "separate people from their government." In fact, it was "too evident to be questioned," he said.

---

[334] The Writings of George Washington from the Original Manuscript Sources, 1745-1799. John C. Fitzpatrick, Editor. Mount Vernon, October 24, 1798.

Dick Morris

One of President Bill Clinton's former advisors, Dick Morris, made a startling admission on the Fox News Channel in 2009 when talking to Sean Hannity about the New World Order and a global currency.

Morris began: "There is a big thing that's going to happen in London at this G-20, and they're hiding it, they're camouflaging it, they're not talking about it. The coordination of international regulation. What they are going to do is to put our Fed and our SEC under the control, in effect, of the IMF."[335]

Hannity: "Oh, come on. You believe they'll do this?"

Morris: "That's what was in the draft agenda. They call it 'coordination of regulation.' What it really is, is putting the American economy under international regulation. And those people who have been yelling, 'oh the U.N. is going to take over—global government...'"

Hannity: "Conspiracy theorists."

Morris: "Conspiracy theorists...they've been crazy, but now...they're right! It's happening!"

Hannity: When Geithner said he would be open to the idea of a Global Currency last year, those conspiracy people had said and suggested that for years. You're not wrong."

Morris: "What they always do at these conferences is they have the center show here, and the side show they don't want you to pay attention to. The center show is the size of the stimulus package, but the real show is international regulation of the financial institutions which is going to happen under the IMF control. A few years earlier Morris had revealed why, despite being a personal friend of the Clintons and working as Bill's advisor, he cut all ties with them, saying, "I finally parted company with Hillary Clinton when I saw how she was using private detectives to investigate the women who were linked to her husband to cow [intimidate] the women into silence so that he could get elected president."[336]

Cass Sunstein

President Obama appointed a Harvard law professor named Cass Sunstein to head up the Office of Information and Regulatory Affairs which is an executive office of the president responsible for issuing policies regarding information technology, privacy, and information regulation. Sunstein's Orwellian philosophy of how the government should handle information technology was detailed in a white paper published in 2008 titled *Conspiracy Theories,* where he argued that the government should ban "conspiracy theories" or "impose some kind of tax, financial or otherwise, on those who disseminate such theories."[337]

---

[336] *Hillary: The Movie* (2008) produced by Citizens United

[337] Sunstein, Cass R. "Conspiracy Theories" Harvard University - Harvard Law School (January 15, 2008) page 14

He took things further than the typical political rhetoric by actually proposing that government trolls inundate the comment sections on "conspiracy" websites, videos, and social media accounts with outlandish comments in order to derail the discussion and introduce issues into the conversation in hopes of tarnishing the image of such websites, videos, or social media pages.[338] He even suggested government operatives should attend meetings and events organized by "conspiracy theorists" saying, "We suggest a distinctive tactic for breaking up the hard core of extremists who supply conspiracy theories...whereby government agents or their allies (acting either virtually or in real space, and either openly or anonymously) will undermine the crippled epistemology of believers by planting doubts about the theories and stylized facts that circulate within such groups, thereby introducing beneficial cognitive diversity."[339]

Aside from going after "conspiracy theorists" (translation: prominent independent media outlets who have successfully bypassed the editorial control of the mainstream media), Sunstein also set his sights on the Second Amendment and with a straight face lied to a group of students at the University of Chicago Law School saying that "The Supreme Court has never

---

[338] Sunstein, Cass R. & Vermeule, Adrian "Conspiracy Theories: Causes and Cures," 17 *Journal of Political Philosophy* 202 (2008)

[339] Sunstein, Cass R. & Vermeule, Adrian "Conspiracy Theories: Causes and Cures," 17 *Journal of Political Philosophy* 202 (2008) page 15

suggested that the Second Amendment protects an individual's right to have guns."[340]

Of course his claim about the Second Amendment couldn't be further from the truth, because its sole purpose is to authorize individual citizens to have guns. In his lecture he went on to predict that in the future the Second Amendment would be repealed and the right of citizens to own guns would be eliminated.

In 2014 Sunstein published a book titled *Conspiracy Theories and Other Dangerous Ideas*, where he warned that conspiracy theorists were dangerous anti-government terrorists. Of course what he means by "conspiracy theorists" are people who report on the real reasons for the War in Iraq, or who think the September 11th attacks were a false flag, and anyone who sees the Bilderberg Group as suspicious.

Edward Snowden

In June of 2013, word spread like wild fire around the world that a former NSA contractor with a high level security clearance had stolen thousands of classified documents detailing the technical capabilities of the National Security Agency. 30-year-old Edward Snowden fled the country to avoid imprisonment and was giving asylum in Russia, and the cache of classified documents he obtained revealed the shocking details of how powerful Big Brother had become.

---

[340] *YouTube* "Cass Sunstein Predicts Repealing Right To Bear Arms"

As the Illuminati have been setting up an all-powerful global government, they have also been focused on building an Orwellian society where all citizens are tracked, traced, and databased. While many people reasonably assumed such a system was being built, Snowden's leaks provided irrefutable proof that Big Brother had been born and was more powerful than most people had ever imagined.

The Snowden leaks also proved that the NSA was not just illegally conducting mass surveillance of Americans (and virtually everyone around the world) without warrants, and clearly violating the Fourth Amendment—but they also proved the government's protocols extended far beyond ordinary eavesdropping.

Laptop computers were routinely intercepted from UPS during shipment after being purchased from online retailers like Amazon and then fitted with special hardware, including micro cellular modems so their hard drives could be accessed even if the computers weren't connected to WiFi or an Ethernet cable. (This operation is called INTERDICTION.)[341]   We also learned that the government has the ability to manipulate online polls on websites (UNDERPASS); they restrict YouTube videos from going viral or have them removed for phony "terms of service violations" (SILVERLORD); or, if they want,

---

[341] *USA Today* "NSA Intercepts Computer Deliveries" by Raphael Satter, Associated Press (December 29, 2013)

make certain videos receive massive views to make it appear as if they've gone viral (SLIPSTREAM).[342]

They've intercepted millions of webcam feeds and scanned the people chatting over them with facial recognition systems to identify them (OPTIC NERVE);[343] they collect naked and compromising photos of people so they can be blackmailed or publicly humiliated by releasing them (LOVEINT);[344] and they even have the ability to record and store every single phone call in the entire world. Not just the record of who called who and when, but the actual audio of all calls (MYSTIC).[345] They can also spoof anyone's email address and send emails under any identity (CHANGELING), not to mention spoof any phone number. This is just a sample of their capabilities, and of course this is all done under the umbrella of "National Security."

This technology allows the government to have "turn key tyranny" power and with the flip of a switch they can

---

[342] *TechDirt* "Latest Snowden Revelations Suggest GCHQ Is Just Like 4Chan Trolls, But With More Firepower" by Mike Masnick (July 14th 2014)

[343] *TIME Magazine* "U.K. Spy Agency Stored Millions of Webcam Images" by Denver Nicks (February 27th 2014)

[344] *ABC News* "LoveINT: Given Immense Powers, NSA Employees Super Cyber-Stalked Their Crushes" by Lee Ferran (September 27th 2013)

[345] *Washington Times* "NSA program MYSTIC culls 100 percent of phone records from foreign country" by Douglas Ernst (March 18th 2014)

target anyone, anywhere in the world. Not only can they physically locate you and bug you through cell phones or webcams in the area, but the NSA operatives can find out everything about a target, from your most intimate communications sent though text messages or emails, to obtaining personal photos, to uncovering health problems, shopping habits, eating habits, political views, friends, family, acquaintances, personal finances, gun ownership, etc., etc.

This power is so incredible that no man can resist abusing it, and in the final phase of the New World Order, the Illuminati and their inner circle of government agents will come down on dissenters with a digital iron fist and make them disappear down the memory hole like something right out of George Orwell's *Nineteen Eighty-Four*.

Orwell ominously wrote, "The telescreen received and transmitted simultaneously. Any sound that Winston made, above the level of a very low whisper, would be picked up by it; moreover, so long as he remained within the field of vision which the metal plate commanded, he could be seen as well as heard. There was of course no way of knowing whether you were being watched at any given moment. How often, or on what system, the Thought Police plugged in on any individual wire was guesswork. It was even conceivable that they watched everybody all the time. but at any rate they could plug in your wire whenever they wanted to. You have to live— did live, from habit that became instinct—in the assumption that every sound you made was overheard, and, except in darkness, every movement scrutinized."[346]

Checkout my previous book *Big Brother: The Orwellian Nightmare Come True* if you'd like to read my analysis of Orwell's novel and how it eerily parallels our world today. Orwell didn't just accurately forecast the invasive Big Brother surveillance system, but also ominously warned about our current dumbed down and heartless society; endless wars perpetuated to justify reducing civil liberties; and the erosion of the language and the breakdown of families and relationships in order to shift people's obedience and reliance to the State.

[Author's Note: Please take a moment to rate and review this book on Amazon.com or wherever you purchased it from to let others know what you think. This also helps to offset the trolls who keep giving my books fake one-star reviews when they haven't even read them. Almost all of the one-star reviews on my books are from NON-verified purchases which is a clear indication they are fraudulent, hence me adding this note. This has become a huge problem for author's on Amazon and at the time of this writing, they haven't done much to combat it, so I really need your help on this ASAP! Thank you!]

---

[346] Orwell, George — *Nineteen Eighty-Four* page 2

"Ex-Illuminati Members"

Similar to government whistleblowers or career criminals turned into informants who reveal the closely kept secrets of their organization, a handful of people have come forward over the years claiming to have been involved with the Illuminati in one way or another, and offer up what they claim to be insider information about the activities and goals of the network. Most of these people are complete frauds and are simply con artists trying to sell books and lectures, or just enjoying the attention from the conspiracy community since many people believe their stories—hook, line, and sinker.

In my previous book, *The Illuminati: Facts & Fiction*, there is a detailed analysis of John Todd and William Schnoebelen, who are two of the most popular men who have made such claims, but there are also others whose stories have spread far and wide on the Internet like urban legends, so in this book we'll take a close look and determine whether or not there is any legitimacy to them.

So far none of the alleged "defectors" have offered up any kind of evidence to back up their claims, but instead have only told tales based on the publicly known information about the history, beliefs, and activities of the Illuminati. None of the "former members" have ever revealed *any* new information that wasn't already published in literature widely available in the conspiracy culture. But if you read through some of the comments on any of the YouTube videos featuring their claims, you will see that a very sizable percentage of the audience wholeheartedly believes these individuals and see them as heroic whistle blowers who "escaped" their dark past and are now on a mission to "expose" the Illuminati.

For an astute student dedicated to the truth and who doesn't approach these people's stories with confirmation bias—and if one has diligently done their own research—the inaccuracies and fabrications stick out like sore thumbs. For those who are new to investigating the Illuminati, or to those who are quite gullible, these "former Illuminati members" only serve to confirm their greatest fears. Most of these "defectors" are simply gifted storytellers presenting publicly known information from a first-person perspective as if they themselves actually witnessed it or participated in it. Some of these people are perhaps mentally ill and may actually believe what they are saying, but the evidence proves one after the other to be fake.

Let's take a close look at some of these individuals' stories so we can prevent them and future hoaxers from deceiving people who are trying to find answers and accurate information regarding the Illuminati and the New World Order.

Doc Marquis

Joseph "Doc" Marquis (born on October 26th 1956) is allegedly a former U.S. Army medic which is how he says

256

he got his nickname "Doc," and is one of several self-proclaimed "former Illuminati members" who says he was born into an Illuminati family but now is dedicated to "exposing" them.

"Doc," who claims to have been raised as a seventh generation witch, says when he was three-years-old his family brought him to a special ceremony and dedicated him to Lucifer in a satanic baptism.[347] For the next ten years, he says, he was in the "outer court" of the Illuminati which he described as a satanic seminary school where he supposedly learned about the philosophies and secret symbols, and what he claims are the "eight nights of human sacrifice" that Illuminati members allegedly celebrate.

According to his story, when he was thirteen-years-old he was "fully initiated as a member of the Illuminati"[348] after signing his name in his own blood in a book made of lamb skin which he called the *Book of the Dead*, which just so happens to be the name of an ancient Egyptian scroll containing information on how to navigate through the afterlife in order to enter into Heaven.

Four years later, when he was seventeen, "Doc" says he underwent another initiation ceremony and became what he called a Master Witch, or a High Druid Priest, which granted him "automatic authority over a region of the United States" where he was in charge of over 1000

---

[347] Prophecy Club: *The Arrival of the Antichrist* presentation by Doc Marquis (YouTube video at 1:52 mark)

[348] Prophecy Club: *The Arrival of the Antichrist* presentation by Doc Marquis (YouTube video at 2:46 mark)

other Illuminati members.[349]   This, all before he even graduated high school!   His superiors, he says, then ordered him to join the United States Army in order to help the Illuminati infiltrate the armed forces. Within two weeks of being stationed at Fort Lewis in Washington he says he had twenty people recruited for the Illuminati, and just a couple months later says he had more than a hundred more![350]   In reality, the actual Illuminati most likely consists of no more than a few hundred men, but when "Doc" Marquis was just seventeen-years-old, he says he was "in charge" of over 1000 of them!

During an online lecture produced by Prophecy Club, he says he practiced human sacrifices eight times a year and had "constant communication with Demons."[351] Marquis claims to have personally witnessed dozens of human sacrifices before he "got out," but no law enforcement agency has ever expressed any interest in him and have never considered him to be a suspect or a witness to any murders whatsoever. Trash television, on the other hand, gave him a platform to spread his nonsense in the late 1980s. He was once a guest on *The Oprah Winfrey Show* where he was talking about all these supposed murders and said, "The thing is, we didn't body bag these people afterwards. We'd just take them [and],

---

[349] Prophecy Club: *The Arrival of the Antichrist* presentation by Doc Marquis (YouTube 4:13 mark in video)

[350] Prophecy Club: *The Arrival of the Antichrist* presentation by Doc Marquis (YouTube 5:33 mark in video)

[351] Prophecy Club: *The Arrival of the Antichrist* presentation by Doc Marquis (YouTube 6:21 mark in video)

throw them in the woods, on the side of the road on a highway. Somebody's going to find them."[352] Of course, no one ever has because these "victims" don't exist.

The "eight nights of human sacrifice" that Marquis claims to have celebrated was concocted from the eight festivals that Pagans celebrate (or Sabbats as Wiccans call them) which are commemorated throughout the year on solstices, equinoxes, and the four mid-points in between —none of which involve human sacrifices. I'm certainly not saying that Satanists don't commit human sacrifices still to this day, because such occurrences have been well documented,[353] but the closest Marquis has come to one was watching a horror movie.

Local authorities would have taken him into custody for questioning if there was even a shred of evidence to back up his claims and no one involved with such crimes would dare speak about them out of fear of being arrested. Obviously in the 1980s, before the Internet, the average person could not easily confirm or disprove most claims made about the Illuminati and the occult, and very few people knew much about the subject at all. This is what led to the "satanic panic" in the 1980s when stories like Marquis' were spread through tabloids and trash TV talk shows causing people who didn't know any better to think

[352] *The Oprah Winfrey Show* (June 24th 1987) WLS-TV Transcript #W203

[353] *Daily Mail* "Sickening smile of teen accused of kidnapping, raping and murdering 15-year-old girl in 'satanic ritual'" by Michael Zennie (February 11th 2014)

Satanists were abusing children and sacrificing people in communities across the country.

"Doc" says that in between committing his evil deeds, he was repeatedly asked by Christians if he wanted to go to church or if he knew Jesus, and for whatever reason—despite being a "high level Illuminati master," he decided to go to church on Easter Sunday in 1979, where he realized he was a "sold out slave of Satan," became a Christian, and "left the Illuminati."[354]

In one of his video lectures titled *Arrival of the Antichrist* he can be seen giving the usual history lesson about Adam Weishaupt and the formation of the Bavarian Illuminati, their structure and goals, and shows the all-seeing eye on the back of the one dollar bill while telling the audience to pull out their wallets to look at the dollar themselves as if this was some major revelation.[355] The eye on the back of the one dollar bill has become so elementary and Illuminati 101 that most middle school students are now aware of it, but back in the 1980s and 90s when Marquis began giving his lectures, things were quite different.

After his discussion on the one dollar bill symbology, he goes on to cover the well-known quotes from Pike's book, *Morals and Dogma,* and then shows the interesting designs in the street layout of Washington D.C. and then complains about the government, the dumbing down of

---

[354] Prophecy Club: America's Occult Holidays, presentation by Doc Marquis

[355] Prophecy Club: The Arrival of the Antichrist presentation by Doc Marquis (YouTube)

America, the Constitution, the demonization of Christians, etc., etc… Of course he concludes that the Illuminati is going to declare martial law and is setting up a New World Order for the reception of the antichrist.

When conducting my research into the Illuminati and coming across Doc Marquis' claims of being a former Illuminati member, I painfully listened to his lectures online, which, like nearly every other self-proclaimed "former Illuminati member" didn't reveal a single shred of information that wasn't already widely known. Not only that, but many of his claims are clearly ridiculous to anyone who has basic knowledge about the Illuminati conspiracy.

For example, he says that they place a $10,000 bounty on anyone's head who tries to leave.[356] After he "left the Illuminati" he says they tried and failed to kill him at least six times![357] The Illuminati can assassinate world leaders and other heads of state, but they've failed over a half dozen times to kill this guy? Absurd.

Of course there are no police reports or news stories about *any* of these alleged murder attempts against him and since the Illuminati is the most powerful secret society in the world, they would have no problem killing anyone, especially no-name loser like "Doc" Marquis.

He sells a DVD called *Frontmen of the Illuminati* which consists of nothing more than a poorly produced

---

[356] *The Oprah Winfrey Show* (June 24th 1987) WLS-TV Transcript #W203

[357] *The Oprah Winfrey Show* (June 24th 1987) WLS-TV Transcript #W203

home video of him sitting at a table showing different photos of symbols and people while talking about the Illuminati. The information on a website selling his DVDs reads, "Doc Marquis is a former Satanist who was trained in the Illuminati Plan before he came out of the coven to become a Christian. In 1992, Doc was hired by the Boston Police Department to train their homicide detectives how to spot evidence in a crime scene that the perpetrator was a practicing occultist. Doc also has appeared on the following TV shows: *Oprah Winfrey*; *Geraldo Rivera*; *Hard Copy*; and *Inside Edition*. He is the author of numerous books, video tapes and audio cassette series and has appeared as an expert witness in a number of documentaries."

His claim of having worked with the Boston Police department has not been verified and to think that this man would be hired to "train" homicide detectives is laughable, particularly after having claimed to have murdered a bunch of people in satanic rituals! I guess the police just decided to forgive him of all those supposed murders!

Marquis has also claimed to have degrees in sociology, and history, and once claimed he would soon be getting his doctorate in psychiatry from Baptist Christian University in Shreveport, Louisiana, but it was later revealed he wasn't even attending the school. He then said the school would be accepting a book he was writing on the occult as his doctoral dissertation!

Marquis wrote several books (as does every supposed "Illuminati defector") hoping to make a few bucks off the conspiracy community. Marquis and other "Christians" who claim to be "former Illuminati" members like Bill Schnoebelen and John Todd—while being complete phonies—may, in their own mind, actually believe that they are helping people learn about the Illuminati conspiracy. There is, after all, a massive conspiracy, and these individuals do actually expose *some* of it, but their fabricated pasts and long lists of lies about being personally involved with the Illuminati—when they clearly don't even have some of their basic facts straight —shows that men like Doc Marquis are not only frauds, but quite pathetic and shameful as well.

Leo Zagami

Another man claiming to be an Illuminati defector who went on to give interviews and lectures about the nefarious plans he learned while supposedly "inside" the secret society is Leo Zagami (born in Rome on March 5th 1970). While other alleged defectors claim to have become born again Christians after "leaving the Illuminati" and say that Jesus helped them realize they were on the wrong path and found support from Christian audiences, Leo Zagami instead has taken the New Age angle. He insists the Illuminati hold "the truth" but are a corrupt group of enlightened ones who have hijacked the Mystery School teachings so he decided to leave the Illuminati in order to preach their secret philosophy to the masses.

To help spread the "enlightening truth" kept suppressed by the Illuminati, Leo Zagami claims to have started a new "religion" called Matrixism that's based on the popular Matrix movies! He says he started this new "religion" in 2004 to commemorate the 100th anniversary of the "deliverance" of Aleister Crowley's *Book of the Law*, the short blood thirsty book Crowley claimed was dictated to him by a demon while he was visiting Egypt in 1904. Yes, Zagami is a fan of dirt bag Aleister Crowley, whose philosophies he considers "the truth."

His website described his new "religion" as, literally having been inspired by the *Matrix* movies, but insists it was "conceived by an anonymous group in the summer of 2004 [and] has attracted over 16,000 adherents."[358]

The explanation goes on to say, "*The Matrix* trilogy, along with related mass media products such as video games, is generally considered to be the 'sacred text' of the movement."[359] He literally says *The Matrix* movies and video games are "sacred texts" of his "religion." He also says the "faith" can be traced back to a book called *The Promulgation of Universal Peace*, published in 1922 that consist of a series of speeches given by Abdu'l-Baha, the founder of the Bahá'í Faith. All of this information, he says, comes from his knowledge of being an "Illuminati Grand Master" himself.

Zagami's website claims that he is, "a high-ranking Illuminati Grand Master, who gained considerable attention in the conspiracy research community between

---

[358] LeoZagami.com

[359] http://www.leozagami.com/index.php?
option=com_content&view=article&id=44&Itemid=55

2006 and 2008 as a defector and whistle-blower."[360] He once went by the name Khaled Saifullah Khan after having supposedly converted to Islam, but later changed his name back to Leo. He claims that his goal is to now organize "the Knights Templars of the Apocalypse" to fight the Illuminati, and says this "group" has recruited 12,000 troops from the U.S. Military, CIA, FBI, etc., who are going to stop the "Dark Illuminati plans."[361]

In Leo's mind, the main enemies of humanity are: The Jesuits, which he calls "the head of the serpent"; Zionists, who he says are "the economic arms of the Vatican New World Order"; the United Nations which is "a corrupt organization in the hands of the Jesuits and their Zionist allies dedicated to enslave mankind"; and "all religious fundamentalist because organized religion in all shapes and forms is a legal mafia manipulated by the Vatican and Jerusalem in the hands of corrupt individuals who work for the elite families and their intelligence services to keep our race in ignorance and superstition in the end of times."

Despite Leo's strange and rambling history and his new "religion" that he created based on *The Matrix* movies, and his claiming to still be involved with the "good" Illuminati and the "Knights Templars of the Apocalypse" and other undercover "Illuminati Resistance" members in the CIA, FBI, military, and police; and despite revealing no new information about

---

[360] Ibid.

[361] Ibid.

the workings of the Illuminati—some completely gullible fools actually believe that he actually was, or still is involved with the secret society.

Leo Zigami's claims never gained anywhere close to the traction of other supposed "defectors" before him such as John Todd or Bill Schnoebelen, because he's not a gifted storyteller like some other hoaxers. And we were well into the information age by the time Leo decided to step on the scene (in 2006), whereas John Todd started his talks in the 1970s, and Bill Schnoebelen in the early 1990s before the Internet was fully utilized by most people who can now quickly fact check claims online. Even with this resource at people's fingertips, however, a shocking number of people still believe the stories from "ex-members" like "Doc" Marquis, Leo Zagami, John Todd, and others.

Many people enjoy conspiracy entertainment or *conspiratainment* as I call it, and have little to no concern about actual facts or the truth. They simply love the sometimes cleverly concocted tales by people who are inspired by actual events or conspiracies and then manufacture a sometimes entertaining conspiracy mythology based on grains of truth. It's sort of like a good science fiction story that's based in part on actual technology and then extrapolates into a fantasy designed to entertain the audience.

Supriem Rockefeller

A man calling himself "Supriem Rockefeller" and claiming to be a member of the famous Rockefeller family created a bit of a stir on the Internet in 2010 after announcing that the Rockefellers were launching a plan to fund the building of the Third Temple in Jerusalem, in what was called the "Temple Now Project." The Third Temple refers to the rebuilding (again) of Solomon's Temple in Israel, which was originally destroyed in 586 BC by the Babylonians, and later rebuilt only to be destroyed again by the Romans in 70 AD. Christians believe that when the temple is rebuilt for the third time, it will signify the fulfillment of one of the final prophecies concerning the rise of the Antichrist and the return of Jesus.

Currently, a Muslim mosque called the Dome of the Rock stands on the ruins of the temple, and the only way Solomon's Temple can be rebuilt on that spot is if Israel destroys the mosque and occupies that part of the land. This is why the "Rockefeller" announcement of supposed plans to build the Third Temple caught so many people's attention.

A few official sounding websites published a press release about the "Supriem Rockefeller" plan without attempting to verify his identity or the supposed plan's legitimacy. With sites like CNNMoney.com and MarketWatch having the press released posted, that was all the evidence many conspiracy blogs needed to run with the story that one of the final Biblical prophecies was about to be fulfilled thanks to the Rockefellers.[362]

---

[362] *World Net Daily* "Will Rockefeller build 3rd Temple?
Internet abuzz with report of biblical proportions" (02/03/2010)

None of this was true, however, and "Supriem Rockefeller" didn't exist. The man behind the hoax was identified as a high school dropout named Kris from Louisiana, who was born in 1975. While living with his mother he worked as a cashier at a fast food restaurant and tried to make money by gambling and selling ringtones on various websites.

After he was fired from his job for allegedly stealing, the thirty-four-year-old then started going by "Supriem Rockefeller" online and saying he was the secret son of David Rockefeller Jr. "Supriem" posted online about how he was authorized to finalize the New World Order and "revealed" that the Rockefeller family had descended from the Annunaki, the supposed ancient race of aliens, who are believed by some to be responsible for the creation of humans.

It appears his "Temple Now Project" hoax was an attempt to receive donations from people who wanted to support the plan, hoping to fulfill Bible prophecy. One press release claimed he would be "raising funds to go towards building the Third Temple in Jerusalem in strict coordinance with The Temple Institute, Rabbi Hiam Richman and The Palestinian National Interest Committee (PNIC)," and his mission was to "build the Temple and to create a One Israel-Palestine state."

What made this hoax believable for some, aside from the Christian prophecy of the Third Temple, was the very real Jewish plan to one day accomplish this very task. Ever since 1987 a non-profit Jewish group called the Temple Institute has been working to do just this. In fact, in 2008 they announced they had the High Priest's garments already made along with dozens of other items they plan on using in "sacred rituals" once it is rebuilt. Of course the Temple Institute had nothing to do with "Supreium Rockefeller," but he cleverly included their name in his press release to add an aura of credibility to his claims, since they are a real group working to accomplish this very goal.

This hoax didn't last too long and his Facebook page was soon deleted, but many Jews and Christians continue to await the actual rebuilding of the Temple, an event that will be seen by Christians as one of the Bible's final prophecies being fulfilled because in this Temple it is believed the Antichrist will announce himself to be "God" and order the people of earth to worship him as such.

In the 1970s, 80s and 90s, Illuminati phonies were able to pull off their scams with a remarkable amount of success, and while the Internet can put an end to most of these scams rather quickly today, countless people are simply lost in the sea of information available on the web and continue to spread Illuminati hoaxes far and wide, believing every word. These are the same kinds of people who believe that every time a famous celebrity dies from a drug overdose, car accident, or health problem—they think they were actually "murdered" by the Illuminati or faked their own death. If you search YouTube for keywords like "Paul Walker Illuminati Sacrifice," "Michael Jackson Murdered by Illuminati," or "Tupac killed by Illuminati," you will find literally hundreds of videos with millions of views and countless comments from people who are 100% convinced the Illuminati is behind *every* celebrity death.

The "Supriem Rockefeller" Third Temple hoax is not the first time that someone has posed as a member of the famous Rockefeller family. A man who called himself Clark Rockefeller (real name Christian Karl Gerhartsreiter) was sentenced to 27 years in prison for murdering his landlord's son which put an immediate end to his elaborate scam.[363] Gerhartsreiter even fooled his own wife into thinking he was a Rockefeller for years by taking extreme measures to hide his real identity. To accomplish this he had his wife file her income taxes as an individual instead of jointly as most married couples do, so his real name wouldn't have to be on the couple's tax returns, which she most likely would have noticed.[364] He even forged their marriage license to avoid having her see his actual name.[365]

Another man calling himself Christian Rockefeller (real name Christopher Rocancourt) actually swindled tens of millions of dollars from rich people in New York in the 1990s through fake investment scams after they thought he could increase their wealth because they believed he was a Rockefeller.[366]

---

[363] *ABC News* "Fresh Details on Mystery Man Clark Rockefeller as Trial Opens" by Michele McPhee (May 26th 2009)

[364] *Boston Globe* "'Rockefeller' Seeks Dismissal of False Name Charge" (March 13th 2009)

[365] *Vanity Fair* "The Man in the Rockefeller Suit" (January 2009)

[366] *CBS 60 Minutes* "The Counterfeit Rockefeller" (April 18th 2003)

Svali

The list of people who have come forward claiming to be former members of the Illuminati are mainly men, but in 2006 a woman calling herself "Svali" popped up on the Internet claiming to come from an Illuminati family in Germany who then relocated to America when she was very young. "Svali" said when she was a kid she was told that she was "special" and that the Illuminati had big plans for her. At 12-years-old she underwent her "initiation" at the Vatican, as she claimed all the leadership in the Illuminati do, and by the time she was twenty-two, she was the youngest person in the "Illuminati leadership council" in Southern California.

"Svali" said that secret Illuminati meetings were held three times a week in Escondido, California, which is a lower income area inland where no wealthy or powerful members of the Illuminati would ever go, let alone choose to live. I have personally lived near this area for over 15 years and have friends who have lived in Escondido and I've seen the city with my own eyes many times. It's primarily a Mexican ghetto and would be the last place in the world the Illuminati would ever think about going.

The security for these "Illuminati" meetings, she said, was a "spy" who had climbed up into a tree with a walkie talkie to spot unwanted visitors and would then radio ahead to the group so they could "leave within five minutes." I guess the group would just run off into the woods if the person in the tree saw anyone unexpected rolling up to the house! You'd think the Illuminati's security detail would be a bit more sophisticated than someone climbing into a tree with a walkie talkie! Her claims get dumber by the second the more she tells her story.

The source of the information coming from Svali appears to lead back to a man named Greg Szymanski who wrote (or may continue to write) for a little known website called ArcticBacon.com, one of countless amateur websites that contains posts about the Illuminati, the Jesuits, and other conspiracy issues. "Svali" allegedly reached out and contacted him with her claims, so he then interviewed her in January of 2006 on his virtually unknown Internet radio show. Audio of the interview can found on YouTube if you can force yourself to listen to more than 30 seconds of her incoherent rambling.

In the interview she said her adult co-conspirators would, "get up in the middle of the night to attend meetings," and while the adults were doing their thing, the kids were "learning how to march and shoot guns and were being trained in martial arts." She claims her initiation at the Vatican included a child sacrifice and throughout the interview she was very scatterbrained and had a hard time explaining her story, which isn't even remotely convincing. Greg the interviewer ate it up though, and seemed to believe every word she was saying, as did a measurable number of people on the Internet who happened to come across her story.

When she was allegedly hanging out with the Illuminati, she claimed to be a "head programmer" involved in mind control programs but never offered up any details about what her supposed responsibilities were and couldn't even articulate the basic concepts or history of mind control.

Svali isn't even a clever hoaxer like some others before her, and appears to be a mentally deranged person just looking for someone to pay attention to her. It's also possible that Greg Szymanski, the man who first interviewed her, actually crafted the Svali hoax himself by working with a female friend to concoct the entire story so he could be the person to have the "exclusive" interview and forever be linked to her as the person who first "broke her story."

His website is just one of countless virtually unknown sites in the sea of conspiracy theories online so it makes no sense why a "former Illuminati member" would reach out to him since there are a large number of fairly prominent conspiracy websites that cover such topics. She did try selling an e-book titled *Breaking the Chain: Breaking Free of Cult Programming,* but it's not even listed in any of the major e-book stores and seems like a failed attempt to try to make a few bucks by selling a PDF file from a website.

I can attest to the fact that I have received multiple e-mails from different people making extremely bizarre claims such as being stalked or harassed by cults and the rambling and incoherent nature of their emails clearly show that they are from mentally disturbed and insane people sounding very much like this woman.

Actual Illuminati members are educated, intelligent, and well-spoken people. They are very persuasive and convincing—none of which can be attributed to Svali, whose stories are so convoluted they're hard to follow as she jumps from thought to thought. How did she eventually "escape" the clutches of the Illuminati? Well, she said she left the organization because she started to realize, "what I was doing was wrong." Now that she is a "former member" she is a born again Christian and has repented of the activities she claims to have participated in. Today, the woman says she's a "diabetic educator" living in Texas with her husband and two children.

The bio on the website of the man responsible for conducting the interview reads, "Greg is first and foremost a satirist, a writer and a reporter," so he was likely just playing a role and trying to have fun with conspiracy theories by producing a new Internet urban legend of conspiracy theory fiction about the "woman who left the Illuminati."

Brice Taylor

A woman calling herself Brice Taylor (a pseudonym) published a book in 1999 titled *Thanks For The Memories: The Truth Has Set Me Free! The Memoirs of Bob Hope's and Henry Kissinger's Mind-Controlled Slave* where she details what she says is her account of being a CIA mind control victim who was used as a sex slave by the Illuminati.

David Icke, a popular conspiracy writer best known for his theories that the Illuminati are an alien race of shape-shifting reptilians, is listed as an endorsement on Amazon.com's listing of the book, as well as Ted Gunderson, a former FBI Agent from Los Angeles who said, the book "confirms facts furnished by many other witnesses."

With endorsements by such heavy hitters in the conspiracy world as David Icke and Ted Gunderson, many people are inclined to believe her claims, but upon even a brief analysis of the book, the woman's story quickly goes from being hard to believe, to being completely ludicrous and impossible by any stretch of the imagination.

The first wobbly leg of this story comes when we learn Brice Taylor is just a pseudonym and the authors' real name is Susan Lynne Eckhart Ford who admits that from a young age she suffered from multiple personality disorder. "But as I began to heal and remember more of my hidden past, I realized that ritual abuse was merely the mind control trauma base my ritually abused, programmed pedophile father, Calvin Charles Eckhart, and others used to condition me for participation in the still active top secret Project Monarch, the Central Intelligence Agency's white slavery operation that is related to MKULTRA and its numerous sub-projects," she writes.[367]

"The result of many years of trauma, intentionally inflicted on me by my father and others to create within me multiple personalities, was that I was transformed into a programmed, totally robotical slave that could not remember to think or tell what happened to me, due to the mind control and sophisticated programming I was under. I was used frequently in child and adolescent prostitution

---

[367] Taylor, Brice - *Thanks for the Memories* page 1

and pornography. By my pre-teen years, I had many personalities specifically programmed to be the perfect sex slave—a 'presidential mode' with government mind files and a photographic memory equipped to deliver (most often through sexual encounters) messages, some cryptic, to top government officials, entertainers, and other world figures."[368]

She writes that when her memories started coming back to her at the age of thirty-five she, "began having vivid, detailed memories of being used both as a sex slave and human mind file computer to some of our nation's highest level government officials in and out of the White House."[369] She then goes on to list Presidents John F. Kennedy, Lyndon Johnson, Gerald Ford, Ronald Reagan, George Bush, Jimmy Carter, as well as Henry Kissinger, Nelson Rockefeller, Bob Hope (the popular entertainer), and many others as men she says all abused her.

Taylor says that while meditating she began to remember things all the way back to when she was *four months old*! (Not four years old, four *months* old.) She says her father worked as a welder who owned a welding shop in Los Angeles, but was somehow also secretly working for the CIA as a mind control programmer. "My father began the rigorous training and intentional torture required to shatter my base personality with the goal of

---

[368] Taylor, Brice - *Thanks for the Memories* page 1

[369] Taylor, Brice - *Thanks for the Memories* page 2

creating many separate individual personalities for training and use by others as I grew older."[370]

Her mom too, she says, was under mind control and "was listening to music she was told to listen to in order to keep her memory of our actual life locked deeply within her subconscious mind, while the programmed reality of herself and our 'perfect happy family' was kept alive through programmed phrases in the music."[371]

Most of the book consists of lengthy and rambling tales of alleged abuse by such a long list of people, both famous, and ordinary people in her community, that it reads like a parody of a poorly written horror story. The people involved in the conspiracy include her ballet teacher, her doctor, her dentist, her choir teacher, her next door neighbor, the people at her local church (who she says all had tunnels under their homes connecting them to each other and also leading to the church); the owners of the local bowling alley were also in on it, and of course the Freemason Shriners, and even the owners of a local gas station! They were all sacrificing children and shooting snuff films or involved with the "CIA's mind control program" she says.[372]

The list of her alleged abusers and human-sacrificing CIA Satanists she was involved with just goes on and on. Prince Philip, Prince Charles, and even Sylvester Stallone

---

[370] Taylor, Brice - *Thanks for the Memories* page 4

[371] Taylor, Brice - *Thanks for the Memories* page 6

[372] Taylor, Brice - *Thanks for the Memories* page 9

are on her seemingly endless list of abusers. Sylvester Stallone, she claims, directed several bestiality films where she says she had sex with dolphins and other sea creatures! Other celebrities such as Jane Fonda and Barbara Streisand were also under mind control she says, and Elton John was aware of such things and tried to help the victims with the lyrics in his music.

Aside from listing half the people in her community as being "in on it," and a dozen presidents and celebrities, she also names some very odd places where she says everyone sexually abused her or "programmed" her with mind control. One of these supposed places was Disneyland where she says her father introduced her to Walt Disney himself when she was five-years-old, who then made her look into a View-Master box containing dead cats and dead people.

"Brice Taylor" said she would also meet Henry Kissinger there at Disneyland where he would "program" her using CIA mind control techniques. One of these "programming sessions," she said, needed to be done in front of a carrousel for some unknown reason. "I also continued to be taken to Disneyland for base programming for my new government mind file system," she wrote.[373] Who would have thought the CIA was using Disneyland as a secret mind control center? Like I said, her book reads like a bad parody of a horror story written by a teenager.

She goes on to claim she was also taken to various McDonald's around the country and "programmed there

[373] Taylor, Brice - *Thanks for the Memories* page 30

too." And of course she says she was also taken inside the National Archives, the State Department, NASA, the Pentagon, the Federal Reserve, the World Health Organization, and other military bases around the country —and insists she was "programmed" at every one. Why her handlers would need to take her to the Federal Reserve Bank to "program" her using mind control techniques isn't said, and these claims are clearly ridiculous and the result of another over-active imagination of a clearly insane person, or by a horrible storyteller fabricating such tales hoping to sell a ton of books to the conspiracy community.

She wrote that she was even told that in a few years she would be killed and her services wouldn't be needed any longer. Why would her handlers inform her that they would kill her at some point in the future? Wouldn't they keep this to themselves and lead her on? After all, if she knew she was going to be killed soon, wouldn't this give her even more reason to betray them and escape before this happened? The more of Brice Taylor's story you read, the more absurd it gets, well beyond the point of nonsense.

The book is self-published because I'm sure that not even a small fringe conspiracy publisher would invest their money in such a worthless piece of garbage filled with fictional delusions. Near the end of the book , as expected, she starts talking about the elite's plan for a New World Order. Then there is a "suggested reading" list which includes the staple books of New World Order and Illuminati literature such as *None Dare Call it Conspiracy* by Gary Allen (published in 1972), *Tragedy and Hope* by Carroll Quigley (published in 1966), as well as books by conspiracy authors like David Icke, Texe Marrs, Fritz Springmeier, and other titles about mind control, the CIA, and brainwashing.

The question remains...why would this woman make up all these horrific things that she says happened to her? What would compel a woman to write such a book? I speculate that the only truthful part of the book is that perhaps she was sexually abused as a child, but not by any of the political figures or celebrities she mentioned, but at the hands of a relative or perhaps even her own father. She may feel justified and achieve some degree of healing by venting her anger and betrayal in a fictionalized book where she has projected that the perpetrators of her abuse are men in high positions of power within society. It's also likely that she wrote the book purely as "conspiracy fiction" hoping to pass it off as factual to the often gullible conspiracy community.

The reason some people believe her claims is because there are grains of truth (albeit tiny miniscule grains) since the CIA did do horrific mind control experiments in their MK Ultra program, and they did drug, hypnotize, and torture people in those experiments trying to create mind controlled slaves. In 1994 the US government awarded 77 people $100,000 each in financial compensation for experimenting on them,[374] but Brice Taylor (whose real name is possibly Sue Ford) never even

---

[374] *Canada.com* "Woman sues Ottawa over CIA brainwashing at Montreal hospital" (January 11, 2007)

went to court over her allegations and was not one of the recipients.

A few years before Brice Taylor's book was published, another woman named Cathy O'Brien released a book titled *The Transformation of America* where she had claimed to be a test subject for the CIA's MK Ultra program, and a "sex slave" of the Illuminati's top politicians. O'Brien even claims to have been taken inside Bohemian Grove. It's most likely Brice Taylor was inspired by Cathy O'Brien's book and hoped she could cash in by making similar claims. While Brice Taylor is clearly a fraud, Cathy O'Brien's claims are a bit more believable (but also possibly fabricated), and are analyzed in detail in my previous book *The Illuminati: Facts & Fiction* if you are interested in reading about them.

"Jess LaVey"

A man calling himself "Jess LaVey" saying he was the son of Anton LaVey, the infamous founder of the Church of Satan and the author of *The Satanic Bible*, threw his hat into the conspiracy entertainment ring around the year 2000 and got himself a small amount of attention on a few Internet radio shows who eagerly took the bait and gave him a platform to spread his nonsense.

"Jess LaVey" not only claimed to have been the son of Anton LaVey (whose real name was Howard Levey by the way), but also said he climbed the ranks of Satanism all the way up to the Illuminati. In one interview "Jess" claims, "I never could forget the counsel of thirteen, they were very wicked looking men. When I reached the age

of twelve, my father told me I had to go before them...
They warned me of what could happen to me if I did not
do as they suggested. George H.W. Bush Senior was one
of these men. I stood before them and told them I was not
going to follow their ways and I was not going to take my
dad's place, and that there was nothing they could do to
me....I told them I believe in a higher power and that
higher power said in His Word that no harm can come to
me."[375]

After he refused this "invitation" to the Illuminati, he
says they castrated him as his punishment. He also talked
about the Kimball-Cherokee Castle in Sedalia, Colorado,
a 1450s style castle built in the 1950s on a 3,100-acre
ranch in Colorado where, he claimed the Illuminati meet
every year to do human sacrifices. "Satanists come
together and do unspeakable things...To think that Bush
and his whole family is a part of this kind of thing is hard
for some people to believe. The whole Bush family is
Satanists...I have met Bush Jr. once when he came to a
ritual at the castle once with his father....He is a very cold
man for Satan. Like a lethal weapon."[376]

Other "insider" satanic "leaders" have come forward
over the years, mainly in the 1980s and 90s such as Mike
Warnke and Stephen Dollins, trying to use their supposed
"satanic credentials" to boost their new career as Christian
evangelists, but most were never involved in any

---

[375] YouTube: Interview with "Jess LaVey"

[376] Ibid.

organized cults or groups and wildly exaggerated the supposed activities they claimed to have participated in.[377]

In 2002 John W. Morehead of the Watchman Fellowship, a group that monitors the activities of cults, was given a copy of what "Jess LaVey" claimed to be his social security card which was clearly fake and when the number was run for a background check it was proven to be invalid.

"Sadly, many have claimed to be LaVey's child in order to gain financial support from churches and to give credibility to their ministries allegedly addressing Satanism and the occult," Morehead told Charisma Magazine in 2002.[378]

Anton LeVay, Aleister Crowley, Helena Blavatsky, Manly P. Hall, and other real occult insiders have revealed plenty of details to see exactly what is going on in various Satanic groups and secret societies, but conspiracy con men seem to keep coming up with the idea that they can make some money by claiming to have been an "insider" who is offering a "first-hand account" of what they have allegedly seen and done.

The interviews "Jess LaVey" did can be found on YouTube and after listening to one for about five seconds, any sane adult should obviously be able to tell he is making up his story pretty much as he goes along and doesn't even have the faintest hint of legitimacy. Anton

---

[377] *Cornerstone Magazine* Issue 98 "Selling Satan" (1992)

[378] *Charisma Magazine* "Alleged son of Anton LaVey fails to prove identity" (7/31/2002)

LaVey (again whose real name was Howard Levey) had two daughters and only one son; a boy named Satan Xerxes who was born in 1993.

George Green

A supposed former investment banker named George Green claims to have once sat in on secret Illuminati meetings where men were making "god-like decisions as to who lives and who dies" and contemplated "dropping neutron bombs" on major American cities to reduce the population in accordance with the Georgia Guidestones. "I actually sat in on the meetings. I was in the game big time. In fact, I was making such a mess, they decided rather than kill me, which they could, they invited me in to the inner group and asked me to be the finance chairman, and at that point, I probably would have been secretary of the treasury or whatever they wanted to do with me."[379] The financial chairman of the Illuminati, huh? This I gotta hear about!

In his interview, which can be seen on YouTube, Green talks about the World War Three looming in the Middle East, a coming one world currency, FEMA concentration camps, the coming economic collapse of America, the planned extermination of the majority of the world's population to save the earth's natural resources for the elite, and rattles off a list of well-known plans of the Illuminati. Green doesn't reveal an ounce of new

---

[379] *YouTube* "This is how they plan to KILL us - Elite Insider George Green"

information whatsoever and like many others, just talks about the same old widely available claims while presenting them from the perspective of a supposed insider who says he literally sat in on the meetings. Of course he too is trying to sell a book titled *Chaos in America,* which never gained much traction.

If George Green actually did attend any of the Illuminati meetings, he would be able to at least reveal *some* previously unknown details about their plans, but instead he just recycles the same old material that has been floating around the Internet and patriot circles for many years. An interesting phenomenon in the information age is that if you claim to have some kind of Illuminati "scoop" and throw the video online, people are going to find it and people will believe it.

Aside from the typical Illuminati talking points about the Georgia Guidestones, FEMA camps and the collapse of America, George Green goes straight into crazy town and says the Illuminati have been making "synthetic people." He's not talking about secret cloning programs, which most likely exist—he claims that most presidents have been "replaced" by these synthetic clones! That's right. He says our major world leaders are all grown in an Illuminati lab and are just pretending to be real people.

To "prove" this is happening he points to the movie *Boys from Brazil*, a 1978 film about Nazi scientists creating clones of Hitler to rebuild the Third Reich. This cloning technology, he says, was given to us by the "greys" (aliens), and he says he knows this because while working in the Air Force he claimed to have "top secret" clearance which gave him access to some dead Nordic-

285

type aliens called the Pleiadians who came to earth from the Pleiades star cluster.

While aliens may actually be directing the Illuminati, and top secret human cloning programs most likely do exist, George Green's presentation is so poorly executed and unconvincing, it reeks of a hoax from the very moment he opens his mouth. And again, he hasn't provided a single piece of new "evidence" that wasn't already widely known by most conspiracy researchers.

Not to mention nobody has been able to verify any part of his supposed background as an "investment banker" or having any kind of "top secret" security clearance in the military. But then again, we're living in a world where countless people believe Tupac faked his death which just goes to show that some people will believe just about anything, no matter how crazy it is, despite zero evidence, and defying all logic and common sense.

Kevin Trudeau

Kevin Trudeau is a man that almost everyone in America has seen on TV (whether they know his name or not) over the course of twenty years pitching various products on infomercials such as health supplements, anti-aging cream, and methods to get "free money." He is an extraordinary salesman who could sell ice to Eskimos, as the cliché goes, and has been labeled the "infomercial king" due to the massive hours of airtime and the large number of different products he has pitched over the years.[380]

As a follow up to his bestselling book *Natural Cures 'They' Don't Want You to Know About* (2005), he published *More Natural 'Cures' Revealed* (2006) where he claimed to have been a member of a powerful secret society, hinting it was the Illuminati—and through his supposed membership in this society, he learned how the world really worked, including how drug companies were suppressing natural cures for diseases in order to allow them to sell more drugs instead of helping people to be cured.

Trudeau alleges that because of his drive for wealth and his knowledge of the human mind, he was approached by members of "the Brotherhood" secret society and recruited by them to join. Trudeau wrote, "As a member of this secret society I have sat in private meetings with heads of state from countries around the world. I have attended secret international business meetings where business leaders, politicians, and media moguls coerce together to create the new world order with global control over individual people everywhere."[381]

Sounds a lot like the Bilderberg Group, doesn't it? During an interview on the Alex Jones Show in 2009, a very convincing Trudeau discussed his knowledge of the Bohemian Grove and other secret societies, and stated

---

[380] *ABC News* "Infomercial King Kevin Trudeau Loses On $38 Million Appeal" by Alan Farnham (December 20th 2011)

[381] Trudeau, Kevin - *More Natural 'Cures' Revealed* (2006) page 11

that he had friends who attended the Bilderberg meeting that year in Greece and that he had personally "sat in on meetings" where the elite talked about reducing the world's population by killing off "the dumb people."[382] Later in the interview he mentioned "what we talked about at Bilderberg" prompting Jones to interrupt him for clarification asking, "Did I hear you correctly, were you at Bilderberg?" to which Trudeau answered, "Yeah, I was in Greece, because I have friends who were there...All I can say is that I was in the area, and many of the people that were there and who are members are in fact people I converse with on a regular basis."[383] Of course Trudeau's name has never appeared on a Bilderberg attendee list and all this was building up to his latest money making scheme, the Global Information Network, which I'll get into in a few moments.

A member of this "elite Brotherhood," Trudeau says he worked covertly for the wealthiest families on earth and during his alleged involvement, he says he made hundreds of millions of dollars and lived a life many could only dream of. "Members of this society includes politicians, captains of industry, news journalists, celebrities, musicians, writers, scientists, law enforcement officials, movie stars, and more," he says.[384]

---

[382] *The Alex Jones Show* (May 26, 2009) Guest Kevin Trudeau

[383] Ibid.

[384] Trudeau, Kevin - *More Natural 'Cures' Revealed* (2006) page 13

In his book *More Natural 'Cures' Revealed*, he goes on to write that after he became a member of this "elite secret society," he discovered they had two groups, and that one was evil, and the other good, and both were using the organization's advanced knowledge and power to influence the world. "I was on the dark side doing evil; now I have repented, changed my ways, and turned my life around...Now I am going against the masters that I once served. I am telling people the truth about Big Pharma, the food industry, the oil industry, governments, and the media."[385]

Trudeau has an extremely checkered past, including a conviction for fraud and larceny which resulted in him serving two years in prison in the 1990s.[386] He was also banned by the Federal Trade Commission from selling products like health supplements and beauty creams on TV and fined $37 million dollars for making false claims in infomercials about his book *The Weight-Loss Cure 'They' Don't Want You To Know About*.[387] He found a major loophole however, and continued selling books and audio recordings because these items weren't seen as "products," but were considered information, thus protected by the First Amendment right to free speech.

---

[385] Trudeau, Kevin - *More Natural 'Cures' Revealed* (2006) page 13

[386] *ABC News* "Infomercial King Kevin Trudeau Ordered to Jail" by James Hill (September 18th 2013)

[387] FTC.gov "Judge Orders Kevin Trudeau to Pay More Than $37 Million for False Claims About Weight-Loss Book" (January 15, 2009)

In *More Natural 'Cures' Revealed*, he claimed that his prison sentence in the 1990s wasn't really because he was a criminal, but instead, "The society needed me to go to prison for a very specific mission."[388]   So what he means apparently, is that this all-powerful "Brotherhood" wanted him to commit credit card fraud and larceny because they "needed" him to go to prison for a "mission." He goes on to write that during his sentence he spend most of his time not in a prison cell, but hanging out at the Officer's Club at Edwards Air Force base eating "the finest food in the club," all because he was a member of this Illuminati-type secret society![389]

As if Trudeau's claims weren't already hard enough to believe, they get much, much stranger. He also wrote, "I have been to Area 51 in Nevada. This is where much of our technology has been developed. Area 51 houses most extraterrestrial artifacts, including a working spacecraft and dead alien bodies. I have seen these things with my own eyes."[390]   He actually says he has been inside Area 51 and saw the aliens with his own eyes! I guess they have a family and friends night and even give tours to infomercial pitchmen!

Trudeau keeps his discussion on his alleged involvement with the Brotherhood and aliens brief in his *More Natural 'Cures' Revealed* book, but states that

[388] Trudeau, Kevin - *More Natural 'Cures' Revealed* (2006) page 12

[389] Trudeau, Kevin - *More Natural 'Cures' Revealed* (2006) page 12

[390] Trudeau, Kevin - *More Natural 'Cures' Revealed* (2006) page 11

unless he is the victim of an "unforeseen accident," he will discuss this "secret society" in detail in a future book he planned to write.

At the end of 2009, Trudeau launched a new infomercial for an audio series titled *Your Wish is Your Command* where he claimed to teach magical methods of the "law of attraction" found in *The Secret*, the popular DVD produced by Rhonda Byrne, released a few years earlier which discusses mystical ideas about how your own thoughts and beliefs can metaphysically alter your physical reality.

The new infomercial was designed to look like an ordinary talk show with Trudeau as the guest and can be viewed in its entirety on YouTube. He starts of by saying that when he was 15-years-old, he was exposed to "the Brotherhood" secret society which he says took him in and taught him how to use *The Secret* and enabled him to make millions of dollars before his eighteenth birthday. In high school, he was actually voted most likely to succeed when he graduated in the class of 1981 from Saint Mary's High School in Lynn, Massachusetts.

Instead of simply regurgitating *The Secret's* "law of attraction" philosophy, Trudeau cleverly mixed secret societies in with his sales pitch, since he likely knew a growing segment of the population were highly interested in researching them.

In the infomercial he says, "Quite frankly, these are the same techniques that members of Skull & Bones have learned from Yale University; the Bilderberg Group— some people may be familiar with some of these organizations—the power elite. When you get to the highest level in Freemasonry, the 33rd degree level of Freemasonry—these are secrets of these various associations and societies on how to—we call it manipulating energy—it's really just how to beam the frequency in your brain of what you want so it will come into your life."[391]

He went on to say that all the popular self-help books, such as Napoleon Hill's classic, *Think and Grow Rich*, and Norman Vincent Peale's *Power of Positive Thinking*, were missing the "key ingredient" which makes these mystical ideas work, and only his audio program would reveal them. During part of his sales pitch he even says, "If a guy is watching this right now and doesn't get the *Your Wish is Your Command* program, they'll always be a loser."

The host asks him why the wealthy people in the past didn't want others to know this information (a scripted and preplanned question, of course) to which he answered, "When you're in Skull & Bones, the secret society, or the highest levels of Freemasonry, or the Bilderberg Group or the Trilateral Commission or the Council on Foreign Relations, or the Brotherhood—like I was a member of—you're basically a part of a group that believes 'we want to keep this information to ourselves, we don't want competition.'"

He later claims he left "the Brotherhood" in 1999 because he didn't believe that the information should be kept from everyone else and tells the audience that if they

[391] Your Wish is Your Command Infomercial with "host" Skip Linderman on "A Closer Look" (11:52 mark of interview)

"call today" they'll get his 14 CD program at 70% off the "regular price" of $1,000. "I would just really encourage people to take advantage of this secret knowledge on how to have, be, or do whatever they want." He also says he has received death threats from "the Brotherhood" for revealing these "secrets," but apparently they have enough power to rule the world but couldn't successfully assassinate a TV pitchman!

Trudeau then started offering people a membership to "a very elite society" which he called the Global Information Network, a supposed network of former Illuminati members, Skull & Bones members, Bilderberg Group insiders, 33rd degree Freemasons, Bohemian Grove members, etc., who all left those organizations to start GIN with him to help reveal their insider secrets to the world! Trudeau's Global Information Network is not to be confused with Global Information Network, Ltd., a non-profit news agency started in 1986 in New York City which specializes in news from Africa.

While Trudeau is an extraordinary salesman, he is a terrible teacher and a pathetic motivational speaker. As part of my research on Trudeau I have actually listened to all 14 CDs, approximately one hour each, as I sat painfully waiting for something of any value to be said, but there was nothing. For most of the 14 hours I was extremely bored and had to force myself to keep listening, and occasionally I sat in awe at Trudeau's marvelous ability to sound like he was about to reveal something of incredible importance but never actually getting to the point. Through the entire program he just kept regurgitating a wide variety of popular analogies that have been used by self-help gurus for decades.

The website, GlobalInformationNetwork.com described his organization as being, "conceived by a group of individuals from around the world who are the highest ranking members of several private societies, associations, clubs, and groups whose membership has been exclusive to the privileged elite class of the world,"[392] including supposed members from just about every Illuminati connected secret society and organization you can think of. The website originally actually listed the Illuminati, Bohemian Grove, the Bilderberg Group, Skull & Bones, Freemasons, the Council on Foreign Relations, the Trilateral Commission and more, saying that members from all these groups had defected and were now part of the Global Information Network's secret council.

The website went on to claim that, "For the first time in human history, the highest ranking members of these secret societies have encouraged the formation of a new, private, member only group that allows people who do not qualify to become members of the above listed societies to join together and be exposed to the same secrets revealed and taught to members of those societies and clubs."[393]

The site went on to say that a New World Order is forming that "is designed to increase the gap between the

---

[392] Original explanation from www.GlobalInformationNetwork.com

[393] Ibid.

wealthy and the average working man" and that "GIN does not agree with this movement" and they believe "EVERY person has the right to know the secrets of creating the life they want and enjoying freedom, pursuing happiness, and achieving all their dreams and desires."

"Members" of GIN apparently got several CDs and books shipped to them each month to further their education on the "law of attraction" and other Illuminati secrets. What did you have to do to "join" this secret society of Illuminati defectors who were ready to reveal their insider secrets to the world? All you had to do was pay $1000.00 down and $150 a month, each and every month after that! Once you were a "member" you could get a $200 commission for every one of your friends you suckered into signing up as well. Each new member was given an affiliate code that was used as a "secret invitation" to the Global Information Network, which they gave out to others who they hoped would then sign up, earning them $200 bucks.

When I first began investigating GIN, there was a section on their website to "join" their "society" that asked for the "invitation affiliate code," so I simply typed in *Kevin* as the code which was accepted because I was then taken to the payment page asking for my credit card number to pay the $1,000 initiation fee, which of course I didn't pay. I also tried *Trudeau* as the affiliate code, and it worked as well. GIN was so "exclusive" that I guessed two of their secret passwords in two seconds!

Buying "Illuminati secrets" didn't end there though. After paying a $1000.00 down payment and a $150 each month, new "members" were only given access to the first of twelve different levels within the "society." To rise to the next level and learn more "Illuminati secrets" to success, each person had to pay more and more money with payments exceeding $10,000.00 dollars!

When I first began looking into the website, there was a section for a description and "member benefits" for each level but all the details, including the costs, were marked "classified information," except for the $1,000 initiation fee to join the first level.

The site claimed, "Members must qualify for each membership level by meeting specific requirements and being approved by the Global Information Network membership acceptance committee. Each higher membership level in GIN gives the member additional classified benefits, substantial cash bonuses, and other financial and monetary rewards."[394] I had a sneaking suspicion that in order to "qualify" for the next level, all you needed to do was pay a large amount of money without your credit card being declined.

The site said that the "requirements" for the next level would be revealed in the previous level, but insisted that although the "benefits" were "classified and confidential," they, "may include cash bonuses of over 1 million dollars, all-expense paid exotic vacations, one-on-one mentoring with high level GIN members, monthly residual payments

---

[394] Ibid

of over $100,000, luxury automobiles, private jets, and more."[395]

A YouTube video advertising the Global Information Network had the following description, "For the first time in the history of mankind, the Illuminati is opening their doors to qualified people." This video was created by someone who signed up as an affiliate and was trying to lure people to join so they could get their $200 commission through the website's affiliate program designed to pull in new "members." As absurd as this all sounds, as P.T. Barnum said, there's a sucker born every minute.

The GIN website boasted, "Affiliates could potentially earn hundreds of thousands of dollars in commissions," but included a disclaimer saying, "Individual results will vary. There are no guarantees that you will make any sales or make any money as an affiliate."

If this didn't sound like a good enough reason to pay the $1,000 initiation fee, they claimed that, "members could be given hundreds of thousands of dollars in surprise bonuses" as they qualify for various levels within the GIN membership organization and could get, "All expense paid trips to exotic locations around the world, luxury automobiles, private jet trips, and more," a claim which was immediately followed by another disclaimer saying, "Legally we are required to say that there are no guarantees that you will earn money as an affiliate or a member of the Global Information Network."

---

[395] Ibid.

And if this still didn't sound good enough to get someone to join, they insisted, "This is just the tip of the iceberg. Surprising as it seems, the majority of member benefits are not discussed here. The most significant members benefits are confidential and only revealed to members."

The site claimed that members would have access to, "experts, the powerful and affluent, celebrities, professional athletes, authors, scientists, politicians, successful business people, doctors and medical experts, leaders in various fields, plus many others."

Basically, Trudeau was trying to sell a ridiculously expensive membership [$1,000 down—later reduced to $500—and $150 a month] to join his own "secret society" that he made to appear was comprised of former Illuminati members. Trudeau carefully crafted an image of being an insider affiliated with groups like the Illuminati who was "leaking" the secrets to the average Joe who also dreams of being rich and powerful or who wanted to be a part of the Illuminati themselves.

He even advertised a special pay-per-view video "seminar" mid-2012 where he claimed he would reveal the secrets of December 21st 2012, which, you may recall, was supposedly the date that the Mayan Calendar indicated would be the end of the world. In a video posted on his YouTube channel promoting his pay-per-view "special," Trudeau said, "There is something coming, significant, December 21st 2012...We now have the data. I now have the data authenticated. I now have the data verified through multiple sources. Something significant that you need to know is going to happen on December 21st 2012."[396]

He went on to say, "I'm going to be revealing in a two hour webinar, exactly what is going to happen December 21st 2012. This is information you and your family need to know. It is information that you categorically 100% need to know. You need to know this. It is vital." Gullible fools thought he got this "data" from his Freemasonry, Bilderberg, Bohemian Grove buddies who supposedly made up the "GIN Council."

Trudeau is, in my opinion, an extraordinary liar and con artist and has fabricated his alleged connections with the Illuminati and the Bilderberg Group just like so many others, but added his own ingenious twist by creating his own "secret society" and selling "memberships" to suckers who thought they were going to get rich quick. If only Trudeau would have moved to Hollywood decades ago, he could have perhaps earned hundreds of millions of dollars as an Oscar winning actor and may have avoided his many legal troubles.

I'm sure that *some* of the information in Trudeau's *Natural 'Cures'* books, and "getting out of debt books," is legitimate and useful, and perhaps has helped a fair number of people get healthier and manage their finances better. But the extraordinary claims of seeing alien bodies in the Area 51 hanger, and being recruited for an elite

---

[396] YouTube.com "Kevin Trudeau reveals 2012 Mayan Calendar TEOTWAWKI, Planet X" (posted April 2nd 2012 on Official Kevin Trudeau YouTube Channel)

secret society when he was 15-years-old and having to go to prison for a mission to help them are truly ridiculous.

And anyone who was dumb enough to buy into his $1,000 (or later reduced to $500) "initiation" fee to join his "elite society" which he claimed had members of the Illuminati and Bohemian Grove as a part of it, then those people are truly gullible fools who were blinded by their own desperate hopes of becoming rich without having to work hard.

Trudeau's claims of being affiliated with an elite secret society and his carefully crafted Global Information Network scheme clearly, in my opinion, shows him to be concerned more with fooling gullible people out of large amounts of money than helping anyone get cured from any disease.

While he may discuss various useful home remedies in his "Natural Cures" books, and tout them as 'cures' for diseases, many health professionals have expressed concerned that people with real illnesses may have taken his advice while abandoning traditional medical treatment for what may be very serious diseases. The fact that Trudeau has been a pitchman for a wide variety of products, almost all of which play off people's basic desires to be healthy, look beautiful, or to get out of debt, shows that he has a knack for presenting supposed easy solutions to difficult problems.

Finally, I should point out that in his *More Natural 'Cures' Revealed* book where he first claims he was a member of an elite secret society and offers cures for all kinds of diseases, on the page immediately following the *Table of Contents*, is a disclaimer with a paragraph reading in part, "This book is considered by some a work of fiction, yet inspired by a true story. The truth is sprinkled in to spice things up. On occasion, names, dates, and events have been changed or made up for fun." It goes on to say the book is, "for entertainment purposes only."[397] How clever of Trudeau for including this legal disclaimer which hardly anyone even noticed, which attempts to protect him from the legal ramifications of the claims he is making. Since when is a book containing "cures" for diseases "entertainment?" It's shameful.

So basically if you believe Trudeau's wild tales of attending Bilderberg meetings and being connected to the Illuminati, may I remind you that in his own words he admits that it is all for "entertainment purposes only."

After I posted several videos on YouTube exposing Kevin Trudeau beginning in 2009, some of his supporters posted angry comments on the video and on my Facebook page saying things like, "Maybe you're the one working with the Illuminati to try and discredit him for leaving them in the first place and exposing the truth."

Another of the countless crazy comments by the gullible GIN members said, "Kevin Trudeau and his friends have dossiers of the crimes of the Illuminati all over the world and if anything happens to the GIN council it will be released to every news agency."

In March of 2014, Trudeau was sentenced to ten years in prison for violating his court order not to make

---

[397] Trudeau, Kevin - *More Natural 'Cures' Revealed* (2006) page vii

deceptive claims on infomercials.[398]   Court documents revealed that his Global Information Network took in over $100 million dollars in just a few years,[399] all the while Trudeau claimed to be broke and didn't pay a single penny towards his $37 million dollar fine the Federal Trade Commission levied against him.[400]   One court document states, "Trudeau denies having any personal property other than $2000 worth of clothing, but spent more than $15,000 in one trip to a high-end men's clothier in Zurich [Switzerland] only months before he filed the 'sworn' statement.[401]

In court it was revealed that GIN technically listed in his wife's name, a Ukrainian girl, twenty-three years younger than him (who some speculate was possibly a "mail order bride") as the named officer and director.[402] During court proceedings she "took the fifth" when asked

---

[398] *USA Today* "TV Pitchman Kevin Trudeau Gets 10-Year Sentence" (March 18th 2014)

[399] *KSHB Kansas City* "As infomercial king Kevin Trudeau heads to jail, his secret global club faces uncertain future" by Ryan Kath (October 17, 2013)

[400] *Chicago Tribune* "TV pitchman Kevin Trudeau Sentenced to 10 Years in Prison" by Jason Meisner (March 17th 2014)

[401] Trudeau Civil Case Document 713 07-15-13 (DX25 at 6; FTCX 90 at 103)

[402] Case: 1:03-cv-03904 Document #: 481-1 Filed: 07/13/12 Page 8 of 22 PageID #:6777

how she met Trudeau.[403]   Court documents reveal Trudeau was accused of hiding assets in a variety of ways including a convoluted ownership structure of various companies, off-shore trusts, and even using casino chips.[404]

A major key to Trudeau's book sales were his infomercials which appealed to a sizable segment of society who weren't very tech savvy, like many baby boomers and senior citizens—many of whom were facing declining health and desperate to try something hoping for a cure for their ailments. If, instead of ordering his books using the 1-800 number from the infomercial, they would have looked up the books on Amazon.com, then they would have seen many of the reviews were one star, and many of them ripping Trudeau for his outlandish claims and criminal past.

It is for these many reasons that, in my opinion, Kevin Trudeau is the biggest Illuminati hoaxer in history and is virtually unmatched by anyone in his ability to deceive people and put a fresh new spin on the ancient art of selling snake oil. At his sentencing, Trudeau told the judge—who called him deceitful to the core, "If I ever write a book again, if I ever do another infomercial again, I promise no embellishment, no puffery and absolutely no

---

[403] Case: 1:03-cv-03904 Document #: 713 Filed: 07/15/13 Page 3 of 35 PageID #:11594 (FTCX 14, Babenko Dep. 96:16-97:3, 100:3-24.)

[404]Case: 1:03-cv-03904 Document #: 481-1 Filed: 07/13/12 Page 14 of 22 PageID #:6783

lies."[405] And if you believe that, I've got a bridge to sell you!

Mark Cleminson

Mark Cleminson is a Seventh-day Adventist Christian who says he was born into an Illuminati family and at the age of twelve was able to bend spoons, move objects, and even levitate himself through telekinesis! Cleminson claims to be a descendent of Pope Clement, and says he once worked for IBM allegedly making "hundreds of thousands of dollars a year" but left that job in 2001 for whatever reason to apparently "expose" the Illuminati. His parents attended a Roman Catholic Church as a cover for their occult "Illuminism" he says, and his father and grandfather were supposedly raised by Jesuits in the "Himalayan Mystery Schools."

A few of his interviews can be found on YouTube where he duped a couple small Christian groups into talking with him. In the videos he looks presentable, wearing a suit and tie, appearing to be in his mid-forties, although his delivery is extremely dry and boring and consists of the typical "my life was threatened when I left" claims. First of all, the Illuminati doesn't "attempt" to kill someone. If they want you dead, there's any number of ways to do it, from the CIA's frozen poison dart guns, to swabbing poison on the door handle of your car that will be absorbed into the skin and cause an

[405] *Chicago Tribune* "TV pitchman Kevin Trudeau sentenced to 10 years in prison" by Jason Meisner (March 17th 2014)

undetectable heart attack, to walking next to a target and spraying them with hydrogen cyanide (HCN) or cyanogen chloride (ClCN) gas or other poison that will induce a timely death and be attributed to a heart attack, stroke, or other natural causes.

Cleminson says that shortly after "leaving the Illuminati" he was at a secluded property his family owned in upstate New York when "twenty or so" men in "full regalia masonic gear" gathered at the property next door in order to "intimidate him" and "threaten him for leaving." He says as he walked over to confront the men, who he said he recognized as his former associates, all of a sudden the Egyptian god of the underworld Anubis appeared to him standing twenty feet tall in the woods. "You can have my body, but you can't have my soul," he says he told the demon, which caused it to vanish.

His story lacks details and is so vague and unconvincing it appears at times that he's making it up off the top of his head as he's telling it. But, like agent Fox Mulder in the popular 1990s TV series *The X-Files*, so many people "want to believe" that they turn off their critical thinking and absorb every word he and other "former Illuminati members" say because it reinforces their current world view and makes them feel as if they are special for discovering these "little known truths."

Regarding his supposed ability to "bend spoons," with his "telekinesis" Illuminati power, this is one of the oldest parlor tricks in the book which is accomplished by using one pre-bent spoon and a second spoon handle that's been cut off from a different spoon by removing the head, and then by holding both pieces in one's hand and making it look like they're only holding one spoon, magicians make it appear as if the spoon is bending.

Cleminson may have dabbled in New Age philosophy and witchcraft on a personal level, unaffiliated with any organization, and then later found interest in Christianity, but his claims of coming out of an "Illuminati family" trained by the Jesuits and "Himalayan Mystery Schools" is preposterous and purely an attempt to tap into the anti-Illuminati sentiment by portraying himself as another supposed insider who is revealing their plot. Of course in the hand full of interviews gullible suckers conducted with him, he never once revealed a single detail that wasn't already widely known in conspiracy circles, and what little information he did offer up consisted of little more than claiming "the Rothschild's control the banking industry."

Maybe he did work at IBM, and was possibly fired for any number of reasons—in my opinion, probably for incompetence—but as far as having any affiliation whatsoever with the Illuminati, or having anything more than a basic understanding of them, Mark Cleminson completely misses the mark.

In August of 2014 I received an e-mail from someone who said they graduated high school with Cleminson twenty-five years earlier and was in the same circle of "jock friends" growing up. This person, whose name I won't mention, happened to see my YouTube video about Cleminson and reached out to me to let me know what a "liar and a fraud" he was, but that's pretty obvious to anyone with any common sense.

Conclusion

Even skeptics and debunkers have to admit that oftentimes no matter how "crazy" many so-called "conspiracy theories" sound, there are often undeniable truths at their foundation. It's a full time job to separate the facts from the fiction when talking about conspiracy theories or the Illuminati since there is so much disinformation, misinformation, half-truths and hoaxes out there. I hope this book has helped you in your quest for the truth and shown you solid, verifiable information and helped you see through much of the B.S. that's floating around out there.

For over ten years I've been tirelessly researching this material and carefully assembling the pieces of the puzzle to create an accurate picture of this monumental mystery. Even the most adamant "debunkers" have to admit that at the core of this massive conspiracy are many disturbing truths that cannot be ignored.

A writer for the New York Times who aimed to "debunk" Illuminati conspiracies in his 1983 book *Architects of Fear*, had to admit, "Elitism has always been the dark side of illuminism; the revolutionary vanguard that seizes control because it *knows* what's good for the people, the philosopher-king who knows the truth, the technocrat who *knows* how to run societies and wars—all try to hoard the light at the top of the pyramid. Reason, which can be used to rescue man from churches and kings, can also be used to enslave him with dogmas of its own. Knowledge is power that can be abused."[406]

Elitists and Big Government New World Order promoters want people to believe that rights come from the government, instead of from God. The United States Declaration of Independence says "All men are endowed by our Creator with certain unalienable rights," which means our rights can't be taken away, and are permanent from the moment we are born. No society can vote to eliminate them—no government can charge you money in exchange for granting them—they are inherent, irrevocable, and unchangeable. The State (the government) is God in the New World Order, and that's why most bureaucrats and the mainstream media portray presidents as modern day Pharaohs who they want you to believe are the only God you need. The Illuminati want the government to be the ultimate authority, not God. They want your loyalty to be to them, not to your family, community, or religious dogma. The law is considered the Gospel. The government is your protector, provider, and teacher. *It* knows what's best for you.

Because of the 24-hour cable news and satellite networks, the Internet, and social media—many people are inclined to think that we are able to quickly resolve all the world's problems since we are instantly informed about them, but this information age seems to be a double edged sword. On one level, this technology informs us about major events or problems, but at the same time, it usually prevents people from taking action to actually

[406] Johnson, George – *Architects of Fear* Page 222

resolve them. The term *narcotizing dysfunction* refers to the theory that because of modern media, when people are informed about a particular issue they substitute taking action to resolve it, for simply knowing about it.[407]

Most people feel that by posting information about a particular issue on social media that they have "done something" to help by "getting the word out" but this "slactivism" as it has been called, often has little to no actual effect. People can post all day long about earthquake victims needing help, but if nobody gets off their computer or puts away their mobile device to actually *do* anything to help them, then all of their talk is futile.

This is similar to the bystander effect which explains the phenomena where almost everybody assumes that someone else is taking action to resolve a problem, resulting in nobody taking action because everyone thinks someone else will do it or is already working on it.[408]

Terrible tragedies like airline disasters, terrorist attacks, or other high profile crimes get constant news coverage for a short news cycle often lasting no more than a few days and then the next big scandal or tragedy is put on the front pages and runs its brief cycle, and then that too disappears from people's minds as they are occupied by the next "top story" and the cycle endlessly repeats itself, with people's focus quickly jumping from one

---

[407] The term was first identified in the article Mass Communication, Popular Taste and Organized Social Action, by Paul F. Lazarsfeld, and Robert K. Merton.

[408] *Psychology Today* "What Is the Bystander Effect?"

tragedy to the next with the vast majority of people never actually *doing* anything about it. This endless barrage of sensationalist stories keeps most people in a virtual hypnotic trance, preventing them from ever looking beyond the tip of the iceberg in terms of what's really going on in the world.

Cultural Marxism creates an invisible pressure that prevents most people from breaking away from the crowd and keeps almost everyone following the herd and subscribing to the norms of society and afraid to question the deeply engrained patterns of their peers.

Since esoteric information is hard to contain these days, and bits and pieces of it occasionally leak out, sometimes the mainstream media has to do some damage control to prevent the masses from waking up to the magnitude of the reality we are experiencing. Sometimes scholars and college professors are rolled out by mainstream media in an attempt to discredit "conspiracy theories" and hoping to keep people from peeking behind the curtain.

One such "debunker" named Michael Burkun wrote a book titled, *A Culture of Conspiracy*, where he ridicules "conspiracy theories" that he says almost always include "ridiculous" claims such as the [supposed] "systematic subversion of republican institutions by a federal government utilizing emergency powers; the gradual subordination of the United States to a world government operating through the United Nations; the creation of sinister new military and paramilitary forces, including governmental mobilization of urban youth gangs; the permanent stationing of foreign troops on U.S. soil; the widespread use of black helicopters to transport the tyranny's operatives; the confiscation of privately owned guns; the incarceration of so-called patriots in concentration camps run by FEMA; the implantation of microchips and other advanced technology for surveillance and mind control; the replacement of Christianity with a New Age world religion; and, finally, the manipulation of the entire apparatus by a hidden hierarchy of conspirators operating through secret societies."[409]

He actually lists these events as "ridiculous conspiracy theories" when a brief examination of current events reveals that they're basically all obviously true. Burkun also tries to associate "conspiracy theorists" with "anti-government right-wing extremists" like Timothy McVeigh.[410]

Another popular "debunker" is Daniel Pipes, who just so happens to be a member of the Council on Foreign Relations and the founder of Campus Watch, an organization that some say was set up to harass scholars who are critical of Israel.[411] Pipes, who is the author of *Conspiracy: How the Paranoid Style Flourishes and Where It Comes From,* says "I have yet to see a clandestine effort by these so-called secret societies to gain power and to harm other people, or to fulfill their

---

[409] Barkun, Michael - *A Culture of Conspiracy* page 39-40

[410] Barkun, Michael - *A Culture of Conspiracy* Preface page ix

[411] *San Francisco Chronicle* "Professors Want Own Names Put on Middle East Blacklist by Tanya Schevitz (September 8th 2002)

own ambitions to gain power."[412] In his book, there isn't a single mention of the Bilderberg Group or Bohemian Grove, not a single word, not even once.

Pipes even ridicules people for being concerned about implantable microchips saying that some people fear one day, "tiny microchips will be inserted into American's buttocks to keep track of each person's whereabouts and activities."[413] He actually said conspiracy theorists are worried about the government implanting tracking devices in their butts! I guess he never heard of the Verichip or other implantable RFIDs or bioelectric tattoos, or wearable WiFi enabled devices or NFCs that are growing in popularity. Implantable and wearable tracking devices are very real, but Pipes attempt to trivialize the legitimate concerns about such technology is clearly ridiculous.

Furthermore, Pipes states that only conservatives and Republicans are conspiracy theorists and says Democrats and liberals are all simply too smart for such nonsense. Pipes writes, "With uncommon exceptions, the conspiracy theorists on the Right consist of skinheads, neo-Nazis, and other yahoos who express vicious ideas about Jews and batty ones about secret societies. Most of them suffer from a lack of qualifications; many have little education and work at menial occupations...In all earnestness, right-wing authors cite as sources the *National Enquirer*, a

---

[412] *History Channel* "History's Mysteries: Secret Societies" (2001)

[413] Pipes, Daniel - *Conspiracy: How the Paranoid Style Flourishes and Where it Comes From* page 8

grocery store tabloid, and other publications with no pretentions to accuracy."[414]

Regarding liberals and Democrats, however, Pipes claims, "The Left offers densely reasoned economic analysis and presents an idealistic vision. The one presents a face contorted with malice; the second offers a smile and a hope."[415]

Pipes also tries to paint "rightwing" conspiracy theorists as mostly anti-Semites. He quotes a supposed "study" on the American Militia movement, saying "leaders are careful to talk about 'international bankers' or the 'Federal Reserve' or the 'Trilateral Commission' or 'eastern elites.' But these are code phrases, carefully picked by the leadership to pull people into their movement without greeting them with overt anti-Semitism and that militias even if they call it something else and never mention Jews, they are referring to Jews."[416]

He even says that the Illuminati is good! "The Order of the Illuminati represented his [Adam Weishaupt's] effort to build a just community within a corrupt society

[414] Pipes, Daniel - *Conspiracy: How the Paranoid Style Flourishes and Where it Comes From* page 159.

[415] Pipes, Daniel - *Conspiracy: How the Paranoid Style Flourishes and Where it Comes From* page 161-162

[416] Pipes, Daniel - *Conspiracy: How the Paranoid Style Flourishes and Where it Comes From* page 142

and to modernize Germany through the discipline of a secret society."[417]

In a History Channel special titled *Secret Societies*, Pipes concludes, "Basically all the conspiracy theories about secret societies wanting to take over the world are wrong."[418]

Many people who criticize "conspiracy theorists" claim that we all have a "confirmation bias" which is the tendency for people to favor information that supports their current worldview or hypothesis—which in many cases is an accurate assessment of conspiracy theorists, but this certainly isn't the case for me. For several years after the 9/11 attacks on the World Trade Center, I fully believed the official account of what happened and I believed the conspiracy theory about Iraq having weapons of mass destruction that they were prepared to use against us at any moment. It was only when faced with growing evidence to the contrary that the American government's lies started to slowly unravel, allowing me to see things differently.

Since searching for the truth is difficult and painful, not to mention time consuming, most people never even start out on the journey. Instead they turn their mind, body, and soul over to the mesmerizing mainstream media, or to celebrity news or sports entertainment, so I congratulate you on your determination to be different

---

[417] Pipes, Daniel - *Conspiracy: How the Paranoid Style Flourishes and Where it Comes From* page 62

[418] *History Channel* "History's Mysteries: Secret Societies" (2001)

and for taking the road less traveled. I hope I've been able to provide you some of the answers that you've been seeking, because I too have a burning desire to know the truth and we are on the same path.

In this book we've covered a variety of evidence, ranging from the original writings of the Illuminati, to how they were discovered, what their plans are, and tracking them to their Skull & Bones, Bohemian Grove and the Bilderberg Group offspring. We've seen some little-known insider revelations, looked into their philosophies, symbols, and more—which when carefully assembled form an undeniable picture proving the Illuminati is still alive.

I wish you well on your journey wherever it may take you from this point forward. If you found this book valuable in your quest please review it on Amazon.com or whatever e-book store you got it from to help support my work, and I encourage you to check out some of my other books which I'm sure you will find interesting as well. I doubt you'll ever look at the world the same way now that you've peeked behind the curtain and seen *Inside the Illuminati*.

25527129R00181

Printed in Poland
by Amazon Fulfillment
Poland Sp. z o.o., Wrocław